A whole new country!

Arvind Banavaliker

Published by Arvind Banavaliker, 2024.

A WHOLE NEW COUNTRY!

First edition. March 21, 2024.

ISBN: 979-8224160662

Written by Arvind Banavaliker.

Table of Contents

for Priya, Raj, Maya and Alia and

in never failing memory of

Pratibha and Sujata

AUTHOR'S NOTE

Because it deals principally with India, this book (product of about 10/15 years' labor) after completion was sent to a well-known Southeast Asian publisher for offer to readers in India and elsewhere. The publisher advised that several paragraphs in the book might offend the sensibilities of the Indian government. This was news to me because that was never the intention of the book and I refused to make any changes. I countered that the book was my submission to the country and its people! It was not directed against the Indian government or its people. Instead, I was critical of the "conditions" obtaining there and these began long before Indian independence, Indian governments and Indian Prime Ministers. A quick study of the Contents would have confirmed the historical nature of the book, its emphasis on modern science and technology as a vehicle of change and the attempt to bring communities together – not drive them apart!

The book, therefore, is addressed to the Indian reader. Of the three largest economies in Asia, Japan, not China, was the first to get off the mark. China has followed spectacularly in our own times. It hurts me, therefore, that India still remains a laggard and this was one of the chief reasons for writing the book.

What interest can it have, therefore, for US readers and those in other countries? I think that what happens in India – presently the second largest and soon to become the largest populated country in the world – would be of great consequence for current and future generations in the US, Europe and elsewhere. This would be true for obvious reasons but there is one special reason and it is this: President Biden has said that it has long been his dream that the US and India, two large democracies, become true allies. The US is already one of the larger economies in the world but India still remains a developing country. If India was to become a developed country and was able to do it in a proper democratic way through the agency of science and technology, it would not only redound to the benefit of both countries but - do I dare say this? – it also could help considerably in the cause of world peace.

A further reason for interest would be because the book sets out what the author feels is truly required in transforming any developing nation and here not only is the receiving nation itself involved but also all those who aspire to help her.

Preface

The doctor and I were chatting at the local DMV (motorcar licensing authority) while waiting for the renewal of our driving licenses.

"What do you do?" the doctor asked, very slightly ostentatiously.

"Doctor, when I was a young man no one explained to me that biology did not involve study of mathematics. So I never became a doctor but then...I proceeded to do the next best thing!"

"What was that?", he said.

"Doctor, you see your patients one at a time. I decided to be different...I decided to invite all of India's people into my consulting room at the same time. It did get a little bit crowded but doctor, I think I have found the answer to India's illness".

Some friends object to the word "illness". But illness it is and my view is that unless we bravely square up to the fact, how do we tackle it and how do we put it right? Because it is possible to put it right. So this book is partly about the illness but mostly about the cure.

Also, some months ago, in considering the recent, spectacular development of China, I wondered why that country, although a serious latecomer, had done so well in the last thirty or forty years while Russia, which used to be a superpower had, during that same time, in a manner of speaking, squandered its advantages.

Wanting to really know the reasons, I picked up "Deng Xiaoping and the Transformation of China." by Ezra Vogel and found to my complete surprise the discovery in his country by this Chinese leader of the very same illness which, I believed, afflicted India and which I had struggled so much to write about and get accepted by my friends, readers and listeners.

The rapid development of China is now an accepted fact. But think of China as being flanked by two countries – one which preceded China itself in development by as much as a hundred years and another, our own, on the other side, which still lags behind. This book is about developments in all three countries - and a lot else.

Introduction
What the book is about

First, let's get one thing straight. Is India a poor country or isn't it? The trouble is that if one takes the former view, many people immediately come down on you like a ton of bricks. Never mind the evidence all around you or even sometimes the sad fact of India's per capita GDP of UD$ 2200/-. This kind of economic level certainly does not qualify us to be a developed country or even a middle income country. And it is not only a question of poverty. There are certain consequences which flow from it which also have to be addressed.

I debated this matter in my mind for quite long. I kept on thinking that unless we faced up to reality, how were we even going to devise a solution. Then, on a chance visit to Washington,DC some four years ago, I reached a decision. In that city, off Constitution Avenue, there is a large, beautiful statue of Albert Einstein by Robert Berks. One of the plaques adorning the place contained the following quotation:

"The right to search also implies a duty, one must not conceal any part of what one has recognized to be the truth"

After that, although the decision was a painful one, my mind was made up.

It is actually the business of economists to explain matters of poverty and prosperity. But this is precisely the trouble. Economists as a group and many books on economics look at the problem from an economic standpoint only. Some do admit that India's poverty is essentially a cultural problem but few go on to study it as such. This is what we attempt to do in this book

Before you have advanced very far into the book, you will realize that my own explanation for India's backwardness and consequent poverty is simply that we have been left behind after the coming of modern science and technology (also referred to as MoST from now on.) This too may be considered by some as a quite obvious statement to make. But wait. I did not say "left behind in modern science and technology" although this also is true. I said "left behind after". There is a difference and how this difference is critically important for a true understanding of India's condition, I will try and explain in the course of the book.

We cannot, of course, stop at merely explaining away India's problems. We must try and do something about it. Therefore, this is also a book about a cure. I start by looking at India's symptoms, I then diagnose India's illness and finally, I suggest the treatment or the cure. It is for the reader to judge whether the cure is acceptable in theory and whether it will work in practice. My claim is that it is the only cure and that there is no other and that, sooner or later, it is going to be forced upon us.

If this be so, then, as a nation, we have to learn about modern science and technology. I actually mean learn how to learn it. Now, if you are one of those who already feel greatly excited by modern science and technology and especially the general reasoning behind it and are able to tie it all up together into one piece, then you must go about studying or pursuing it in your own special way. Your own way is, of course, the best way. In that case, this book may perhaps read easily for you like a narrative. It is also possible that you may benefit from some of the explanations provided and the techniques shown in parts of the book. For the large majority, however, those who are apprehensive of the prospect of embarking on a study of science and technology, even an overview of the subject, or those who consider the task as being simply too formidable, this book may yet provide a way.

For such people, including those who have so far been connected with the arts or the humanities or with the professions such as law or accountancy, people in administration or general management and even those students of science who have been involved with one specialty or the other and are curious about how a general study of science can help to build bridges between subjects, this book may be of interest.

Part One, Chapter 1, therefore, gives an account of India's problems and how, in my opinion, we became a backward country in the first place. Chapter 2 offers an analysis of where we went wrong and specifically how we missed out by way of modern science and technology. In Chapter 3, I assert that this missing element would need to be supplied if a rapid recovery was to be staged and a proper course set for the future.

Part Two, on a personal, individual level, is by way of an intellectual journey which may prove useful to some readers .Here Chapter 4 discusses what science is and isn't. Chapter 5 shows how it is possible nowadays without difficulty to become broadly familiar with different branches of science. In Chapter 6, we try to show how this even enables us, when desired, to cross over into the humanities. Chapter 7 lists various "Western" ways which we take for granted and shows how they happened to come about. The claim is made that if you simply follow a certain path, the initial fruits begin to rain on you.

In Part Three, Chapters 8 and 9, now once again on a national plane, we indicate how it might be possible to get our message across to the people at large in a process of economic and cultural rejuvenation of individual and country.

Because the subject is vast, this book only traces out how; it does not and cannot develop every theme fully. It is left for the reader to do this. That's the whole point of the book. It is impossible to set out one single way which every person will find satisfactory. Better that we should explain past happenings, show what is missing, provide guidelines and allow every person to develop his or her own way.

Once you have become familiar with the broad idea of science, you will yourself attempt to use it as a general purpose tool. In Chapter 4, under the acronym OTEST, we show how science can help you organize your own knowledge, how it results in transformation of the individual, how modern science and technology is the true engine of growth in a nation, how it can be used to straddle science itself and the humanities and finally, how it is capable of bringing about nothing less than a total transformation of society.

A brief word about nomenclature. The sub-title "India's problem" in the Contents page presented some difficulty. I needed to point out that, of the three large countries in Asia, Japan and China had now both got off the mark and that India had still to get going, fully and properly going. I began by calling it "the problem of India" but that somehow gave the impression that there was a standing problem which was India and that was definitely not my intention.

"Modern science and technology" because, as explained in the book, science has been with us for a long time and it was necessary to point to the difference between old science and technology and modern science and technology.

The book's sub-title says modern science and technology will transform you and your nation. I wanted to make clear that every individual would be affected but also and more importantly, that there was a certain inevitability about it. Also that within that inevitability and sometimes pushing it, individuals might themselves benefit from certain techniques/ways mentioned in the book.

The book is couched in simple language and is addressed to the general reader. Specific situations from everyday life are taken and set up for illustration. No special training of any kind is necessary. No scientific or mathematical background is called for. All that is required (if some of the recipes are to be followed) is a fondness for reading and a curious mind. Hands-on experiments in school or college laboratories and visits to modern exploratoria where visitors can actually manipulate machines to understand the general principles of science are two different ways of bringing home the meaning of science to people. However, I feel reading about science is not only a quicker, more comprehensive, less expensive way but also is essential for a general overview of the subject. The late Nobel Prize winner Dr. Harold C. Urey appeared to think similarly. In his introduction to the Junior Pictorial Encyclopedia of Science, he says :

"Moreover they should read. In the last years there has been a great emphasis on children performing experiments. Many times they spend a great deal of effort preparing demonstrations for science fairs and contests of various kinds. This has probably gone too far. It is essential that boys and girls do enough experiments to learn how to use laboratory apparatus but it is a mistake to believe that they can do original scientific work or that they can learn from these specialized experiments the broad knowledge which should be theirs as they go on to their advanced education. It is important that they should acquire a factual background in science. This can be done only by spending more time reading...."

If reading is so important for children and for our young people still to complete their formal education, imagine how much more important it is for older persons, those who have passed through the portals of school and college but who must now seriously reflect about the problems of their country and then must begin the task of resolving them.

Prelude to Chapter 1

Wish to know how the idea of this book came about? If so, here goes: I had graduated in Economics in 1950 from a Bombay college without, I must confess, any real knowledge of the subject. Not knowing what I should do in life, I next joined Government Law College in Bombay. Many of my classmates, in later years, became some of the legal luminaries of India but although I liked the subject when in college, I did not exactly fancy life as a full time lawyer. My father was an engineer in the Telephones Dept. of the government but was due to retire in a few years and when that happened, I knew that as the only son (I had my mother and three sisters) I would have to be the bread-winner for the entire family. Unlike these days, there was acute scarcity of jobs in Bombay at that time and especially for one without contacts of any kind. I somehow got a job as a medical representative for a pharmaceutical company. Apart from salary, this type of company paid a goodly allowance when one travelled on work. This enabled me to set aside an amount equal to the lowest fare I needed for the journey by ship from Bombay to London.

I arrived in England in 1953. This was barely eight years after the War. There were already plentiful jobs in London but none apparently for people of the skin tone I carried with me all the time. I found it slightly infuriating that these people had been our erstwhile masters in India and now were still the bosses here. What was it that we were lacking as a people? However, other British people were very hospitable.

After six months, I was coming dangerously close to the end of my funds. One day, when passing Tavistock Square, I saw a board which told me it was the office of the National Union of Students (NUS). On an impulse, I walked in and asked if they might have any openings for me. They enquired instead if I would I be interested in a position available in the Farm Camps Department right there in their own office? For me, this was a heaven-sent opportunity. The job also was very interesting. Every year large numbers of students from different parts of the Continent (Norway, Sweden, Denmark, France, Spain, Germany, the Netherlands etc) would come to England, to work on different farms picking up potatoes, strawberries and other fruit.

This enabled them to make enough money to travel around elsewhere in Britain usually to improve their English. My job was to arrange for a sprinkling of each of these groups so that we built up a mini United Nations in the various farms. I loved the work. After some months in the office devoted to organization, I decided to visit a camp in Oakham, then Rutland county, for on-the-spot inspection! I was 23 years old and happily joined in with the students in the exhausting field work that they did and in the clean but barracks-like conditions in which they lived.

One moonlit night, when about ten or twelve of us were walking back to the camp after watching a movie in Oakham town, the discussion somehow turned to "who was the most important man of the century?". A British girl spoke up immediately: "Oh Winston Churchill, of course!" This seemed like a good choice but a German boy – to this day I remember his face vividly in the moonlight– said hesitantly but quite clearly – "I think it was Mahatma Gandhi". Everybody turned towards me and I was obliged to say a few words about Gandhi. But in my heart, I knew that I did not really know very much about Gandhi. I was only 16 when he was assassinated in India in 1948. I always only thought of him as a quaint, half-clothed old man. I resolved to do something about this immediately on returning to London. As luck would have it, on my very first visit to the bookstores on Tottenham Court Road, I came across on the pavement itself a used copy of "Gandhi" by Romain Rolland which I have with me still. This was the book that introduced Gandhi to European readers. It also introduced Gandhi and India to me. It was ironical that I had to come all this way to London to not only discover but to fall in love with the very subject of India. From Gandhi to Nehru and from Nehru to Patel, the three Founding Fathers and following that, many of the stalwarts of the independence movement in India. My encounter with slight racial discrimination had probably prepared me for the experience. (They rightly speak with pride about the Founding Fathers of the US. In my opinion, the founding fathers of our nation, were equally great. To this day, more than fifty years later, I experience goose pimples and tears roll down my cheeks when I read even extracts from their lives).

What did I study in London during my four years there? Exactly nothing! Not for want of trying, though. I flapped about, simply couldn't figure out what course of study I should follow. Nor did I find anyone I could trust to properly advise me. From the small employment department of the NUS, I had learned that there was a position available in a travel agency called Cox and Kings in the Haymarket, near Piccadilly Circus. This company had seen its best days but was still prosperous enough to continue to have an office on a prominent street in downtown London. Right next door to Burberrys which also in those days seemed to belong to a bygone era. It was only many years later that I suddenly realized that Cox and Kings had been started in 1758. Hello! This was one year after the battle of Plassey when Robert Clive had somehow managed to get the better of Siraj-ud-daulah in Bengal. Of course! They were travel agents to the British Army in India and therefore, in a manner of speaking, probably the oldest travel agency in the world.

Despite my impecunious circumstances in London, I always bought and read the London Times newspaper. One reader contributed a letter to the Editor where, in dissecting that year's budget, he showed an excellent grasp of public finance. The next month, the same writer marvelled at Sherpa Tensing's feats in mountaineering in the Himalayas. I was amazed at this and longed to be such a person.

I returned to India in 1958, helped by a 50% discounted first class ticket which one of the steamer lines gave me as a reward for the business I had brought them.

Within the first few years in India, I happened on an article on Jawaharlal Nehru in an issue, of all things, Playboy magazine. It was an excellent piece and carried a lovely photograph of Nehru smoking a cigarette with a cigarette-holder. (In a subsequent issue, the magazine explained that they had been deceived into believing that Nehru had given the interview – it was a compilation by someone of his statements culled from various sources!) There I read Nehru say that if one wanted one's life to have any meaning, all that was required was to attach oneself to some noble cause – any good cause. I reasoned to myself: what better cause than that of the suffering millions of India?

So this is how I embarked on a study of poverty. Before long, I realized that this was a fruitless pursuit and that I would have to take a different approach if I was to get anywhere. How I hit upon that approach and how I discovered for myself what the solution might be to India's poverty problem is related in Chapter 2. But before that it is necessary to give a brief outline of the enormous size of the problem itself and of the many standard explanations that are given for it.

Part 1
(historical setting)

Chapter 1
INDIA'S PROBLEM / symptoms

"They tell the story of the Sikh who, returning to India after many years, sat down among his suitcases on the Bombay docks and wept. He had forgotten what Indian poverty was like." – V.S. Naipaul, An Area of Darkness

Mass poverty of the kind seen in rural Tamil Nadu and elsewhere cannot be viewed as a pocket phenomenon or as a mere aberration of the system. It is a reflection of the total malfunctioning of the economic order. - John K. Galbraith, quoted in C.T.Kurien, "Rural Poverty in Tamil Nadu," Poverty and Landless in Rural Asia (Geneva:ILO,1977)

• multiple cure for long standing illness • the numbers • public health • belief v. understanding • cholera and commonsense • how science works on society • how irrationality impedes: blindness • the world of ritual • agriculture is industry! • too early to say? • measured growth or are we faltering? • colonialism as culprit • the Hindu route, the Islamic state • the luxury of religion • from liability to asset • is corruption the villain? • multiplier

defect! • the opiate of religion • problems of wealth, problems of poverty • past glories • the central question

When we see widespread poverty of the kind mentioned by Naipaul, one is forced to ask if such poverty is only a pocket phenomenon, a mere aberration of the system—or whether it is, to quote Galbraith, a reflection of the total malfunctioning of the economic order? In other words, is it episodic or are we suffering from a certain kind of continuing illness?

Or are these surface impressions only? Are these conditions purely temporary? There are many in India who resent that we should speak in this manner; a large number are earnest, well-meaning people who cannot bear to entertain the thought that there could be something desperately wrong with their country and object to regarding it as a illness. This would be understandable if the country were prospering and doing well for itself or even merely marking time before it really got going. However, if the indications are clearly otherwise, despite the gains of recent years and especially if one goes back in time by several hundred years relative to other countries, surely there can be no harm in postulating the matter and examining it carefully.

Some others might reply that this basic reluctance to see one's shortcomings is itself one of the failings of Indians, probably arising out of a sense of loyalty to what was once unquestionably a great civilization. I myself am inclined to this view, and I will try and show why this too happens and even why it can be expected to happen. So, dear reader and fellow citizen, try and keep an open mind and allow me to attempt to make a case that there is dire need for change, that it is now time for change, and that it is possible to change.

So let's begin. Imagine for a moment that there is a grave illness in a family. The patient is in critical condition. The doctors are unable to understand. A specialist is sent for. He examines the patient. Having concluded his examination, he puts away his stethoscope and shuts his bag. There is a solemn expression on his face. The family elders follow him into an adjoining room. The doctor says something like this: "This patient is suffering from a serious illness. If neglected, it could prove dangerous. Luckily there's hope. A remedy exists but just this one remedy – there's no other."

multiple cure for longstanding illness

What would you say to such a diagnosis? Too good to be true? On top of this, the doctor tells you that this medicine:

- is simple; not extraordinary

- isn't unusual or novel; is right there, staring you in the face

- is comprehensive, brings about a general sense of well-being

- isn't instantaneous but can begin to show results quickly even when offered to large bodies of individuals

- is sweet-tasting and enjoyable to take

- inexpensive, and needs little by way of resources

- is personal, self-administered, and individual; and finally:

- is irreversible—once it acts, there is no real possibility of relapse

What would you say when offered such a solution to the problem of India's illness? Unbelievable? Impossible? Well, it's true. Modern science and technology (MoST) can be the solution to India's accumulated problems. What's more, it is the only solution. I explore in this book the outlines of what we regard as modern science and technology and how it can help in dealing with our country's ills and I invite you to decide for yourself whether this claim is true.

Of course, there is no magic potion. Change will not happen overnight. The process is long, slow and sometimes arduous but we can be certain that we are headed in the right direction and that initial results will begin to manifest before long.

the numbers

India is a country of about 1352 million people but we produce only about 50% more wealth each year than Australia, a country with a population of 25 million. The U.K, with a population of only 66 million, has a gross national income roughly the equal of ours. Switzerland has only about 8 million people and has a GNI which is one fourth of ours. And, of course we are way below the big, rich nations like the USA, Japan, Germany, and so on.

With GNI calculated on a per capita basis, India is nearly at the bottom of the league among the countries listed here. To my mind, the figures in Table 1 are indicative of a fundamental problem.

Table 1

Country	Population (million)	Gross National Income (US$ billion)	Gross National Income per capita (US$)
2018			
Australia	25	1,329	53,190
Austria	8.8	436	49,250
Canada	37.1	1,662	44,860
Germany	82.9	3,935	47,450
Japan	126.5	5,231	41,340
Switzerland	8.5	712	83,580
Netherlands	17.2	884	51,280
United Kingdom	66.5	2,748	41,330
USA	327.2	20,563	62,850
China	1,392.7	13,184	9,470
INDIA	1,352.6	2,734	2,020
Bangladesh	161.4	282	1,750
Nepal	28.1	27	960

From U.N.World Development Indicators, source World Bank national accounts data

This initial impression is confirmed if we look at various key indicators of development as listed in Table 2. The first and most important step in a country's development is literacy. Comparison with not only developed countries but even with present day China shows that we are way behind. (The Chinese actually regard illiteracy as a kind of blindness. They call it "word-blindness")

Table 2

Key indicators of development

Country	Life Expectancy		Adult Literacy Rate
	Male	Female	
Australia	81	85	*
Austria	79	84	*
Canada	80	84	*
Germany	79	83	*
Japan	80	87	*
Switzerland	81	85	*
Netherlands	80	83	*
UK	80	83	*
USA	77	81	*
China	75	78	96.4
INDIA	67	70	72
Bangladesh	71	74	72

+ From The Economist Pocket World in Figures, 2019 Edition

* we assume 100% literacy

Table 3

Country	India	China	UK	Denmark	Australia	Japan	USA
Doctors/ 100 pop.	0.8	3.6	2.8	3.7	3.5	2.4	2.4
Telephone line/ 100 pop.	1.8	14.7	50.9	27.3	33.9	50.2	37.7
Mobile tel subs / 100 pop.	85.2	97.3	120	122.3	110.1	130.6	122.9
Cars / 1000 pop.	17	97	510	420	562	478	380

From The Economist Pocket World in figures, 2019 Edition

public health

There is probably no better single indicator of the true well-being of a people than its general physical well-being. Let us therefore look at conditions in India from the point of view of public health.

Blindness. There are 37 million blind people in the world. Although India's population represents only about 18% of the world's total (about 7 billion in 2016), there are 12 million blind persons in our country—or, nearly 33% of the world's blind. In other words, every third blind person in the world is an Indian. A further 8 million Indians are blind in one eye. About 40,000 children lose their sight each year to malnutrition, of which night blindness, although easily preventable with Vitamin A, is the first stage.

Leprosy. There are 12 million leprosy patients in the world. Of these, as many as 4 million are in India (once again, nearly 33 percent).

Tuberculosis. Pulmonary tuberculosis is said to be India's biggest health problem. Our total number of cases is anywhere between 9 and 10 million, and as many as 500,000 people die of this disease each year. The annual loss in terms of income is reported to be about Rs. 1000 crores.

Filiariasis. (tropical, parasitic disease affecting lymph nodes/vessels and causing swelling of limbs and other body parts). Filiariasis is said to have existed here from the 6th century BC. At present, 14 million people suffer from it and 304 million Indians living in areas where the disease is common are considered to be at risk. Filiariasis and elephantiasis present significant sociological problems as well.

Amoebiasis. (parasitic infection of colon because of contaminated water or food) is also widely prevalent. Approximately 250 million of the 359 million people infected in Asia are in India.

Iodine deficiency. 40 million people are affected by iodine deficiency and millions more exposed to endemic goitre (swelling of neck due to enlargement of thyroid gland).

In addition to all this, we experience periodic explosive outbreaks of cholera, typhoid, hepatitis and encephalitis, especially following large fairs and festivals as well as after natural disasters.

All this does not make for a particularly flattering portrait of our country even at present. But the position of India's children, our hope for the future, is even worse. As long ago as 1989, E.R. Ramkumar wrote that India "may have reached a point of no return as far as the mental and physical health of at least one fourth of our children is concerned." 60 to 80 million children went through life with impaired physical and mental faculties and this resulted in a great loss of manpower. Also, there were a further estimated 20 million mentally retarded children whose ranks were swelling alarmingly. His conclusion was that "forty years after independence, a third of our child population continues to be unlettered, unattended and exploited."(1)

Ramkumar's article was written nearly three decades ago, and our position hasn't improved. The Economic Times of 3 April 2002 carried a statistic that one out of every two children in India under three years of age was either underweight or already stunted.

Now, add to this mix the non-communicable diseases which are becoming major health problems. In its 28 July 2002 issue, the Economic Times reported that India had the highest rate of heart disease in the younger age brackets in the world, with an estimated 10% of the adult population suffering from coronary artery disease. Eight years later, in 2010, P.C.Reddy of Apollo Hospitals asserted that "by 2050, India is likely to be the heart disease capital of the world... the incidence is five to seven times more than that of the western world." (2)

India had an estimated 41 million diabetes patients in 2010 and this figure was expected to rise to 70 million by 2025. (3) Then there is obesity, chronic urinary tract infection (especially in girls), and of course, HIV and AIDS. We have also been called the lung disease capital of the world; in 2002, India had 15 to 20 million asthmatics out of a worldwide 100 to 150 million people. (4)

And we haven't considered mental illness yet. Estimates of people with mental illness vary. The New York Times of December 4, 2014 says that the 2011 census puts the figure of Indians suffering from mental illness or intellectual/developmental disabilities like Down syndrome at more than 2 million. However, the Human Rights Watch estimate is significantly higher: 1.5 million people suffering from intellectual disabilities and 70 million from mental illness. There are only 43 state-run hospitals in all of India, and an unknown number of private facilities.

What an utterly depressing picture! Do we hold the politicians responsible (a common enough choice)? Do we blame our successive Governments? Can we blame the British for bequeathing such a general state of affairs to us? Or should we really blame ourselves for having permitted these incredible conditions to occur, having allowed them to continue and for even now having become inured to the fact?

However, there's no sense in losing heart. We'll never get anything done if we lose heart. So let's look at the positive side of things. These are gigantic problems to be sure but no problem lacks a solution – and the way to go about solving these problems is to understand each disease - by way of science, naturally (that is critical) - and then begin the task of tackling them with science again guiding us every step of the way. If we made even a minimal 10% progress every year, we would have solved each of these problems in 10 years! Think of the tremendous legacy we would be leaving for our children and the inspiration it would give them for the future as the new never-say-die Indian nation!

belief v. understanding

As a people, we instinctively ascribed these illnesses to Fate. We called them afflictions from God. Blindness, deafness, speech impairment were visitations from God. There was little we could do in these matters. Some regularly attributed disease to sins or misdeeds in past lives.

Leprosy was something terrible, nothing less than a maha rog. Smallpox was the province of Sheetaladevi (from sheetal, meaning cold, calm, pleasant-feeling as a counter to the heat generated within the body). Even today smallpox is called devi in Marathi and Mata in several other Indian languages. Villagers in their thousands still flock to the temple of Sheetala Mata near Jaipur for protection from smallpox although this disease was stamped out in India by vaccination in 1975 (part of a world-wide campaign spearheaded by the World Health Organization (WHO) (5)

Not that in earlier times this kind of misconception or fear also existed in the Western world. For example, influenza (or flu, as it is popularly called), as recently as 1918-1919, during the great influenza pandemic, is reported to have caused the death of 18 million people in India. (6) More people died of influenza during this epidemic than in the First World War itself. The name of the illness comes from the Italian word influenza, meaning influence. Influence of what? Influence of the stars, is what Europeans actually believed!

Similarly, malaria, as the word suggests, was thought to be caused by bad air until a British doctor in India, Sergeant Major Ronald Ross, demonstrated in 1898 that the malarial parasite was something actually passed on to humans by mosquito bites.

But diseases and epidemics were not controlled or eradicated in Europe by pure chance or by invocation to God. It was only because of knowledge gained in the physiological and biological sciences that progress became possible.

cholera and common sense

Sometimes, the advance was achieved by plain, ordinary reasoning. Take the case of cholera. Cholera had been known in India for centuries but no attempt had ever been made to understand the disease. It was in England that cholera first came to be understood, and that too in a novel and most interesting way.

In 1854, cholera broke out in the Soho district of London. Dr John Snow, a physician in Soho, placed a map of Soho before him and simply marked the streets/places where deaths were known to have occurred. This simple exercise pointed to a public pump on Broad Street as the likely source of infection. All Dr Snow did was to persuade the local authorities to take the handle off the pump, and within a few days, the epidemic had subsided!

However, there were still some deaths which fell outside this simple pattern. For example, a lady living in Hampstead, some five miles away from the area, had also died during the outbreak. It turned out that she had always liked the taste of the water from the Broad Street pump and used to send for it regularly. A man in Brighton, about 200 miles from London, had also died. In his case, it transpired that he had a brother living in Soho. The Brighton resident had received news of his brother's illness and decided to visit him, but his brother was dead by the time he arrived. Before returning to Brighton, this gentleman had had lunch in Soho with a shot of brandy mixed with water from the Broad Street pump.

Today, John Snow is known as the founder of the science of epidemiology. His evidence was instrumental in building for London one of the finest sewage systems of any city of its day, something, it is said, which is serving the city well up to the present time. Simple advances in knowledge of this kind brought about large investments in public infrastructure like water supply and sewage systems – facilities woefully lacking in many Indian cities even today. Notice, therefore, the different levels at which study, mapping and discovery of cholera took place. For us in India, on the other hand, it was easy to automatically attribute this and other diseases to curses handed out by God.

The actual organism that causes cholera remained undiscovered until 1883, and only as recently as 1960 was it discovered that the disease brought about death through dehydration of the system and consequent shock. When we eat, nutritive substances pass from the blood vessels to the tissues. But when cholera sets in, the process is reversed. Substances now pass from the tissues to the blood vessels in such uncontrollable quantities that extreme nausea results, with continuous vomiting, diarrhea and bowel movements. This causes dehydration and can result in death.

The case of plague is similar. For centuries, this had been a killer epidemic even in the West. By the early 17th century, people in Europe had begun to fear plague when they saw dead rats in the streets and in homes. Only much later, when the microbe was finally identified by the Pasteur Institute of France in 1894, did they learn that the cause was fleas infected from dead rats.(7) But even after Russian physician W.M.Haffkine actually developed anti-plague vaccine in Bombay in 1899, Lokmanya Tilak was sceptical of the Government's compulsory vaccination programme, objecting to quarantine measures for the population of cities in Maharashtra as an interference by the British rulers in the religious and domestic matters of their subjects! (8)

Charting a path and mapping out disease is one form of scientific inquiry. Our approach to the problems of public health, whether based on faith (automatic ascription to God) or following the ways of science, itself reflects the way culture moulds and conditions our minds. Therefore, however we consider our economic condition, whether we judge by economic parameters or by figures concerning health and disease, it does appear that India suffers from a fundamental illness. Later in this chapter, we quickly examine and then try and answer the ready explanations (and there are many) put forward for our condition.

how science works on society

How exactly does science work on society? It does so in two different ways:

first, by the application by individuals of reasoned, logical, rational thinking; and second, by the influence of technology on their habits, attitudes, values and behaviour. These two factors shape the minds of a country's people and determine their actions. In the absence of these factors, an entire country's thinking can become suspended in a general air of unreality, with increasing impediments to its material progress, finally resulting in social disorganization.

In developing countries like India, we may be surrounded by the outward trappings of science and technology but we fail to realize that science also constitutes a deep cultural influence on people. Like religion, science determines what we think and what we do.

Unfortunately, while the function of culture-determinant is readily accepted for religion, the role played by science is not so widely known. Science is generally thought of by the lay person as the appliances or the articles of science, not as a process or a method or as an approach to thinking. Exactly how science affects a person's thinking and his culture is often not acknowledged at all or is at best obscure.

Even in European countries, the special role of science was at first not recognized. Because of England's explosive growth in the seventeenth century and consequent chaotic conditions, there began a vigorous search for order. Various alternatives were considered: Science was one model. Latin – still the language of mathematics and theology – with its regular grammar, spelling conventions and systematic style was another. Again and again during the next hundred years or so, English writers would look back in vain to Latin for inspiration and authority. (9)

For India, science should indeed be considered as a model. We need to understand that logical, rigorous thinking based on reality helps us see things in proper perspective and helps us take the right steps in attempting to solve the problems of our country. We need to accept that blind faith, myths, ritual, tradition, superstition, old people's tales mislead us, act as barriers to correct action, make us turn too readily towards Providence and often end up compounding our problems instead of solving them.

For this initial chapter, our three examples are taken first, from health and medicine, next from the sphere of culture and lastly, from agriculture/industry. These examples are chosen at random and treatment for each is attempted on a separate, different plane. In showing how treatment can be applied, a brief description of existing systems is also given.

how irrationality impedes: the problem of blindness

Let's begin with the problem of blindness in India. As we have noted, there are nearly 12 million blind people in our country. In addition another 13 million or more suffer from visual impairment. In other words, we have more people affected by blindness in our country than the entire population of countries like Austria or Finland or New Zealand!

Aside from the fact that blindness is a shattering personal experience, it is time we realized the colossal loss in economic terms that this represents for our country. A reader of the Economic Times worked out in 1990, based on an average working life of 32 years and a 1989 per capita income of Rs.3760 per annum, that the loss of income for 9 million blind persons was of the order of Rs 3384 crores! Even if we considered half the blind population as overaged and beyond an effective working life, the annual loss came to Rs. 1692 crores! This was about two decades ago. Imagine what the current loss would amount to.

Many people in this country, educated and uneducated, continue to believe that blindness is an act of God and that there is little that man can do about it. I remember an interview on Bombay TV some years ago where a doctor lamented that newborn twins had recently been brought to him with cataract (or was it glaucoma?) in the eyes. The parents flatly refused an operation, saying that it was God's handiwork and should not be interfered with!

In Europe too, in the Middle Ages, they thought similarly. Many said to themselves: "Why have eyes been given to men if not to know the true shape, size and colour of objects in the external world? Were not mirrors, prisms and lenses devices for making visual lies?" Devout Christians wanted nothing to do with this trickery. (10)

In our country, we often hear the claim that some baba, rishi, sadhu or godman has within him the power of restoring eyesight to the blind. If anyone was truly to possess this rare ability, it would indeed be a boon for this unhappy country. The cruel reality is that in spite of a multitude of babas and other assorted spirits, we continue to have in India nearly one third of the world's blind.

Some few years ago, I happened to be visiting a well-known multinational pharmaceutical company in Mumbai. The receptionist, an educated young lady, was busy explaining to a colleague that a lady with occult powers who had taken up residence in the Shiva temple at Ambarnath, near Mumbai was able to cure blindness with mantras and invocations. The receptionist even carried with her an article from a vernacular newspaper which testified to this. (This holy lady was also later the subject of a write-up in India Today). I must have shown complete disbelief because she pressed me to explain. When she insisted, the following conversation ensued:

Do you agree that blindness is the opposite of vision? I asked her.

Yes, she replied.

You know that you need three things for vision, the eye, the object being seen and the medium, that is, waves or particles of light.

Yes, she agreed slowly.

Do you realize then that we are all partially blind for nearly half of each 24-hour day, that is, during the night because one of the items is missing? She said it hadn't occurred to her.

Do you remember black and white TV when it was first introduced in Mumbai? Now we have colour TV. Isn't it wonderful that we can see on TV, in real-life colour, within seconds, what is happening so far away when we cannot even see at this moment what is happening next door? She kept silent, so I went on: There has to be an explanation for how the eye sees and also for how it sees colour. A lot of work has been done on the physics and chemistry of sight and colour.

The choice was hers. I said to her: Either accept that your TV set is an illusion or accept reality. If you accept reality, then absolutely the first step to take was to prevent present people from going blind. The next step was to try and prevent more blind people from being born. The step after that was to try and roll back existing blindness. But none of this work could properly begin until we understood what blindness was and how it happened in the first place.

I absolutely did not want to be doing this or in any way talking down to this lady. But I was concerned about wanting her to see the contradictions involved. Did she agree with all that I had said? Was she converted? Not a bit of it. She couldn't dispute what I had said but she felt that it was up to each person to believe or not to believe. I cannot say that I was surprised at this reply. I even expect it. After all, one does not change the thinking of an entire lifetime because of a chance discussion with a total stranger. But it may have made her think.

the world of ritual

Our second example concerns ritual. What could be so wrong with ritual, beautiful ritual, some will say. This is exactly what makes India what it is. Surely it can do no serious harm? The intention is not to dispense with ritual. There is undoubtedly something beautiful and Indian about it. But as a nation we must quickly get to understand that it is nothing but ritual. This very necessary distinction is not made in India. Therefore, much ritual today is not only empty but actually harmful because it reveals clearly that we live in an artificial world – a hazy, lazy, involuntary, unthinking world.

A young, woman in Mumbai in her early thirties wakes up in the morning and proceeds to her terrace. She sees the sun rising in the east. She brings her hands together and does a devout namaskar. She waters a tulsi plant in the terrace and circumambulates it a number of times. She then takes a handful of grain and sets it out on the terrace and immediately a flock of crows and pigeons is attracted and begin feeding on the grain. With slight variations, this minuet could be multiplied thousands and thousands of times for men and women all over our country.

On the surface, these actions unquestionably have a beautiful and spiritual quality to them. But what is the reality? What do this woman's actions really portend? Her first action demonstrates that this innocent woman has no liking for ordinary star-gazing. (Why do I say this? Because I myself was no different -except that I didn't do the tulsi plant ritual.) To her, the sun is still something sacred. This is sun-worship in its simplest form. The trouble is that until she understands that the sun is only an average-sized star in a vast firmament peopled with billions of such stars, she will be unable to come to grips with modern science and therefore, as a direct consequence, will be unable to advance herself and thus her children, her family and the country. This is the terrible sequel, difficult though it might be to see it in her very innocent action.

How does this happen? Let's look at it in this way: If you know the basic facts about the stars, the chances are that, sooner or later, you will also become interested in geology and in the story of evolution. This tells you what the earth is, what its place in the universe is, what life is, what the consequence of death is and so on. Then the likelihood is that you will become interested in biology which includes botany (flowers, plants, shrubs, trees) and zoology (birds, animals and fishes). This is how connections take place. One piece of knowledge links up with and leads to another. The process of acquiring knowledge may appear to us to be chancy or fortuitous but actually it is not so. Or at least, we need not allow it to be so when there are definite ways, because of the existence of a whole variety of threads, of inter-connecting with other knowledge.(More on this later.)

If you don't take deliberate, purposeful steps in this direction or even if you decide to be neutral by continuing to practise ritual without questioning it in any way, say, because of blind faith or because your religion prescribes that it is to be so, you are positioning yourself against knowledge. Knowledge will be slow in coming to you and when it comes, it will be accidental or sketchy and perfunctory and will be unable easily to establish connection. When this happens to large masses of people, when an entire nation places itself in such a perilous position and when this state of affairs is allowed to continue year after year for centuries together, ignorance building upon ignorance, is it surprising that stagnation in thinking should set in?

We continue with our example. When our young woman waters the tulsi plant because it is supposed to be holy, she is really turning way from modern botany which claims that no special plant is capable of being holy or unholy. Botany says that it all depends on the circumstances, upon the usefulness or otherwise of the plant to man. In this scientific age, if one's approach to Nature is to be based on what one has been told by one's forbears or if we are to go only by what is enjoined by tradition or religion, then, to say the very least, one places oneself in an awkward and uncertain situation.

This lady's knowledge of plants is unlikely to throw up shoots leading to a passion for further understanding about other plants, other shrubs or other trees. If she were asked, for example, to give the names of the different trees in the very area in which she lives, she would probably find it difficult to oblige. In my opinion, the real reason why we, as a people, have not become truly interested in botany, become familiar with all the luxuriant flowers and trees of our beautiful, tropical country is that we have not yet grown up from our childhood world of tradition and ritual which includes in this case plants, holy and less-than-holy.

Similarly, when crows and pigeons flock to her terrace, these happen to be the very birds which constitute such a nuisance in large cities like Mumbai. It points to a lamentable lack of acquaintance with modern zoology. Once again, the sad fact is that unless we truly interest ourselves in this subject, we really cannot begin to benefit our millions of cows or buffalos or goats (all vital to India's economy) or get started on bird-watching or go on to ornithology or otherwise become deeply interested in the flora and fauna of our country. Empty ceremony and ritual is not a crime but it is symptomatic of a deeper, much more subtle malaise, one with important, even serious educational and economic consequences for our country.

Once again, do we blame this innocent woman for thinking as she does? Most decidedly not! This just happens to be the way in which her world-view has been formed. Everything is seen and determined from this one special prism only. Each one of us carries such an outlook shaped for us in many different ways from childhood all the way up to youth and adulthood: by our upbringing, the thinking and example of our parents, our religion, our peers, other cultural influences, our education, our job experience and so on. We acquire a set of values, beliefs, judgments, understandings, expectations that are peculiar to us, that are our very own cultural property and that we would not want changed – except if we ourselves were to decide that change was called for. Therefore, change must come from within and must take place only on our own terms. It is difficult for outsiders to force change. In our hurry to change things, we tend to overlook or ignore this important human reaction.

I again asked myself: Is this being really petty? Trying to examine the thought processes of this woman. Can it really count or is it immaterial? But these are urgent times. We have a long way to go and much ground to cover.

agriculture is industry!

Our final example, along slightly different lines, comes from the field of agriculture and industry. We are a predominantly agricultural country, with nearly 50 to 60% of our large population still dependent on agriculture. The practices which our farmers follow are very traditional, and their work does not yield anything more than a subsistence living. Because they are illiterate or uneducated, they cannot break out of the bonds of age-old custom and tradition. They do not seem to be able to develop the drive or the desire to acquire literacy. It's a vicious circle. Everything is accepted without questioning and with a sense of resignation. There is no great indignation at their economic condition. There is no hope of a better life. This contributes to a general culture of despair and despondency. It would not be unfair to say that as a group they are the among the largest repositories of blind faith, myths and superstition in the country. They are fatalistic in their beliefs. All is considered to be part of God's will. The only concession to modern times is that if God is unable to come to their rescue then there is at least the Government of the day, on which they therefore lean heavily. I am not arguing that Government should not assist. Since we know that they cannot help themselves and because we recognize how they have come to be this way, there is urgent need for Government action. The sad fact is, however, that these people have reached a stage where they are totally dependent and are incapable of lifting themselves out of poverty.

Logical, scientific thinking can point the way out and provide the means for the ending of poverty. The very first thing to understand is that world agriculture, which remained more or less unaltered for two thousand years has changed dramatically during the last few hundred years. You wish to study the soil? You have the science of soil mechanics. You need to understand and classify seeds? You are helped by the science of genetics. If you require irrigation, you need cement for canals, steel for pipes and electricity for pumps. Finally, you need modern means of transport to move agricultural and other produce quickly to markets. Agriculture, which for centuries together was different from industry (the Physiocrats in France in the 1750s claimed it was the true foundation of all growth), had itself become an industry. All this happened because of modern science and technology. (11)

Actually, rural India is itself already leaning towards industry. An article in the Economic Times (February 20, 2009) tells us that about a fifth of the non-farm rural workforce is employed in agricultural establishments while four-fifths work in non-agricultural establishments. A New Delhi think tank is quoted as saying: "Such a transformation –away from agriculture – is actually desirable for India as over 60% of India's population cannot live off just under a fifth (19%) of the country's GDP in agriculture."

Starting out this way, a total transformation of Indian agriculture itself could be aimed at. In India we have more and more farmer suicides and further farmers appealing to the President for permission to commit suicide, suggesting utter helplessness, while the Economist (August 28, 2010) reports that Brazil has revolutionized its farms in the last thirty years.

In the USA of the nineteenth century, about 50 percent of the population was engaged in agriculture. In the early decades of this century, 20 percent of the population was in agriculture. Today as little as about 1.65 percent are employed in agriculture. Thus, out of every one hundred persons, less than two are required to meet the entire food needs of the country. In addition, the US also exports in a large way to other parts of the world.

When California on the west coast of the United States was first settled by immigrants, they stayed away from the staple food crops of the rest of the country like wheat, rice, corn, and so on. Instead, they developed fruit crops. Within a few years, California had become the largest fruit-producing area in the whole world. These fruits included almonds, apricots, avocados, sweet cherries, dates, figs, grapes, grapefruit, kiwi, lemons, melons of 5 types, nectarines, oranges, peaches, pears, plums, pomegranates etc. Today California boasts of as many 214 different agricultural products including 35 field crops, 68 different types of fruit and 86 types of vegetables.(12)

None of this would have been possible without being helped, especially in the latter years, by the sciences of modern botany, modern zoology and modern geology. Today again, with the computer industry and the bio-technology industry to add to agriculture, California, with a population of 38 million people (about one third the size of Maharashtra), is the seventh largest economy in the whole world! Drive and creativity, supported by knowledge of modern science, takes the place of fatalism and passivity as in India.

Look at the possibilities in India itself. Mr. K.L.Chugh, Chairman, ITC Ltd., speaking at the annual general meeting in July 1993 said:

India has 60 million hectares under irrigation, compared to just 47 million in China, and yet our food grain production is only 180 million tonnes, whereas China produces two and half times as much. Nothing illustrates the divergence between promise and fulfillment than being the second largest producer of rice in the world, we are just 54th in yield; the second largest producer of wheat and 38th in yield; ranked no. 1 in groundnut production, we are 72 in yield; the second largest producer in rapeseed and 33rd in yield; the third largest in tobacco and 42nd in yield. In fruits and vegetables too, our position is as dismal. With a 7% share of world production in the former and an 11% share in the latter, we tragically process less than 1% of our total production commercially. In contrast Brazil processes 70% of its fruit and vegetable production, Malaysia 83% and Philippines 78%. (This was two decades ago but it will indicate to you what I mean.)

But again, this too is not going to be enough. We now need in addition better transportation, reliable cold chains, perhaps more contract farming arrangements and certainly reliable power availability in the rural areas – all will create jobs and all are available only through the agency of science.

Application of reasoned, scientific thinking by an entire nation is essential for a turnaround. The absence of such thinking, due to custom, ritual and tradition, all sentiments often disguised in the garb of religion, has led to a nation of frozen minds. And unless the minds in a nation are liberated and set free, nothing of importance will be achieved. This is why I have set out to show in some detail that one leg of our road to progress can be determined very simply by the manner in which we do our thinking.

From the Economist of March 13, 2010, here's a fresh look at Indian agriculture – and especially its possibilities for the future:

"Indian policymakers should see agriculture as a source of growth, not votes.

Indian agriculture can comfortably feed the country, but that remains the sum of its achievement. (India) freed industry first (but) has barely reformed agriculture... they regard a state warehouse bursting with grain as a sign of success, and imports of wheat as a mark of defeat. Politicians' outbursts against hoarding and speculators have stymied the development of storage facilities and commodity markets; concern to protect farmers from exploitative merchants has slowed the development of contract farming. India still fixes prices and subsidizes inputs when public money would be far better spent on infrastructure."

And now here are some of the general explanations commonly offered for our poor economic conditions :

too early to say?

There are those who say that the present poverty and backwardness are only the birth pangs of a nation. They argue that independent India is less than 75 years old and that in the life of nations, this is too short by any account. They consider any comparison with older nations as unfair. There is some merit in what they say. Our existence as an independent nation is only a small portion of the time we spent even as a colonized country. The progress made in 70 years is clearly impressive but these gains have been largely cancelled out by the more than quadrupling of the population and by the sheer complexity of the problems that have arisen since. The problems are more in number, the nature of the problems is different and more involved, the frequency is greater. Can we see our way out of this muddle? Most people would agree that we were off to a good start but that our progress, in many ways, has been slowed down after the first twenty or thirty years or so. The mid-course corrections which should have been made were never made until change was forced on us in 1991. In any case, it is difficult to convince supporters of the birth-pangs theory that we have not achieved enough –except to point out what could have been achieved instead and even what can be achieved from now on within whatever time is left to us.

measured growth, or are we faltering?

Others say that, as with growing children, one should not generalize. Nations, like individuals, grow differently, each at its own pace. The circumstances for each nation are different. It is not surprising that India, with its own special problems, should take longer than many developed countries and also longer than other developing countries which became independent at about the same time. The trouble with this line of reasoning is that one can be smugly satisfied with whatever the rate of progress might be. There is no room for criticism, no impatience to be shown, no targets to be set – until there is collapse of the whole, unreal, all-too-fragile structure and by then, of course, it is too late!

colonialism as culprit

To many people, the answer is simple. It is the 250 years of colonialism that reduced India to the rank of one of the poorest nations in the world. If not for the British, we, like them, would probably have muddled through and even if not one of the richer nations, would at least have made our presence felt and become much more prosperous than we are today. After all, they say, we do have in India several thousand years of unbroken civilization. All that the British really achieved by interposing themselves in our affairs was to interrupt our development, alienate us from our own way of life and make us uneasily, yet hopelessly, dependent upon a strange, foreign culture. We have fallen between two stools. There was serious drainage of wealth from India. Add to this the psychological effects of British rule in India and the result has been, as Mahatma Gandhi called it, an emasculation of the Indian people.

Colonialism undermined the very confidence of the Indian people in themselves. A greater calamity for the growth and development of any nation cannot be imagined.

Again, one cannot entirely reject this line of reasoning. Although British rule in India conferred many benefits on this country, there can be no question that we have had to pay a bitter price for them. Were the benefits brought by British rule outweighed by the extravagant cost we have had to bear? We cannot set out in detail here either the advantages or the disadvantages but if the backwardness of the country is to be attributed to colonialism alone, then should we not ask whether there were no signs of incipient backwardness to be seen before the coming of colonialism and also ask if none are to be seen today although more than 70 years have passed since independence?

If Indian culture and civilization was strong enough to have prospered on its own, should it not have been strong enough to withstand both the appearance and spread of British rule in India? It was clearly incapable of doing this.

It would appear that we were routed on our own home ground. Better to be critical with oneself than to readily attribute blame to others. If we really wish to learn from the experience of colonialism in our country, we must be honest and unsparing in our analysis of ourselves and consider carefully why colonialism became possible in the first place. At one time, around say 1914, over 84% of the world's land area was European-dominated. (13) So colonialism did include India but was not restricted to India, suggesting that a much larger explanation is called for.

the Hindu route, the Islamic state

If developed Western nations follow the Christian religion, why cannot we have a Hindu state in India? Then our split personality will be healed, our sense of identity restored and we can really begin our journey towards progress. Hindu because the majority of the people in this country (85%) are Hindus. However, this glosses over the fact that a substantial minority (15%) are either Muslims or Christians or belong to other religions. Apart from the fact that they are not likely to submit to Hindu dominance and Hindu institutions, it is not at all certain that the Hindu way of thinking in all matters is likely to solve our innumerable problems. There is already a Hindu state in existence; this is Nepal. Nepal is much worse off in economic terms than even India. As we have seen, its GDP per capita annually is only US $670 as against India's already low US $2200 per year.

Can Islam provide the answer? More and more states in West Asia and South and South East Asia would appear to think so. Forced by strong currents of fundamentalism, nation after nation wants to become an Islamic State. Pakistan, Bangladesh, Afghanistan and now Indonesia are only the most recent examples.

It is one of the purposes of this book to show that religion cannot provide the answer. Whether that religion be Hindu or Muslim or Sikh, it will be our endeavour to show that it is not possible to run a modern industrial state on the basis of the tenets of any religion. To want to do so is, to me, a clear contradiction in terms. Therefore, also, to attempt to rebuild developing nations on the basis of religion or some kind of fundamentalism, is a promise that cannot come true.

the luxury of religion

If it is our argument that modern industrial nations cannot be built on the basis of religion, how is that developed nations, nations like the USA, Britain, the Western European nations, Canada etc. have people who profess the Christian religion? The answer is that each of these nations was built on the basis of modern science and technology and not on the basis of religion. It couldn't have been otherwise. From the very beginning, religion did not, indeed could not, provide support; in fact, religion frequently obstructed their efforts at nation-building and had increasingly to be ignored or contested until such time that development had taken place, the nation-state had been installed, secularism had become the order of the day (in practice, if not always constitutionally) and religion again could be permitted, at least in free societies, to whoever chose among its peoples to follow religion. Religion was not banished as such. It wasn't possible or necessary to do that nor will it be necessary in our case. It just means that although religion existed side by side with efforts at development, its role got increasingly constrained and that of science and technology increasingly expanded until a point was reached, as at present in all these nations without exception, where leadership, direction and determination is provided by non-religious bodies, non-religious laws or by people in non-religious capacities and only spiritual advancement is sought from the clergy or the Church.

Difficult to believe? One small but telling example. Later, we will show how religion could not have provided the answers. The example is this: If, say, three to four hundred years ago, during for example, the time of the Renaissance, you would have said to anyone that he or she was being creative, you would actually have been guilty of blasphemy. Because, at that time, "creativity" was an attribute belonging only to God. (14) In the five hundred years before 1600 the words "heresy" and "blasphemy"struck terror into the European soul. (15) Creativity could not be said to have belonged to man. The idea of creating something new, something undiscovered—innovation, as we know the term today—itself did not exist. Knowledge consisted solely of a capturing of the old and what had already been experienced before. (16) There was no such thing as new knowledge. This is the extent to which science and technology has changed society.

from liability to asset?

Perhaps the biggest single obstacle for most Indians in accepting the seriousness of their condition is the fact of India's large population. This is the readiest explanation, the one most easy to fall back upon. As we know, the population has more than quadrupled since we gained independence. We now have to provide for much larger numbers. From this position, there's almost a rush to explain that all the progress we have made has been cancelled out by the larger population.

While undoubtedly true, this fact cannot and should not be used as the ultimate argument to show up the futility of progress. After all, the increase could have been foreseen and could have been provided for. It is somewhat like the anti-aircraft gunner explaining that the reason he missed the plane was that his target was moving. In any case, it is impossible to go back to the earlier magnitude of figures. India's quadrupling of numbers is a factor that must seriously be taken into account. It does not benefit us now to explain away India's numerous problems by saying that these are due to the increase in population. If our goals had been clearer and our methods better, we might have slowed down the rate of increase and comfortably provided for the increase.

It is often pointed out that India is not poor because it has a large population but that it has a large population precisely because it is poor. It is the experience of most countries that economic growth brings about population stability and later, population decline. Economic growth brings with it lesser infant mortality but it also leads to better educational standards for parents and to increased standards of living. Parents quickly realize that children represent not just assets but also economic responsibility and they tend to have fewer and well-spaced children.

We have about 65% female literacy in India. This means that practically 1 out of every 3 women cannot even read and write. How then are we to get the family planning message across to them? Without literacy or education how is the woman in our society ever going to acquire the right to space her births?

Consider the case of other large countries like the USA or the erstwhile USSR. They are each roughly one-fourth of our population. By the weight of numbers argument, they should then be about one fourth as poor (in other words, four times as well off) as we are but as we all know, this is definitely not the case. If India's GDP per capita is US$ 2020 per year, the USA should be, say, US 8080 per capita per year. Instead, the USA is about thirty two times richer than we are, the GDP per capita being about US $62850. Exact figures for the USSR are not available but even before its recent break-up, no one would have classified it as a developing country.

Conversely, there are many small countries such as Mozambique or Ethiopia or Tanzania which are poorer than even we are and the nature of their problems is no different from ours. Three such poor countries, countries much smaller in population than India's, namely, Nepal, Bangladesh and Afghanistan, are our very neighbours. So it would appear to be incorrect to say that India is poor only because it has a large population.

Remember that it is also possible to consider our large population as our biggest capital resource. Imagine 1400 million pairs of hands! What can we not do for ourselves if all this energy is mobilized, organized, energized and directed into proper productive channels?

If we have a true understanding of the nature of our problems, determine our priorities properly and correctly decide on the way of going about our objectives, our large population need not be a hindrance and can, in fact, become an enormous, gigantic asset. When we speak continuously of the scarcity of energy resources all the world over and are prepared to harness wind power, solar energy, fuel cells, sea currents and what not, we should ask ourselves whether it is possible to find anywhere a better storehouse of potential energy than 1400 million properly motivated human beings!

is corruption the villain?

Given the conditions of scarcity in India, it is hardly surprising that corruption as a way of life has spread so fast and so deeply. It is no different from other developing countries.

Yet it is astonishing how many Indians consider that corruption in public life is the chief reason for our lack of progress. Corruption would include corruption in Government offices and services, corruption in political life and among politicians individually and a general lowering of standards everywhere. There is no effort to understand that if a public servant is corrupt, it also means that the citizen is prepared to give him what he demands. While this may sometimes be unavoidable because the situation is urgent or because there isn't any other way, there is too often a readiness on the part of citizens to take the line of least resistance, to become, perhaps too easily, a willing party to such corruption. It's a vicious circle. The citizen blames the Government and Government blames the citizen. As corruption increases, it pervades more and more spheres of life. As an individual might get addicted to drugs, so a country quickly gets addicted to corruption and soon it becomes difficult, if not impossible, to lead a life free of corruption. Indeed to claim that such a life is even possible in India at present is to immediately invite ridicule.

Moreover, there is no real attempt to understand that corruption is only a symptom, it is not the cause of the illness. Corruption has become a handy explanation for all that is wrong with India. It obscures the fact that there may be something else which is responsible for India's malady and that, unless this fact is faced and the necessary treatment administered, corruption and a hundred other evils will flourish and cannot be eliminated. In fact, they must be fully anticipated although, of course, they cannot be excused. Later in the book (see Chap.7) we go into short-term and long-term paths to be taken to build a stronger people, a stronger polity – the only enduring way of eliminating corruption.

multiplier defect!

Another popular but facile explanation for our inability to make more speedy progress is that, unlike the homogenous Japanese for example, we Indians cannot pull together. Like the proverbial amoeba, we are constantly dividing into two and presumably each of those two into a further two and so on. Political parties are constantly splitting off into smaller parties, groups are unable to see eye-to-eye with each other, there is an underlying powerful divisive force at work. At one time it was feared that at the rate at which the Congress party was using up the alphabet for smaller, splintered groups, all the letters might be taken up and an additional alphabet have to be requisitioned!

This argument too is unacceptable. In a democratic society, there is bound to be a whole variety of viewpoints. This does not mean that large masses of the people cannot be brought together to work towards a common goal or that people cannot be motivated to see that there is possibly something missing in their society, that impalpable something needing to be identified and then requiring to be put right. Mahatma Gandhi worked single-handedly to bring about a mass movement in India at a time when few people credited him with any chance of success against a mighty empire. With already so much under our belt since independence, our task now in recognizing India's ills and then working to eliminate them is certainly not more difficult of achievement.

the opiate of religion

From luxury of religion to the opiate of religion. How is it possible, some people ask, to bring about change in India since the people are so totally steeped in religion? The feelings of the people 6must be taken into account. Now, there cannot be any objection to a process of slow change if an unlimited amount of time were at our disposal. But is this the case? Other nations are streaking forward. Many nations in South East Asia and many in West Asia (even if it is because of dollar earnings from petroleum technology) are progressing rapidly. China has made spectacular progress. Can India afford to be left behind? If we do not awaken from our centuries-old slumber, India, together with possibly some nations in Africa and Latin America may be the only countries left in the developing world. Then again, will a further long spell of religion solve or even ameliorate our existing problems?

So the process of change must be begun. It happens that there is one thing which is more precious to any individual than even his own religion. It is himself! If the vast masses of India can be persuaded that all their needs, urgent and distant, can only be met by modern science and technology and not by religion, then overwhelming support for change will surely be forthcoming. If food, clothing, housing, education and medicine is truly to reach all our people, then the sooner we recognize the limitations of religion in this regard, the better it will be for us as a nation.

Some claim that Indians are just naturally inclined towards non-materialism, spiritualism, mysticism etc. They will spurn any effort which aims to weaken these cultural traits and will be unlikely to support any move that calls for a different route to be taken. Our reply should be that spiritualism can only prosper when the stomach is full. A hungry man has no appetite for mysticism or non-materialism. Both Swami Vivekanand and Mahatma Gandhi repeatedly acknowledged this. When the basic needs of millions of our countrymen are not even met today, it is, in my opinion, wholly wrong to proceed solely along the path of an empty spiritualism. If the choice is put to the people of India in the clearest possible terms, there is no doubt what their decision will be.

problems of wealth, problems of poverty

If there is so much that is " wrong" with India, why is it that thousands of Europeans, Americans and others from the developed world come to India in search of an alternative way? Those who advance this argument conveniently ignore the fact that for every foreigner who wishes to visit India, there are probably 10, 100 or even 1000 Indians who wish to permanently emigrate overseas! The long lines at overseas consulates is testimony to this fact. Let's admit it. Indians vie with each other and with people from other developing nations to qualify for the ever-shrinking immigration quotas of developed countries. Thousands more attempt to go illegally.

In How the West grew Rich, Nathan Rosenberg and L.E. Birdzell, Jr explain that just as there are problems of poverty, so also there are problems of wealth.(17) No society is perfect. Western societies, which have developed on the basis of science and technology, have undoubtedly generated problems which are characteristic of those societies. When there is an abundance of material goods, it is not surprising that the mind should crave for non-material pursuits. This is the explanation for the few who come in search of spiritual India. However, if it comes to a choice between problems of wealth and problems of poverty, can there be any doubt about what a Western society would choose? Can there be doubt about what we in India would or should choose? After all, when you have problems of wealth, you always have the option of renouncing all or part of your wealth but do you have an option when you are faced with the terrible problem of poverty?

Is it the climate?

It's the climate, some people say. If India was not a tropical country and had a colder climate, we would have had to bestir ourselves instead of being the lazy, indolent people we are today. This too is not a valid argument. Large parts of the USA or Australia or even countries in Southeast Asia with hot and humid climates like ours have proceeded in stately fashion to make themselves independent of the climate. In the USA, when climate got in the way, they invented air-conditioning! And what about Afghanistan and Kashmir, which are cold for a large part of the year and still sunk in poverty? What about Iran and China which can be bitterly cold during winter but hardly qualify as developed countries?

past glories

One way of avoiding the problems of today is to dwell on the greatness of the past. For example, among many other such claims, we are reputed to have developed the airplane long before the rest of the world. What was Pushpak but another airplane, it is said. It is difficult to argue with this type of thinking but I recently was able to essay a different kind of reply.

In the Time-Life book Flight, there is a picture showing a drawing from Joseph Needham's monumental Science and Technology in China. The picture is that of a flying machine with possibly a propeller and later even screw bladed rotors belonging to the period around 1500 BC. Indian enthusiasts then need to be asked whether credit should now also be given to the Chinese for having invented the airplane.

Or would it be more accurate to conclude that the Chinese, like us Indians, by seeing the flight of birds, were visualizing how man could fly and wishing that man could be transported in the same way? Was this not rather different from the science of aerodynamics which makes possible the jumbo-jet travel of today? Would not a multitude of sciences have to be developed in order to make flight possible as a reality? It is highly unlikely that the airplane could have been developed by China or by India without some trace of the attendant sciences remaining to this day.

the central question

To my mind, the central question for us, therefore, must surely be: Why indeed is India one of the poorest countries in the world? So infrequently have I heard this question seriously asked in our country that it does not surprise me that we should never really have looked for a satisfactory answer. Instead, what do we find? We begin by acknowledging that our country is one of the poorest in the world...but at the very next moment, our natural pride and love of country takes over and we delude ourselves into offering all manner of reasons for our condition. Statement made, explanation given! This has now become such a reflex action that it does not occur to us to really ponder why, historically, India should have become a poor nation in the first place!

Chapter 2

WHAT WENT WRONG? HOW INDIA, CHINA AND THE ARAB MUSLIM CIVILIZATION MISSED OUT ON THE SCIENTIFIC REVOLUTION / a diagnosis

Though the Revolution's name is singular, the event was plural. Its core was a transformation of mathematical astronomy, but it embraced conceptual changes in cosmology, physics, philosophy, and religion as well. – Thomas S. Kuhn, The Copernican Revolution

Those men who created the upheaval which we now call the ' Scientific Revolution " called it by a quite different name : the 'New Philosophy'. The revolution in technology which their discoveries triggered off was an unexpected by-product; their aim was not the conquest of Nature, but the understanding of Nature. Yet their cosmic quest destroyed the medieval vision of an immutable social order in a walled-in universe together with its fixed hierarchy of moral values, and transformed the European landscape, society, culture, habits, and general outlook, as thoroughly as if a new species had arisen on this planet." – Arthur Koestler, The Sleepwalkers

The most unparalleled anger which has ever existed since the creation of heaven and earth is exciting all who are conscious in their minds and have spirit in their blood : their hats are raised by their hair standing on end. This is because the largest country on the globe today, with a vast area of ten thousand li, is yet controlled by small barbarians .... Why are they small and yet strong ? Why are we large and yet weak ? Kuen-Fen quoted in Carlo Cipolla, Guns Sails & Empires

---

• what causes poverty? • the newness of prosperity • the turning point • two Revolutions, scientific • ...and technological • forging the tools of science • the case of Japan • what about India? • colonialism, help or hindrance? • the unseen forces of science and technology • secondary imperialism • the mechanization of warfare • technology's influence on culture • science, old and new • why China and India missed out • was India backward or Europe forward? • perceptual before cultural, economic or political • failure of nerve

what causes poverty?

I set myself this question: Why is it that India is one of the poorest countries in the world? To my great surprise, I found that poverty is not something new at all. I discovered that poverty has been with man from the very beginnings of man. To a greater or lesser degree, it has existed in every single country and culture in the world. Indeed, as we shall see, it could not have been otherwise.

Since we are reaching back into the distant past, there are only scanty records. According to Samuel Bernstein (who quotes Angus Maddison), for the period from 1-1500 AD, the GDP per capita for different countries not only was extremely low but continued in that way, unchanged, for centuries together. How could it be otherwise? We began as hunter-gatherers, then went on to practise agriculture, and only later arrived at industrialization (India still remains 50% agricultural by employment). The Industrial Revolution began around 1760 but its fruits did not begin to be enjoyed – and show up in Britain's GDP – until around 1820. (1)

What could be the explanation? This further question started up for me a search, a quest, a voyage of discovery, setting off an entirely new trajectory in my thinking. Always exposed to the sight of degrading poverty in India, I had previously never given thought to what we might call the etiology (causes and origins) of poverty. Perhaps my brief experience of life in England had now made me conscious of the enormous difference between developed and developing countries. My mind began to race as I realized that, contrary to what I had earlier assumed, the rich, developed countries we see in Europe and North America today had not always been that way.

the newness of prosperity

If poverty had always been around, was there anything new, I next asked myself. Yes, indeed, there was something new. This new something was prosperity! Prosperity has been with man for only three to four hundred years. This realization also came as a total surprise and, I must confess, as a particularly agreeable surprise! I still was not clear as to how poverty had been transmuted into prosperity but suddenly the dream seemed realizable. (2)

I found that poverty affected all mankind but only a few countries first broke free from it. In other words, one could also properly say that countries like India and China were not backward, they were still continuing at their own customary pace—it was Europe which had shot forward! And with this realization, do you know what happens? - the solution to a centuries-old problem practically falls into your lap!

the turning point

I searched for some event or events three to four hundred years ago which could have been responsible for bringing about this momentous change, unquestionably, still thinking to myself, one of the important turning points in the history of man. And this was when I first stumbled onto modern science and technology! Earlier, I had always assumed the poverty or comparative poverty of man. Poverty was man's fate, decreed by an unmoved, unconcerned God. Now, suddenly, we were breaking away from poverty and, helped by powerful, new, invisible forces were about to experience a life which would make us far more comfortable than before, at least in a material kind of way. We did not seem condemned to a life of poverty or penury any longer, a feeling or belief which generation upon generation in years gone by had accepted without demur.

We are well accustomed to this in India. The Planning Commission still regularly puts out figures establishing the poverty line in India. There is a culture of despondency or despair (at least before the earlier liberalization but still in existence in many parts of the country) which made it seem unlikely to most people that we could ever lift ourselves up from poverty. It happens that there is an explanation for even this feeling. It also existed earlier in Europe and America and every other part of the world—the feeling is characteristic of all agricultural society. When man was in the hunter-gatherer stage, there were no boundaries to speak of and food and supplies were to be had for the asking. However, when "formal" agriculture began to be practiced, land became the restricting factor and gradually a feeling of limitation set in. Populations kept increasing but land availability was fixed. Only when the Industrial Revolution got going and humans were freed from total dependence on agriculture did this feeling of shortage and scarcity begin to change.(3) In today's knowledge-based society, we have actually come full circle and now people in developed countries have begun to feel that anything, or almost anything, is achievable.

It is difficult for us to imagine it but even the present-day idea of comfort—that is to say relaxation, ease, bodily pleasure—did not exist in earlier times. Change in the meaning of ordinary words can sometimes tell us a great deal about what happens with the passage of time. The English word comfort originally meant something like what we call insurance today, as for example in the sentence: "He is a comfort to his mother in her old age ." (4) Our notion of comfort in the sense of contentment and relaxation developed much later.

Change of this kind in people's thinking as regards poverty does not happen overnight. When it happened in Europe, it probably wasn't even apparent that an important turning point had been reached. As soon as the initial implications became clear, there arose a great deal of opposition to the very idea that man should try to climb out of poverty. Some said flatly that man would be unable to divorce himself from poverty. Others said (and they say it to this day) that prosperity was sinful and that man was born with and should develop the frugal, abstinent, monkish qualities which he had always (supposedly) held so dear.

The Renaissance scholar Petrarch had said that man should not spend time on the vain search for knowledge about "mere things" but should concentrate instead on the investigation of the nature of man himself, considered at that time a far more consequential and weighty matter. (5) Practical inventions in those days were scorned as vile, low, mercenary, and unworthy of (even) being recorded in antiquity. It was thought that "only the tongue was inspired by the Gods, never the hand."(6)

It is one of the great ironies of history that this grudging, reluctant study of mere things should eventually have led to the birth of the giant establishment of modern science and technology and that the resultant superstructure should, in turn, as we shall show, have affected the study of man himself in a most profound way.

This was the climate of opinion which attended the birth of the Scientific Revolution in Europe some three to four hundred years ago. It brought about enormous change in man's understanding of his world. It resulted in a sudden and unprecedented enlargement of his mental and intellectual horizons. There was a true expansion of minds. Nothing like it had happened before. The odds against such a thing happening were also considerable. For centuries, man had been solely dependent on God or Providence. There was no possibility, no desire, even no thought of breaking away.

J.H. Plumb says :

" ...the iron dogmas of theology limited speculation, inhibited change and preference (was given) to argument over observation" .(7)

Man's view of his own condition had become so despairing that inevitably some kind of alternative way had to spring up. The old ways had to give way and something new had to come in its place.

two revolutions: scientific...

A clear distinction needs to be made between the Scientific Revolution and the Industrial Revolution that followed it. Writers Bronowski and Mazlish describe the difference: "the Scientific Revolution between 1500 and 1700 was in the first place an intellectual revolution: it brought men to think differently. Only later was this thought put to a practical use in the Industrial Revolution about 1800." (8)

The word revolution, although nowadays used to describe mostly political happenings, had astronomical beginnings. Revolution means turning or rotation of course, and in its astronomical use it did mean repetitive change at stated intervals but when the word evolved into political usage, it came to involve the opposite meaning namely, irregularity, unpredictability, uniqueness.(9)

After Copernicus in 1543 wrote The Revolution of the Heavenly Bodies, changing man's view of his universe from a geocentric (Earth-centered) one to a heliocentric (Sun-centered) one, the world was never again to be the same. Earlier, man had instinctively regarded himself as the centre of the universe (man divine) while at the same time, rather paradoxically, considering himself wholly dependent on God. Now, the possibility had arisen that the centre of his universe was not Earth at all but was instead the Sun. Man and Earth were to be promptly dislodged from their self-appointed central place in the universe but simultaneously (and again paradoxically), man also became more self-reliant and less dependent on an unseen Providence. How should this have happened? The American writer, Kirkpatrick Sale observes that:

" Far from reducing humans and their earth to an insignificant role in a sun-dominated solar system, [this revolution] rather convinced the 16th century European of the quite wonderful brilliance of the human mind and the beauty of its rationalism...the new astronomy that seemed to reduce man to nothingness (as Egon Friedell points out) made him, in reality, the unveiler, the seer and even the legislator of the cosmos." (10)

...and technological

Now for the technological revolution. How was technology born to science? The notion that man was not necessarily the be-all and end-all of creation was slowly joined with the realisation that he would increasingly have to bestir himself if he was to continue to survive. This ending of passivity or inertia helped along innovative inventions in a whole variety of fields. Of course innovations had existed throughout human history (think of the wheel!), such as those implemented by the stonecutters and masons of the 11th and 12th century in European cathedrals; canals and lift locks; spring-driven clocks and watches; advances in metallurgical engineering; and inventions like the wheelbarrow, the stirrup and the horse collar. But there was to be a significant change from the 16th century onwards. What was this change?

Arnold Pacey (of the Massachusetts Institute of Technology) believes this "change was connected with the intellectual ideals which influenced engineering when mathematical methods were sometimes applied to practical problems for entirely idealistic reasons, because people were excited by the rationalism of mathematics and believed in it as a key to understanding nature. At first, no practical advantage was gained...but the long-term outcome could hardly have been greater because the enthusiasm for using mathematics in a practical context eventually helped to create the basic discipline of modern technology ."(11)

Earlier, the word technology does not appear to have existed. Technology, as we know it today, went by the name of the practical arts or the mechanical arts. It was only in the middle of the 19th century that the word acquired its modern meaning. But in what way was all this different from the work of the time-honoured craftsman? Pacey explains :

"In contrast to the craftsman, the practitioner of a fully-developed technology does all his design work on paper and uses scientific data to calculate the performance of his constructions before they are built.... Like the craftsman, the technologist will have some intuitive insight into his work, derived from experience. But he will usually want to rationalise his insights in scientific language and check them by calculation. The great strength of the technologist's discipline as compared with the craftsman's is that it allows him to design things by drawing and calculation which fall outside the range of previous experience".(12)

forging the tools of science

As the theory of science gained ground and more and more observations of Nature continued to be made, the technology that developed from this progress began to be put to use for the benefit of man. Before the Scientific Revolution (and as we noted earlier), Pacey points out that there were inventions like the flying buttress, the development of the vault in architecture, improvements in water-supply devices, the first weight-driven clocks, the spinning wheel, the silk-reeling machine, improvements in sheep-farming and in mining and so on. (13)

But it was the coming of the twin revolutions, the Scientific Revolution and, consequent upon it, the Industrial Revolution that gave Europe, the place where it first happened, the technical means to liberate itself from the shackles of poverty. These events influenced the mind of European man and provided him with the tools with which to bring about improvement in his material conditions.

Advances in fields such as cartography, ship-building, navigation, and the making of compasses and other instruments now enabled small countries like Portugal and Spain to venture out to the East as well as to the New World.

Speaking about just one of these inventions, this one of early Chinese parentage, Kirkpatrick Sale says :

"It is hard to overestimate the role of the magnetic compass in Europe's technological conquest of the ocean. There were other important navigational instruments—the astrolabe, the cross-staff, the quadrant—but none had the ease and accuracy of the compass, none was so useful on lengthy voyages out of sight of land. It was a borrowed invention, not native—the Chinese had the compass already in the twelfth century and it probably made its way to Europe across the Indian Ocean reaching Italy in the late fourteenth—but like many other borrowings, it was put to particularly good use by a culture just then beginning its restless searches for salvation beyond its shores. In fact, along with other improvements in navigation and ship design in the fifteenth century, it became the centre-piece of a technological superiority that finally enabled the subcontinent of Europe to develop a seafaring power far beyond what its size or population would suggest. Combined with the concerted development of armaments and their installation on shipboard from the middle of the fifteenth century, the compass gave Europe the ability to dominate all the oceans of the world for the next four centuries".(14)

Around the time of the Renaissance, all these separate currents of improvement came together to form a veritable tidal wave and enabled Italy, with scientists such as Galileo Galilei (1564-1642), ultimately to come to the fore. Galileo did not invent the telescope; it was invented in 1608 as a toy in Middleburg in the Netherlands.

Galileo got to know of it, made some minor improvements to it, then trained it at first on ships at sea and later, on the moon and on the planets, Venus and Mars. In Siderius Nuncius (The Starry Messenger), he explained, writing in Latin (not used by many outside the Church or universities), that he saw blemishes on the moon, believed until then to be a perfect, astronomical, heavenly body. Later, Galileo wrote in Italian rather than in Latin and, in doing so, took science to "the people" in a language they could understand. Although he himself was finally to capitulate to the pressure from the religious authorities, science had broken out of its confines and was not to be held back any more.

With advances in mining, in the working of metals, in printing, and in the science of genetics, among other areas, the scene of action moved to Northern Europe and from there to Britain where Isaac Newton (1642-1727) standing, as he said, on the shoulders of giants who came before him, laid the essential mathematical and technical foundation for the Industrial Revolution. Over the next hundred and fifty years Britain went on to become "the workshop of the world", creating an empire which was to last until our own day.

The path from Copernicus to Tycho Brahe (Denmark) to Johannes Kepler (Germany) to Galileo to Newton, therefore, marked the triumphant march in Europe of sciences like astronomy and physics as well as disciplines like chemistry, metallurgy, geology, zoology, botany, physiology and medicine. In 1590 came the microscope; in 1608 the telescope; in 1656 the pendulum clock; in 1712 the steam engine; in 1769 the water frame spinning machine; in 1782 the steamboat; in 1792, (in the US) the cotton gin*; in 1821 the electric motor, in 1827 photography, in 1828 the steam locomotive, in 1837 the telegraph and so on, all in quick succession, each invention treading on the heels of the one before, all based on the principles and logic of modern science. These advances changed the life and the very outlook on life of people in Britain, Italy, France , Germany and the rest of Northern and Western Europe. It was these people who emigrated west to the United States and Canada and east to Australia and New Zealand and it is these countries, therefore, which together with Europe itself, constitute today the chief units of the developed world.

*(In their book, Cathedral, Forge and Waterwheel, Technology and Invention in the Middle Ages", Frances and Joseph Gies say: "Italian craftsmen ginned their cotton with the Indian churkha, acquired from the Arabs, a device not improved upon until Eli Whitney's invention.")

the case of Japan

At this point in our presentation, you may well ask: Does not Japan fall outside of this pattern and is it not, therefore, an exception to our general principle? The answer must be an emphatic no. In fact, Japan is a resounding confirmation of our argument. My excellent but inexpensive digital wrist watch happens to be made in Japan. Among many other things, it splits the second into one hundred parts; my Japanese camera, of course, can split it into two thousand parts! There is nothing Shinto or Buddhist or Tao or Confucian about it. We have to admit that it is one hundred per cent Western science and technology as also is the case with Japanese TV sets, camcorders, radios, VCRs, chips and motor cars.

Some might claim that the basic elements may have come from Western science but that Japan ran with it and expanded on it. Yes but take also another example, the transistor. This was clearly invented by William Shockley in our own times in the USA but imported and made hugely successful by Japan. So embellishment is always welcome but the initial idea has to carry more importance.

Besides, he essential concept of the clock or the watch itself arose in the Western world because "modern science depended on the idea of mathematically measurable sequences and was hampered by the lack of accurate mechanisms for measuring small amounts of time". (15)

In the United States, the industries that modernized first, moving to assembly-line production by the 1820s, were those that produced rifles, clocks and textiles, all consumer products in early 19th century America. (16)

This was long before Japan even got interested in Western science and Western technology.

However, in another sense, Japan is indeed a notable exception. Ahead of and alone among all other countries in the world, Japan acknowledged that the United States, Britain and continental Europe possessed something which it itself seriously lacked. That something was modern science and technology. Approximately 150 years ago, after bitter internal arguments and even battles (including assassination) for and against the culture of the West, Japan decided to take the plunge. Within fifteen to twenty years of the Meiji Restoration in 1868, the country gave itself a new navy, a new army, a new constitution, universal education, land reform, equality of opportunity, new opportunities for industry, for banking and so on. Much of the credit for advancing this view (so far ahead of that of the rest of the developing world) must go to a handful of individuals from the province of Chosho in Japan who, at great personal sacrifice showed how it was necessary to borrow from the West to secure progress.(17)

In a different part of the country, apparently independently, writer, teacher, and progressive thinker Yukichi Fukuzawa (1834-1901) had come to the same conclusion. He is today considered to be the educator of modern Japan. In his autobiography, Fukuzawa describes vividly how he noticed serious flaws in Japanese society and culture that were weakening his nation and how he felt that the answer had to be Western science and a sense of independence (independence in the sense of a movement away from Japanese thought and tradition up to that time).(18)

From about 1900 onwards, large sections of Western industry were transported wholesale to Japan (textiles, chemicals, plastics, electrical power, iron and steel, and so on). (19) This was how Japan developed and it was for these reasons that Japan was able to inflict a crippling defeat on a white power, Russia, at sea at Tsushima, during the early part of the century(1905). It is a grave error to attribute, as many do in our country, Japan's sensational postwar recovery and success to developments dating only from the end of the Second World War. Japan's efforts to become a modern nation with a Western-style economy began long before the War. Were this not the case, Japan, which is only about the size of California, would never have been able to prepare for and then give successful battle for four long years to the full might of both the British Empire and the USA.

what about India?

But what about India? The sad truth is that India missed out on this entire process. While developed countries began to change around four hundred years ago, India remained rooted in its old ways. This is the reason for India's poverty today. Make no mistake about it. For the first half of this four hundred-year period, no one could have been clear, perhaps not even the Europeans themselves, what exactly was going on but from roughly 1850 onwards and in order to save itself from being humiliated like China by the Western nations, Japan went out of its way to secure the benefits and the protection afforded by Western science and technology. We in India, surrounded as we were by what was to become the most powerful and most important Western nation of all, were unable to figure out the reasons for our condition and therefore, utterly unable to secure for ourselves the appropriate treatment for it. The British were swirling all around us. The reasons for our vanquishment stared us in the face but we were unable to see!

It is true that resources, people etc can be controlled and limited in many ways by a powerful, imperialist force but it appears that even the idea had not suggested itself to us. Else, why would we not have begun to work on it after independence had been realized (1947)? Or even now? It seems to me that we still remain befuddled and that the idea is still not clear to us.

China appears to have been no different. In its desperate efforts early in the 20th century, to discover a way to modernity, China actually even thought Beethoven might be the answer! Although undoubtedly strange at first to Chinese ears, Beethoven became (and remains today) an icon to music lovers in that country (20). But Beethoven can hardly be taken as an introduction to the enormous culture which the giant edifice of modern science and technology brings with it. Actually, the answer to Chinese prayers lay right next door to them. When Deng Xiaoping visited Japan in a highly successful visit as recently as 1978, it was apparently the first time an eminent Chinese leader had visited Japan in the 2200 years of contact with that country! In other words, they were looking all over the world but the answer lay close to their own backyard! (21)

colonialism: help or hindrance?

As noted earlier, you have probably heard the argument that colonialism was responsible. It is claimed that had it not been for British rule in India, this country too would have experienced a scientific and industrial revolution. But this is far from certain. Ideas are like free, soaring birds and cannot be imprisoned by colonialists.

The idea that there were new, powerful forces on the horizon capable of re-making nations was not sufficiently understood either in India or in China.

Also, there are examples of countries which did not fall victim to colonialism and they, like us, are still developing. Thailand is one such example. Nepal, Afghanistan, Iran, large parts of China are others. Did colonialism confer any advantages? Perhaps the greatest advantage was that we had commerce and industry (incorporating science and technology) brought to us (or thrust upon us for the benefit of the colonialists themselves) but we nevertheless remained unable to grasp the true lessons that these should have held for us. These cultural lessons (because they are, essentially, cultural lessons), we will try and enumerate in the chapters that follow. Then also, there remains the question that if our ancient civilisation was strong, as we have discussed, why were we not able to withstand colonialism in the first place? In The Unbound Prometheus, David S. Landes, professor emeritus of history and economics at Harvard University, writes:

"In all instances indeed, the failure of the colonial society to stand up to European aggression was in itself testimony to severe internal weakness5888888888888888. Karl Marx saw it very well in the case of India: A country not only divided between Mohammedan and Hindoo, but between tribe and tribe, between caste and caste; a society whose framework was based on a sort of equilibrium, resulting from a general repulsion and constitutional exclusiveness between all its members. Such a country and such a society, were they not the predestined prey of conquest?...India, then, could not escape the fate of being conquered, and the whole of her past history, if it be anything, is the history of the successive conquests she has undergone."

Marx's article about a divided India appeared in the New York Daily Tribune of August 8, 1853; that is, four years before the Indian Mutiny!

In my view, there is but one true explanation. It is a simple explanation but it is supported by evidence in almost any direction you look. We lost and the colonisers won because they had modern science and technology on their side and we did not. We lost although they fought us, with much smaller numbers, in our own country, some seven or eight thousand miles away from home, a distance that meant a great deal more in those days than it does today.

It may be that the British came as traders and stayed on as conquerors but the fact remains that they came to India just as before them, the Portugese, the Danes, the Dutch and the French also came to India. For me it is a minor irrelevancy that they should have come as traders. Of course there was great drain of wealth from India but the reality is that either by themselves or in league with other Indians who collaborated with them, they subdued India. Given the tremendous forces of science and technology which they had working for them, it would have been surprising if, having come, they had not conquered India and established effective rule over the country. Exactly the same thing happened when the Dutch captured Indonesia, the French North Africa and Vietnam, the Belgians took over Congo, the Portugese took over Angola, Mozambique and Brazil (not to mention Goa, which they made the capital of their eastern empire) and the Spaniards captured central America and other large parts of South America (not to mention the Phillipines, from whose king, Philip II, the country even got its name.)

So this was not a singular but a collective " illness". That alone should make us less emotional and more objective in considering the matter.

Also the fact that all the colonizers were Western countries and all the colonized were Asian, African or Latin should have made us at least sit up and wonder.

In the Introduction, we pointed to the difference between left behind in modern science and technology and left behind after. This is more than a mere cosmetic difference. Of the former statement, there can hardly be any doubt. Not many people would object to it. In fact, that is, according to me, the definition of a developing country. However, I also say left behind after because we need to realize that a true description of India's and China's journey was that both countries continued at their own leisurely pace (China too right up until 1949) – and it was the West which had shot forward and left both countries trailing behind. So it was going to be necessary for India and China to win their spurs all over again. Merely bemoaning colonialism, as we have been doing for seventy odd years, will not do the trick. It turns out that it was modern science and technology which felled us but paradoxically, it is the same modern science and technology which will now resuscitate us and put us back on the road to swift recovery.

the unseen forces of science and technology

Exactly how does science and technology help to defeat nations? There are many examples. I will give a few relating to India but also, in order to be better able to show the sweep and the power of these forces, since they are universal and not restricted to India, we will attempt to paint a broader canvas and also give examples from other countries.

As is well known, India was in the 1700s and 1800s one of the leading countries in the world in the area of cotton textiles as well as in iron and steel. India exported cotton goods to many countries, including England. Indian steel was similarly renowned the world over. Pacey writes:

"...while wealthy people in Europe bought Chinese and Indian goods in large quantities because of their high quality, there was no corresponding demand on any large scale for European goods in the East. European bullion was steadily drained away to India and to the treasury of the Chinese Empire.... The cotton cloth brought from India was not only of finer quality than that produced in the West but it was patterned with printed designs in faster and more brilliant dyes. Iron made in India was of a high quality too, even though Indian furnaces were operated inefficiently as compared with those of Europe. Samples of Indian iron were sent to Sheffield because it was excellently adapted for the purpose of fine cutlery and it was difficult to obtain such good iron in England except through imports from Sweden".(22)

Pacey says that at this time India was the greatest exporter of textiles the world had known. Chintz, calico, dungaree, gingham, khaki, pyjama, sash, seersucker and shawl were all drawn from Indian words and have become part of the English vocabulary. (23)

It was, therefore, a particularly cruel piece of irony that the very areas in which India was pre-eminent should have been the industries—textiles, and iron and steel—which sparked the Industrial Revolution in England. For India, the consequences were ruinous. Within less than a hundred years, India not only stopped being an exporter but instead became hopelessly dependent on the textile mills of Lancashire and on the metal and steel factories of the Midlands. If ever there was an example in history of the economic, social and cultural tables being neatly turned on any nation, this was it. Pacey goes on to tell us that:

"...in one type of manufacture after another, the modern industry of Britain produced goods which could be sold more cheaply than Indian products both in India's traditional export markets and throughout much of the sub-continent itself. A complete list of Indian handicrafts and industries which suffered in this way would include: Cotton spinning and weaving, silk weaving, dyeing and calico printing, iron and steel, brass, tool-making, manufacture of agricultural implements, ship-building and glass-making.

...In no case was the disaster as great as in textiles, where India had declined from being the world's greatest exporter in 1700 to being a net importer in the 1850s. By then, India's imports from Lancashire exceeded its own exports by about 8 times. But the collapse of iron and steel making in India was also very marked.... By the 1820s and 1830s, the British could produce their own high-quality iron. British iron-masters had become more interested in finding export markets for their own products. Indian iron-making declined rapidly in the face of this competition." (24)

Let us take the example of India's shipbuilding industry. My granddaughter, herself all of four years old at the time and living in the USA with her parents, related one day on returning from school how she had learned about "The Star Spangled Banner," the country's national anthem. I, visiting from India, contributed the information from my notes that the song was written by Francis Scott Key, a poet lawyer, when he was briefly imprisoned on the HMS Minden in Baltimore harbour during the War of 1812. The Minden happened to have been built by the Wadia shipyards and was launched in Bombay in 1810. Lowjee Nusserwanjee Wadia was a master builder and was busy at that time producing the finest wooden ships in the world, including schooners, graphs, sloops, pilot vessel brigs, frigates, gunboats and steamers. Even the British Admiralty placed orders on his shipyard in Bombay. But this period of shipbuilding came to a total stop in 1884. Why? Because wood and sail had given way to iron and steam! (25) We can call these superior building materials, but it's not just that. Iron had begun to be produced in Britain in large quantities (production increased thirtyfold between 1806 and 1873) and steam was being pressed into service by remarkable advances in the steam engine by Thomas Savery, Thomas Newcomen, James Watt and others.

So modern science and technology changed the building materials { which increased the number of designs) and changed the production system (earlier based on craftsmanship and human skills but now increasingly linked to the machine). Additionally, "... there was synergy between steel and steam technologies. Steam improved the quantity and quality of steel. Higher quality steel allowed for more precise machining as well as higher stress tolerances of pistons and cylinder leading in turn to yet more efficient steam power." (26). These kinds of steps also, of course, helped to expand the human mind and seen in the collective, gradually transformed the ways of thinking of an entire people. This is how "human capital" is created and this is what science and technology, acting together, is capable of doing. We refer to this again later.(27)

Let's take a further example, this time a political one. History books tell us about how the two main forces in India, Hindu and Muslim, joined hands to try to overthrow the British during the Indian Mutiny of 1857. Unfortunately, in the end all their valiant efforts came to nothing. Even if they had succeeded in the rebellion, however, it is at least arguable whether it would have been a boon for all of India. The Hindu side was represented by Nana Sahib of Kanpur and Lucknow, Indian generalship by Tatya Tope, and the Hindu rulers by Laxmibai, Rani of Jhansi. According to some accounts, Nana Sahib and the Rani of Jhansi were themselves resentful petitioners whose petitions had earlier been turned down by the colonial rulers. The Muslim side was represented by the last of the Mughal Emperors, the 82-year old Bahadur Shah Zafar II, whose chief interests in life were music, poetry and hunting.

At the very time when the Japanese were acknowledging that they desperately needed to learn from the West, we were engaged in furious argument with Britain in our own country over the immediate question of cartridges covered with animal grease! Dr. Percival Spear comes to the following conclusion :" The leaders of the revolt were backward looking men whose aims were incompatible. Nana Sahib hoped to revive the Peshwaship and the Delhi leaders, the Moghul Empire. Success would have meant a further war between the two. Their followers had no confidence in themselves or their cause , no ideas of creating anything new.(28)

It is quite possible that had the Indians won, we would have seen not the economic and political consolidation of India but instead, the beginning of possibly a fratricidal war between Hindus and Muslims, the start on a large scale of what we today call communal violence.

In his book (War of Civilisations, India, AD 1857), Amaresh Misra vehemently disagrees. In a contemporaneous article, he offers a wealth of detail showing that the 1857 uprising was not confined to north India as is commonly supposed but instead affected every part of the country. Not just Lucknow, Kanpur, Meerut and Delhi but various other cities in Rajasthan, Maharashtra, Gujarat, Andhra Pradesh, Madhya Pradesh. Even cities like Karachi and Shikapur in present-day Pakistan and Chitttagong in Bangladesh all mounted mutinies against the British. Mishra states that this War of Civilizations went on for over a decade and that more than 10 million Indians, seven percent of the country's population lost their lives, most of them massacred in cold blood by marauding British troops (29) Misra does his best to portray defeat as victory but admits that 10 million Indians lost their lives—a Pyrhhic victory, if a victory at all.

He also claims that a new, indigenous, peasant-aristocratic, Indian-Asian form of capitalism and modernity could have been born. Is this even possible? Western capitalism (with all its merits/demerits) is based on the foundation of modern science and technology and that basic structure remains the same wherever it is practised – whether in Europe, USA, South America or Asia. (In his book, the author begins with India but quickly expands the concept to Asian capitalism.)

I find William Dalrymple's explanation of our defeat in The Last Mughal much more plausible. He attributes it to "lack of strategic imagination, ingenuity and coordination, lack of clear and recognized executive authority, lack of intelligence (human military intelligence), no attempt to persuade independent rajas to come off the fence and failure to establish 'liberated areas' from which they could draw manpower, tax revenue and food supplies." (30)

I would like to add to all this, a marked difference in the quality of "human capital" in the two fighting forces or more particularly, a difference in the quality of officers commanding the two forces. With decades of experience in industrial production behind them, the British already had leadership skills going for them. Thomas Sowell points out that despite Napoleon's derogatory remark that it was only a nation of shopkeepers, Britain already had centuries of experience as a commercial nation before it became an industrial nation. Not just that. It also had experienced a transportation revolution. More people were travelling about on Britain's improved roads and highways even during the years of horse carriages and because of turnpikes, a substantial highway network already had been created by mid-eighteenth century. And then came George

Stephenson's railway locomotive and a developing railroad network from 1830 onwards. Where there were 30 million rail journeys by1845, there were 300 million railway journeys by 1870. So, as Sowell says, "it was not merely things that developed. People developed!"(31)

In other words, in the future, we will have to look to improving the overall quality of our people. Literacy and education is fine but for leap-frog development in people, we have to employ science and technology (as illustrated in later chapters) because this what counts eventually in times of both war and peace.

At the time of the Indian Mutiny in 1857, the British already had nearly 4500 miles of telegraph line in India. Did this further turn the balance in their favour? All of us who today live in an information society, who accept the supreme need for good communication in war , will concede that this bestowed an incalculable advantage on the British. Meanwhile, the first railway in India had opened in Bombay in 1853 and in 1867, the first train was to steam into Delhi station. That same year, Werner von Siemens personally supervised the laying of India's first transcontinental communications link between Calcutta and London. Did we really stand a chance in the face of all this actual and incipient technology?

From the standpoint of history, did we benefit in any way? Is it possible to argue that our defeat turned out to be instead a blessing in disguise? It is customary to look at modern Indian history as two separate periods: first, the period all the way up to Independence and then, the period from Independence up to the time of writing. It's the natural thing to do. However, another very interesting way of looking at Indian history is, as Naipaul suggests, all the way up to 1857 as one period and from 1857 onwards, past Independence and into the present time as another, representing a period of political consolidation of a vast and diverse country and the strengthening of its central government.

Naipaul puts it elegantly:

"The British peace after the 1857 Mutiny can be seen as a kind of luck. It was a time of intellectual recruitment. India was set on the way of a new kind of intellectual life; it was given new ideas about its history and civilization. The freedom movement reflected all of this and turned out to be the truest kind of liberation. In the 130 years or so since the Mutiny - the last 90 years of the British Raj and the first 40 years of independence begin increasingly to appear as part of the same historical period - the idea of freedom has gone everywhere in India"(32)

Was there ever a better, more vivid example of this than when the Hindutva masses in 1992, with the help and encouragement of the State government, brought down the Babri Masjid—and the Central government, failing to make its will felt for one and a half days for perhaps the first time in modern India's history, was only able to gain control of the situation thereafter?

secondary imperialism

We are discussing the unseen powers of science and technology. Having secured a firm base in India, the British quickly began to look for territories elsewhere. Ceylon, Burma, Aden, the Gulf countries all became victims of what has been called secondary imperialism. But perhaps the most spectacular example is that of China.

In his book The Tools of Empire, Daniel R. Headrick relates that it became an irritant for the British that China should export silk, tea and porcelain to Britain resulting in bullion from Britain constantly flowing out to China. There was no corresponding demand in any large way for European goods in the Far East. Was there no way of reversing this flow? The British hit upon the ingenious idea of growing opium in Bihar and Bengal which they would export in large quantities to China. In this venture, Lord Palmerston, then British Prime Minister, received the active encouragement of British merchants in Calcutta and Hongkong. Before very long, they had managed to get the Chinese addicted to opium. Bullion now began to flow from China to Britain. The protests of the Chinese Emperor were brushed aside and the two Opium Wars (1842 and 1854) followed. Headrick relates how in the most crucial battle of all, the British gunboat Nemesis blasted Chinese junks out of the way and steamed up the Yangtse before the Heavenly Kingdom surrendered. "Steam had carried British naval might into the very heart of China and led to the defeat of the Celestial Empire." (33)

When we reflect that it was actually the Chinese who, centuries earlier, had invented the magnetic compass, had discovered gunpowder and who, at the time of Admiral Cheng Ho in the early 15th century had fleets of over 2000 sea-going vessels, (34) it is evident how countries like China and India, once leading civilizations, had fallen seriously behind and become weak and powerless because they were now laggards when it came to modern science and technology.

Headrick even gives an example of the consequences of the absence of technology. How was it, he asks, that in Africa, which geographically was so much closer to the European powers than Asia and the Far East, colonization should have been put off for more than a hundred years? He believes that this development had to await another milestone: namely, biological technology. Earlier European expeditions to West Africa had cost dearly in terms of lives sacrificed, principally due to malaria. With the discovery of quinine, a shield was obtained against this disease and because of this technical development, the penetration of Africa was finally able to take place. (35)

the mechanisation of warfare

As the British continued their march in Africa, they encountered more and more opposition from the African tribes. But the Africans, although larger in number, found themselves severely lacking when it came to the quality of firepower. Guns made with crude methods using cruder cast iron or steel were not the equal of guns made to precise measurements by the Europeans with machines which were themselves part of a machine tool industry. The classic case was probably that of the battle of Omdurman in the Sudan (1898) where 20 British officers and a handful of Egyptian supporters destroyed an army of 11,000 Dervishes with the help of the Maxim machine-gun. The operative word here is machine. With science and technology invading every sphere of life, it was only to be expected that it would eventually also influence the production of guns and ammunition.

technology's influence on culture

We have begun to explore how the presence and continuing development of science and technology brought about an expansion of mind in Europe. We have also seen examples of how the absence of modern science and technology in India led to setbacks and defeat in the areas of commerce and industry as well as in military and political struggle. The continuing absence of scientific thinking and the tools of technology in India, by a curious looping effect, brought about what I can only call a stagnation of mind in our peoples and severely limited our culture. The nature of this illness is so vague, so general and unfortunately so long established that it is usually not even sought to be pinned down. Any effort to do so is like, as the Japanese say, "cutting smoke with scissors".

We will revert to this theme later but for the present, we must only quote with approval the thesis of the Peruvian author, Hernando de Soto (36) , who argues that if his country, Peru, does not work and the USA, Japan, Germany and a few other countries do, then it can only mean that those countries are better than his own. However, even de Soto stops short of the next and even more crucial question. Does it also mean that his people were weaker than the people of those countries? It is only if we brace ourselves and truthfully answer this question that we can go on to the next more important question still, which is how to improve our respective peoples and how to make up for lost time. My submission is that our own position in India is no different from Hernando de Soto's Peru or from all other "developing" countries.

science, old and new

Which brings us to the question with which we began this chapter. Just how did it happen that great civilizations such as China, India and the Arab Muslim civilization, in the final reckoning, lost out and could not give birth to modern science and technology which, as we have seen, was the vehicle which ultimately brought modern industry and commerce and, therefore, power and prosperity to the Western world?

To understand this, it is necessary to understand the critical difference between science and modern science. There is confusion in people's minds on this point. Like poverty, science is also not new and has existed in all nations. China, India and Arab Muslim world were all great repositories of the inventions of science and great contributories to science. As is well known, China was responsible for the first clock, for the compass, for gunpowder, and for a host of other inventions. (Joseph Needham's account of China's science and civilisation goes into 25 volumes!) Similarly, India was renowned in astronomy, mathematics, surgery, the science of medicine and so on. Arab Muslim civilization, on its part, made significant contributions to algebra, agriculture, chemistry, medicine, astronomy, pharmacology, biology, and more.

However, none of these civilizations - China, India or the Arab world - went on to devise the scientific method which called for the rigorous fitting of observation and experiment to conclusion. The result was that inventions and discoveries, which are the cause of growth and progress, came intermittently, haphazardly, serendipitously and not in a methodical or sustained manner. "Science" in all these countries remained just one, large amorphous mass of knowledge which simply existed in the community. Unlike modern science, scientific facts and theories did not generally dovetail into each other or reinforce each other. There were many contradictions and some of these contradictions clearly went against reality itself.

Here are some examples first from Europe itself (because earlier they were no different from us) and then from Arab countries: In Europe during the Middle Ages it was quite common for books to carry illustrations of trees situated on the banks of a lake showing that leaves which had been shed on land became animals and those shed in water turned out to be fish!(37) Even in the Middle Ages, it must have been clear how animals reproduced themselves but the essential thing to understand is that this interpretation of reality actively existed side by side with other knowledge based on myth, superstition, or traditional belief. The Middle Ages was a world of contrasts. Says Dutch scholar J. Huizinga: "the passionate and violent soul of the age, always vacillating between tearful piety and frigid cruelty, between respect and insolence, between despondency and wantonness, could not dispense with the severest rules and the strictest formalism." (38) .

In Europe, for over one thousand years, all manner of theories were actively propagated to show how blood flowed through the septum between the right and the left ventricle of the heart although this was not in the least bit supported by reality. Charles Gillespie, (Swiss physician-writer), writes that:

"[16th-century anatomist] Vesalius investigated the pits himself and could find no passages. 'None of these pits penetrate from the right ventricle to the left...therefore, indeed I was compelled to marvel at the activity of the Creator of things in that blood should sweat, from the right ventricle to the left through passages escaping the sight!' And what is interesting in retrospect is how investigators refrained from finding the answer which is that if blood cannot pass directly from one side of the heart to the other, it must go around through the lungs. When one reads the memoirs, it almost seems to shriek at them from their own discoveries."(39)

In the same way, in Arab countries during the Middle Ages, a giraffe was supposed to be a hybrid of a she-camel and a male hyena although there was not the slightest evidence for such a conclusion. Another zoologist believed it to be a hybrid of the camel and the panther. The rhinoceros was believed to be a cross between a horse and an elephant! (40)

On a broader, philosophical level, India, China and Islam did not, like the Greeks and Romans before them, learn how the world worked from what is now known as inductive reasoning—the collection and synthesis of observations into models and theories. Rather, the ancients described the workings of the natural world using deductive techniques which determined natural law and the shape of the universe from so-called first principles—facts that were assumed to be true, never questioned and used as the basis of all further reasoning.(41)

When this kind of thinking prevailed even in Europe, it should not surprise us that when Galileo in 1610 offered up his rudimentary telescope to the Bologna scholars to see for themselves the existence of the moons of Jupiter, they refused the offer because they were not prepared to accept the evidence of their own eyes!(42)

But Europe had slowly begun to change. The idea of a science based on fact, certainty and reality had begun to take hold. Jacob Bronowski, well known British historian of science, writes that the very idea of research was "an idea which was altogether new to that age. In that way he (Galileo) really did for the first time what we think of as practical science: build the apparatus, do the experiment, publish the results."(43)

The scientific method (the exact and the actual), therefore, and the scientific way of thinking are very much the product of modern science. It took many centuries and involved the life and death of several civilizations before the validity and usefulness of this idea was acknowledged and it was given the respect that it enjoys today. Today, it is the foundation of all science. It connotes complete freedom of thought, freedom from tradition, freedom from religion, freedom from government, freedom unrestricted and untrammeled in any way whatsoever.

why China & India missed out

Scientific method first supplied the intellectual foundation and then detailed mathematical underpinnings were provided by scientists from Isaac Newton onwards. As a result, technology in Europe progressed by leaps and bounds. By way of comparison, Arnold Pacey(44) explains how the totally different ideas and values of the Chinese people seriously hampered the development of technology in that country. I have added notes concerning India in parentheses as the reasons are remarkably (and expectedly) similar in the case of our own country. The emphases are also mine. Pacey says:

1) For example, there was more of intellectual development in the West than in China. In 15th century Renaissance Europe, scholarly study of Roman technical achievements and application of mathematics to engineering provided two powerful incentives for the educated classes to take interest in certain kinds of technology. The names of Alberti (architecture) and Agricola (metallurgy) became well known and there were books on machines from the 16th century onwards. In China, on the other hand, literature on engineering was distinctly small because the constructions of artisans, however ingenious, were often regarded as unworthy of the attention of Confucian literati. If anything, the latter were more interested in agriculture than in machines.

[As regards India, I would merely substitute the word Brahmins for Confucian literati. The contempt for manual labour as against scholarly or bookish study was also present and continues to this day. There was heavy emphasis on agriculture and the philosophy behind machines was, as in China, very little valued or understood]

2) In Europe, mathematics was important not only for itself but for awakened intellectual interest in geometry and the mechanical problems of the engineer. The Chinese developed many branches of mathematics but their interests were never as relevant to practical problems.

[We could say this with even more emphasis about India. After all, Arabic numerals, in use all over the world today, were born in India. India was also the land where the zero and decimal values were invented. However, these developments existed by themselves and did not lead to any systematic application of the concepts to science and engineering.]

3) European builders were prepared to work against Nature. Pacey gives the examples of the Gothic cathedrals, the Versailles waterworks and the Languedoc Canal. He says Chinese architecture was always with, not against Nature. Buildings had a horizontal emphasis, not a vertical one. Collaboration with nature meant that ornamental schemes of this kind were less often turned into major engineering works than in Europe.

[In India also there has been this constant, wearisome emphasis on harmony with nature. Few will disagree with the fact that unquestioned worship of nature never really solved any problems for man. Even today, to very few people is it apparent that, with the coming of modern science and technology, man made a conscious decision to part with Nature or work against Nature whenever it appeared that Nature was working against man or at least, not working for him. Otherwise, would it make sense to say that, for example, smallpox had been eradicated from India and indeed from the rest of the world, from the 1970s onwards because before that it was a scourge which had claimed thousands upon thousands of lives over many centuries.

4) new techniques and new inventions in the 15th and 16th centuries came to have a symbolic value in Europe. They came to be identified with progress. (We should pause to remember that, even in Europe, progress did not always mean what it means to us today. The concept itself did not exist. Earlier, the word progress meant the simple, physical sense of an onward movement in space and then the onward movement of a story or narrative ... (and) neither of these senses was eulogistic (45) Writing about the Middle Ages, Huzinga says:" The idea of a purposed and continual reform and improvement of society did not exist. Institutions in general are considered as good or as bad as they can be; having been ordained by

God, they are intrinsically good, only the sins of men pervert them." (46) ...

" By the late seventeenth or early eighteenth century, however, progress had come commonly to mean advancement to a higher stage, advancement to better and better conditions, continuous improvement," (47)

Europeans began to see their inventions as marking their superiority over ancient Greece and Rome. In China, on the other hand, such things did not have the same significance in their culture. In the West, the clock soon became an everyday convenience, while in China it long remained a toy.(48) Iron smelting, bridge building, flood control, ship design all happened in China before 1400 AD but they existed by themselves and did not have any consequential effects. Later, even when European mechanical inventions were first brought to China "they were not seen as symbols of progress but were regarded merely as novelties or playthings". (49)

[In India too the position was similar. The aristocracy took little interest in European mechanical inventions because of their aesthetic deficiencies ... (but) European novelties, described by the English merchants as 'toys' were very popular with the Mughal aristocracy. European drinking glasses, platters for dainty sweets, a variety of looking-glasses and paintings were much in demand. (50) There is still a basic feeling of discomfort about progress. In its place, there is a philosophy of asceticism or self-denial, a constant harking back to the old, a nagging feeling that the Ram Rajya attained in the past can never happen in the future—- while all the while partaking of and benefiting from the latest gadgets and products of science!)

Francis Fukuyama, of Stanford University, shows how science played a role in all this: "The method that we associate with Galileo, Bacon and Descartes assumed the possibility of a knowledge and therefore a mastery of nature, which was in turn subject to a set of coherent and universal laws. Knowledge of these laws was not only accessible to man as man but was cumulative, such that successive generations could be spared the efforts and mistakes of earlier ones. Thus the modern notion of progress had its origins in the success of modern natural science"(51)

In China and India, there was also the enormous constraint of dependence on an oral or scriptographic culture, as against the West where Johannes Gutenberg had introduced moveable type as early as 1448. Within 50 years of this development, there were already 1500 / 2000 printing presses scattered all over Europe. Typographic culture made possible, in course of time, mass literacy and mass literacy brought in its wake numerous benefits, including a spreading modern science and technology.

These (considerable) benefits included a moving away from group consciousness to individual consciousness; a shift from a "closed world" to "the infinite universe of the new cosmology"; the ability to sustain patenting of inventions or copyrighting of literary compositions; the "awakening of personality" with a new spirit of independence; and a desire to "discover the new" and not, as earlier, only to "recover from tradition."(52) *he printing press "made the Italian Renaissance a permanent European Renaissance...implemented the Protestant Reformation and reoriented Catholic religious practice...affected the development of modern capitalism...implemented western European exploration of the globe...changed family life and politics, diffused knowledge as never before, made universal literacy a serious objective, made possible the rise of modern sciences, and otherwise altered social and intellectual life".(53)

Gutenberg's innovation thus made all of today's developments possible—including, in the end, the subjugation by much smaller European nations of large countries like China and India. For China, the loss was particularly ironic because out of the three constituents—moveable type, paper and ink—needed for printing, two (moveable type and paper) had been invented by the Chinese themselves centuries earlier and only much later introduced into Europe.

Paper was invented in China in 105 AD. It was brought by the Arabs to Europe through Muslim North Africa in the twelfth century, taking the same route that the Muslim invasion into Spain had taken some five hundred years earlier. It arrived in Germany only about 50 years before the re-birth of moveable type in 1448. Ink alone, for moveable type, made with a special kind of oil-paint with linseed oil varnish, was contributed by the experience of the Flemish painters of the Netherlands. (54)

THE JOURNEY OF PAPER MANUFACTURE ACROSS THE WORLD

(by permission from a chart at the Gutenberg-Museum, Mainz, Germany)

BA-GIAO, China	105 AD	VALENCIA, Spain	1151
KOREA	600	FABRIANO, Italy	1276
JAPAN	610	STRASBOURG	1348
SAMARKHAND	751	NUREMBERG	1390
BAGHDAD	793	DANZIG	1473
DAMASCUS	*-	OXFORD	1494
CAIRO	900	MOSCOW	1576
FEZ, Morocco	1100	OSLO	1598
CEUTA, Morocco	-	PHILADELPHIA	1690
CADIZ, Spain	-	CANADA	1803

was India backward, or Europe forward?

We referred to this briefly earlier. India's problems were accentuated by the fact that the two industries most responsible for the Industrial Revolution—textiles and iron and steel—were precisely the areas in which India was most developed and most competitive. The country was now at a distance from the Industrial Revolution and on the other hand, its most prominent industries were rendered totally idle.

V.S. Naipaul believes that successive invasions had so impoverished India and drained its strength that by the 1565 devastation of the Vijayanagar capital, Hampi, India was intellectually dead and therefore, lay helpless.(55)

It is true that the Hindus had suffered a serious defeat in the battle of Talikota in 1565 but the country had withstood many invasions before and could probably have done so again. At that time, the gap between rich and poor nations (or culturally strong and culturally weak nations, if you prefer) was not and could not have been as pronounced as it is today. Naipaul states that after Hampi, India was left with a "headless" population, but I believe that with the assistance of its people India could have recovered its great empire over the next two hundred years. My explanation is, as we noted earlier, that it was not so much that India fell back as that Europe shot forward. It is generally admitted that the two leading economies of the world in 1000 AD were China and India. So, strictly speaking, it is not even accurate to say that they "fell back". Both countries continued at their old, customary pace and it was the Western world which first separated and then strode forward!

Here is an encapsulated account of the kind of advantage that Europe enjoyed:

"In 1512, Copernicus first argued that the earth revolves around the sun. In the following 25 years, Anthony Fitzherbert published the first English manual on agriculture, Albrecht Durer compiled the first German treatise on geometry, Paracelsus published the first book on surgery, Georg Agricola produced the first treatise on mineralogy and Andreas Vesalius issued the first anatomical charts of the human body." (56) In other words, the sluice gates of knowledge had been thrown open in Europe and it was going to be difficult to catch up with her from now on.

Confusion still prevails in Indian minds because some of the high points of Indian architecture and culture were reached during the Mughal period. The Taj Mahal was completed in 1648 and the Red Fort in Delhi and its palace buildings also around then. Such monuments are representative of a strong, rich and creative people. It could not therefore have been, it is argued, that India was already a decadent culture. Had this been the case, European nations could not have known of the fame of India and would not have ventured to come here.

What is not realised is that when Aurangzeb died in 1707, there were in existence two separate curves on a cultural graph—the strong, upward curve represented by a Europe powered by the thrust of modern science and technology, and India's curve, by then downward-moving, announcing that the peak of achievement had been reached and that our best years were at that time distinctly over. Two passenger trains stopped alongside each other at a railway station in the middle of the night but headed in opposite directions!

In an interview in connection with his book, the "Sea of Poppies", Amitav Ghosh argues that it was the period of independence (1947 to 1990) that has made possible the sudden and incredible development that we have witnessed in India, China and other parts of the world.(57) Is this sufficient explanation? China began its open door policy in December 1979. Before that, the country had stubbornly continued down an economic path affected by enormous upheavals like the Great Leap Forward, the agricultural famine of the 1960s, and the Cultural Revolution. Why did it take thirty-odd years for realization to dawn?

India started its liberalization drive in 1991. Why did it take us 44 years? Ghosh doesn't consider MoST (modern science and technology) as an explanation because it is difficult to see. It's not palpable; you cannot put your finger on it. These are unseen forces which can make, break and re-make nations. Nothing exemplifies this more than the history of China and India right up to the present time. Thus, despite a good account of indentured labour ("Sea of Poppies"), I feel Ghosh still fails to ask why the British in India, a mere joint stock company, became our drivers and we Indians became the driven.

perceptual, before cultural, political or economic

Arnold Pacey believes that it was probably colonialism which prevented India from developing its own Industrial Revolution. He points out that in 1851 India got its first textile mill. This was 15 years before Japan. In 1853, India got its first railway. This was 20 years before Japan. Yet by 1910, Japan was becoming self-sufficient in basic engineering industries while India had made little progress in that respect. (58)

This may be true, but I feel that the matter goes much further than that. The colonial period of 150-200 years did undoubtedly inhibit India's development of its own industry but there are other countries which either did not experience colonialism or did not suffer it to quite the same extent as India and are still "developing" today. China, although beginning to suffer much greater humiliation than

Japan at the hands of the Western powers, made only perfunctory, less than whole-hearted, attempts to secure modern science and technology as fundamental tools with which to transform itself. The importance of these tools was still not clear to Sun Yat Sen when he died in 1925. On the other hand, Japan recognized and acknowledged before all others that it was missing something which it could only obtain from the West and thus set about modernizing itself from the Meiji Restoration (1868) onwards.

Can it be that we in India were not truly able to comprehend because we were once a great civilization? Aside from China (which also was very late in coming to the realization) the same seems to be the case with Egypt, Greece itself, Spain, Turkey, Mexico and other countries, all once innovative, dominant cultures but now considered developing, or at best middle income, countries.

I said "Greece itself" above for a certain reason. Greece is acknowledged even today to be the bedrock of Western civilization. We ourselves discussed the Greek Renaissance in an earlier chapter. Then why is Greece today sometimes referred to as the "sick man of Europe."? Because that was then and this is now and as we have seen, a great deal happens to have happened in between. This is best illustrated by the example of the Philhellenes.

The Philhellenes were Western sympathizers of the "Greek khlepts" (half bandits, half rebels against Turkish rule). Their officers, French, German and British, many from the Napoleonic Wars, had tried to instruct the khlepts, unsuccessfully, in modern close order drill at the outset of Greece's War of Independence in 1821.

"At the heart of Philhellenism" says military historian John Keegan " lay the belief that the modern Greeks were, under their dirt and ignorance, the same people as the ancient Greeks...(overlooking) their klepht ways of subsisting by banditry, changing sides when it suited them, parading in tawdry finery, brandishing ferocious weapons, stuffing their purses with unhonoured bribes and never, never dying to the last man or the first if they could help it". Eventually, the Philhellenes were reduced to concluding that " only a break in the bloodline between ancient and modern Greeks could explain the collapse of a (once) heroic culture."! (59)

It seems that for the swiftest possible results, a cultural value determination and an intellectual decision has to be made first and the apparatus of science and technology in the shape of modern industry and commerce and other institutions must follow. In India, possession of a railway or a healthy textile industry or even, for that matter, the rest of the economic and political infrastructure put up by the British, could not set off the process of true, self-generating development. As in China, the precise reasons and tools for growth were not clearly perceived or understood. In my opinion, that realization still has not taken place in India. Jawaharlal Nehru, our first Prime Minister and that also for the initial critical seventeen years was conscious of science - perhaps the only leading politician in India to do so. But even he probably did not estimate the strength of the cobwebs in traditional Indian minds that would need to be gently removed. He happened also to be the only person who could stand up to Mahatma Gandhi (with whom he enjoyed a very cordial relationship) and expect to be heard. Yes, clear perception is required in every country - before cultural, political or economic.

Therefore, it is important that we avoid blaming colonialism for all our problems. There would appear to be something in India's make-up which prevented the country from acquiring the flexibility and response to change which the situation called for, India had begun to fall back in growth and development even before the colonial powers arrived—one reason why it was easier for them to arrive and prevail in the first place! The presence of the British here exacerbated this position in some ways while strengthening it (language, political consolidation, introduction of the railway etc.) in others.

Conversely, there does exist a very good example of a country which was able to resist colonialism and to mount a successful anti-European revolution. These were England's own American colonies in 1774-1776. And so it came about that the United States of America began its existence as a free nation at about the same time that India lost its independence and slipped under the British yoke.

Why should this have happened? Why should India so easily have gone under? Was there any marked difference between the two nations? It is interesting to examine the intellectual sources of the American Revolution and to distinguish them with the state of Indian thought at about the same time. The first thing to be noted is that when the American colonies insisted on independence, it was not because of any history of tyranny by Britain. There was demand for taxes to be paid to the mother country and certain other economic and other questions in dispute but these were not greatly important matters and unlikely in themselves to be the cause of rebellion. What seemed to really irk the colonies was that they considered themselves the equal of Britain in every way and were clearly unprepared to accept a subordinate status. "Policy makers regarded Britain as sovereign and the colonials as subjects because Americans were not taken too seriously.... attitude was again the obstacle; the English could not visualize Americans in terms of equality." (60) The colonies, on the other hand, were not agreeable to being treated as "children" by the " mother country".(61)

Actually, Urs Bitterli, a Swiss professor and well known European authority on colonialism, says in his book "Cultures in Conflict" : "Although England tried to prevent the growth of printing and newspapers in the colonies by keeping a careful watch on the export of printing presses, the first American book, the Bay Psalm Book, was printed in Boston as early as 1640. It was not long before towns like Boston and New York, joined somewhat later by Philadelphia, constituted a class of educated citizens, born and brought up in America, who were fully equal to the English in education, self-confidence and cultivated manners." (62) Thomas Paine's antimonarchist book "Common Sense" was published in 1776 itself and sold more than a hundred thousand copies in 2 months. (63)

Statesmen like Thomas Jefferson studied the constitutions of several European countries, studied the history of the monarchy in England and, influenced by thinkers from England itself like John Locke, came to the conclusion that the king had no hereditary or testamentary right to his rule but instead obtained his powers from the consent of the governed. For its time, this was a revolutionary idea. Jefferson promoted many similar modern and far-reaching ideas: that all men are born free and that all men are born equal; the rights of the citizen against totalitarian control, the importance of a broad-based suffrage, the decent treatment of (American) Indians, the abolition of slavery (at least in theory), the ending of primogeniture, the control of military authority by elected civilians, the separation of Church from State, the need for government to be kept in a plurality of hands and not in the corrupt will of any one man and so on. Jefferson even introduced decimal currency in America but could not have his way with weights and measures, an error for which the United States pays a heavy price to this day. Three of his greatest heroes were Sir Francis Bacon, Sir Isaac Newton and John Locke. (64) His contemporaries were themselves great men like George Washington, James Madison, Alexander Hamilton, John Adams and Benjamin Franklin.

American biographer Fawn Brodie says that Jefferson properly understood the strategic role of the militia, while Cornwallis had "failed to subdue the American interior…All [his] ravaging had resulted not in increased attachment to the Crown but in either a totally hostile countryside area or at best a divided one, with Americans engaged in savage encounters with each other. The terrain and constantly re-invigorated guerilla patriots helped defeat the British."(65)

Compare the intellectual atmosphere in India at approximately the same time. Aurangzeb had died in 1707 after an uncertain reign. Not just the British (1757) but the Persians (1739) and the Afghans (1761 and 1788) had come in as invaders. Historian Fernand Braudel quotes the account of Francois Bernier, a French physician in the Mughal court from the late 17th century until Aurangzeb's death:

"It had been a strange empire, founded on the activities of a few thousand feudal nobles, the omerahs or mansabdars, recruited both inside and outside India. The army itself was the government since the high offices of the regime were chiefly occupied by soldiers. Twice a day, the omerahs paid their respects to the Emperor. Flattery was essential here as at the court of Versailles. The Emperor did not pronounce a word which was not agreed with admiration or which failed to make the principal omerahs throw up their hands crying karamat, that is to say wonders. But what they were doing above all by such visits was reassuring themselves that the Emperor was still alive and that thanks to him the empire was still standing. The briefest absence on the emperor's part, the rumour of an illness or false reports of his death, might immediately unleash the frightening turmoil of a war of succession."

"The high and mighty of Delhi," notes Braudel, "observed a different code of behaviour: they were guided by the precepts of a different world. For what were they but condottieri, like the Italians of the fifteenth century."(66)

Meanwhile, the Mughal ruler Mohammed Shah had a surprising response to Persia's plundering of Delhi in 1739, as described by a secret agent in the Persian army:

"This victory...can be more attributed to God's decree than to the Persian valour in arms, for when the two armies met, neither Shah himself (ie Nadir Shah), nor the last man in his army harboured the slightest hope to withstand the enemy's attacks and considered themselves as prisoners, since the Mughal army was three hundred thousand strong, and only a smaller part of it, perhaps fifty thousand, caused great disaster in the Persian ranks. Even after a successful counter attack by Nadir Shah's army, the situation remained hopeless and the Persians expected even more disastrous attacks from the Indian forces. But suddenly, to the utmost surprise and rejoicing of everyone, the Indian Mughal with his sons, with many Rajas or lords and with his ministers arrived in the Persian camp and surrendered.(67)

Compare this with what Jefferson had to say about fighting the British in America:

"While an enemy is within our bowels, the first object is to expel him.(68) Even William Pitt (Lord Chatham) had this to say in 1777 about the fighting Americans: "If I were an American as I am an Englishman, while a foreign troop was landed in my country, I would never lay down my arms, never-never-never!"(69)

All this suggests a marked difference in the kind of man fighting the British on two, vastly separated continents. Therefore, it does not come as a surprise that the very Cornwallis who himself was roundly defeated at Yorktown (1781) by the militia of the American colonies, albeit with the help of the French, should later have travelled to India and helped to defeat one of our own redoubtable fighters, Tipu Sultan, thereby making it possible for the British finally to remove one of the last few obstacles to their subjugation of the large continent of India.

failure of nerve

One final example will, I hope, convince the reader that the reason for our condition cannot have been colonialism. This is the case of Islam. China and India were early examples but the Arab world came agonisingly close to the acquisition of modern science and technology before, tragically, it also took the wrong turning.

Actually, once again it would be more accurate to say that Islam, like China and India before it, failed to take the right turning at the critical point and doggedly continued on its way as before. If, therefore, the Arab countries also fell behind in the race, surely this was long before the appearance of colonialism or imperialism.

In the course of their observations of nature, as already pointed out, many of the findings of the Islamic men of science did not conform to the facts as believed earlier and especially to the truths as laid down in the scriptures. This happened in many fields but more particularly in the sciences. Rather than going by their own true observations of nature, scholars chose to follow prescribed truths as laid down in the religious books. In the 10th century, a monstrous theoretical and philosophical argument erupted between those who adhered to the rule of theology and law and those who supported science and philosophy. This argument shook the Arab world to its foundations. When the contest was finally over, it became clear that orthodox Islam had won the day and this religion (like others) had, perhaps unknowingly, set its face against modern science and technology.

Historian Syed Hossein Nasr says that the Islamic scholars of that time did not, and could not, "take the step to break with the traditional world view, as was to happen during the Renaissance in the West—because that would have meant not only a revolution in astronomy but also, an upheaval in the religious, philosophical and social domains (70) In the preface which he contributed to Nasr's book, the American scholar Giorgio de Santillana, wrote with foreboding fifty years ago:

"The decline of science inside a great culture is in itself a fascinating study and a terrible object lesson." (71)

I am haunted by these words and they come to my mind every time I see present day photographs of migrants in their thousands drowning in the Mediterranean, Rohingya refugees forced to leave Myanmar and Afghan refugees in their thousands anxious to reach other countries.

Today, many Muslim countries are identified as "developing" nations which, as everyone knows, is only a euphemism for underdeveloped nations. Their populations are increasing rapidly but there is little economic progress. Even the affluent countries in the Muslim world owe their present-day prosperity to the petroleum industry which is, of course, a creature of Western science and technology. Were it not for petrodollar prices, these rich countries would also today be in dire straits.

The world is moving away from fossil fuels. If the oil age comes to an end, Muslim countries in the Middle East, presently already doing poorly, will be in serious trouble. Something fundamental is involved. Tourism and other kinds of investments are mere palliatives. The future lies in understanding the kernel of wisdom contained in the one sentence declaration of Giorgio de Santillana.

Chapter 3
SCIENCE AND TECHNOLOGY AS SOLUTION / treatment

How often in India – at every level – rational conversation about the country's problems trails away into talk of magic, of the successful prophecies of astrologers, of the wisdom of auspicious hours, of telepathic communications and actions taken in response to some inner voice !...When men cannot observe, they don't have ideas; they have obsessions. When people live instinctive lives, something like collective amnesia steadily blurs the past... Like childhood, this golden Indian past is not to be possessed by inquiry: it is only to be ecstatically contemplated. The past is a religious idea, clouding intellect and painful perception, numbing distress in bad times.—V.S. Naipaul, India: A Wounded Civilization

The primary function of reason, as applied to man in society, is no longer to investigate but to transform; and this heightened consciousness of the power of man to improve the management of social, economic and political affairs by the application of rational processes seems to me one of the major aspects of the twentieth-century revolution. —E.H. Carr, What is History?

• how technology acts: jaywalking • the talking machine • packaged motion • the case of the simple spoon • technology as cultural influence (re-visit) • putting it to the people • should we dump English? • communalism • the meaning of secularism •acute bewilderment • RJ vs. BM • applying MoST to communalism • thinking locally, acting globally • Arab Muslim civilization • conclusion

how technology acts: jaywalking

What is jaywalking? We have all heard the term. At one time, the British used the word "jay" (the name given to a species of loud, unruly birds) to describe a rustic who had just arrived in a city, was ignorant of city ways, and—most particularly—did not even know how to cross the street safely but zigzagged or crossed in the wrong places. We have all seen new arrivals in town; those who have trouble understanding the different streams of traffic at an intersection but finally manage to get to the other side of the street although usually not without some difficulty. It may even have happened to us when we first arrived in town or when we visited a larger town or city, say, overseas.

Before long, we have got used to our surroundings, grasped the intricacies of crossing busy streets, and blended in. Earlier, we lacked a skill or understanding because we had no exposure to a certain intensity of technology—and now we have it. Our reflexes and comprehension have quickened, our speed of response has increased, and we now cross the street with a much greater degree of confidence.

the talking machine

We are surrounded by technology on all sides but if you were asked what is the first technology that a child of about two years would encounter and then internalize on his or her own, what might be your reply? In most cities today, perhaps it is the telephone. When the telephone rings, the child, having by this time got over her initial nervousness, rushes to answer the telephone to the exclusion of everyone else in the family and is proudly allowed to do so. The child quickly realizes that this is a method of communication which is different from face-to-face conversation. She learns to put the receiver to her ear and the mouthpiece to her mouth. She learns that it will not do to talk at the same time. She learns to hear before she speaks and to speak before she again hears. She learns to modulate her voice to suit the instrument. Altogether the child conducts herself differently on the phone than when engaged in face-to-face conversation. Would you not agree that multiple psychological changes have taken place in this child as a result of learning to use the telephone? Is it not also your experience that because of her early mastery of the ways of this technology, the child is now a more purposive, a much more confident person?

Just think. There are millions and millions of telephones in European countries and in the USA. Presently, nearly half of the population of these countries has landlines. In India earlier, one had to wait for years together for a telephone connection. Our position has definitely improved with the coming of cell phones: at present, we have 2.6 telephone lines per 100 people and 72 mobile phones per 100. (1)

Can we even begin to understand the enormous head-start which the European or American child received at the very beginning of his life? Can we estimate the early intellectual and psychological disadvantage of our children, now adults, because millions of our nation's homes remained without telephones? Is it not, therefore, an utterly joyful fact that today children in millions of Indian homes, in cities and villages, large and small, should at last be opened up to the confidence-building experience locked up in an unprepossessing telephone?

packaged motion

I look upon the motorcar as packaged motion. If we were to need to single out some machine, some technology which is commonly used by men and women where a fresh decision needs to be made during every moment of its use, it would probably be the motorcar. The windscreen of a motorcar in motion is like a large kaleidoscope. Every second of the time, as with every shake of the kaleidoscope, the picture changes and a fresh decision needs to be made. A pedestrian on the left; a cyclist making an entry from a side street; the changing traffic lights; a bus in the distance thundering its way towards you; perhaps a dog or even cow curled up on one side of the street; a pothole ahead of you; some old ladies about to cross the road (hesitantly or quickly) and the permutations and combinations of all these give a kaleidoscopic flavour to the vision spread before the motorist. Your eye must try and grasp it all, developing your vision right up to the corners of your eyes. Your ears must be alert to the clang of the cyclist's bell or the growl of the taxiwala's engine as he tries impatiently to overtake you. Your nose must take in any smell of possible burning; your sense of touch must feel any possible drag of the car on one or the other side. In short, you must have all systems going. It is because of these enlarged, heightened senses that, once you have learned to drive a motor car it becomes clear to you that, as

Jay Dubashi once asserted, there is a qualitative difference between a car or truck driver and the driver of a bullock-cart.

There are other factors in play. Apart from quickened reflexes and responses, you need certain qualities of the mind which contribute to good driving. Instead of watching only the car immediately ahead of you, you need to watch (through several rear windows) the leader of the pack. You need to develop a sense of anticipation; you need to acquire a feel for the distance to be allowed between the car ahead of you and your own car which, in turn, depends on the speed at which you may be travelling. You need a sense of reciprocal relations, by which I mean an understanding of the dynamics when three cars should be involved: one, say, ahead of yours and the other, third car traveling parallel to yours but perhaps wishing to cut in.

In addition to better reflexes and certain intellectual qualities, you also need a civilized person at the wheel. You need to show consideration for the pedestrian, for your fellow motorist and indeed, for the world at large. It's a rewarding sight in Britain and the US, for example, to see (mostly) a motorist slow down at a zebra crossing while a pedestrian walks across the street with a firm stride accompanied often with a slight nod of the head and a slight raising of the hand by way of thanks. In India, in contrast, one often sees a motorist bearing down heavily on a pedestrian at a zebra crossing or, sometimes, the pedestrian deliberately slowing down traffic out of cussedness and merely to assert his newly discovered rights as a citizen. If the motorist looks after the interests of the pedestrian and the pedestrian looks after the interests of the motorist, both are well served. But when the motorist looks out for himself and the pedestrian does likewise, it becomes a different thing altogether. Do such situations perhaps epitomize the difference between developed and developing country?

In Western countries, it is possible to drive over mile after mile of beautiful road, cambered slightly to either left or right, depending upon how you may be negotiating a curve. By way of contrast, take the case of Mohan (name changed), one of my office drivers in Delhi. Everyone knows that New Delhi is a city of roundabouts. Do what I would, it seemed impossible to persuade Mohan that he should first put the car into a lower gear and then negotiate the curve. Otherwise, I explained, the passenger tended to lurch to one side or the other and this was rather inconvenient. Impossible to make Mohan understand! An idea then occurred to me. Solemnly, I asked Mohan one day whether it was his custom to eat his morning meal before he had his bath or after. No sir, he replied somewhat indignantly, I have my bath first and only then my meal!

Similarly, I said, you must put the car into the proper gear first and only then negotiate the curve. Mohan understood what I was trying to say. There was distinct improvement for a few days but alas, the lesson was soon forgotten and Mohan gradually lapsed into his old ways. Really, how do you explain centripetal and centrifugal forces to dear, barely literate souls like Mohan? How also do you explain to an elderly lady who gets off in the wrong direction from a bus about to stop at a bus-stop, falls down in a heap and starts gesticulating at the driver, that it was not the driver who is to blame!

More could be written about driving habits in India but this is not the place for it. The only reason why we have dwelt on motorcars and driving is to point to the need for the combination of improved reflexes, an important intellectual component and an underlying, sympathetic humanity. We will look at how each of these elements can progressively lead to another and how a combination of these qualities is necessary for any substantive and lasting improvement in the human resources of our country.

the case of the simple spoon

Let us conclude these examples of the effects of technology by taking up the case of the simple spoon. As noted, so much in India have we veered towards a study of man and against mere things that even in matters of eating, we prefer to eat with our fingers and refuse to use implements like cutlery. Some claim that eating with cutlery is not natural, that it somehow lowers the taste of food. Again, this reaction is not new and not surprising. In Europe, when the individual fork was first introduced about the sixteenth century, it was considered to be diabolical. It was argued that God would not have given us fingers if he had wished us to use such an instrument. (2) Nonetheless, use of knife, fork and spoon went ahead.

In our own country, use of the spoon on a large scale has only properly begun in recent years. (Michael H. Fisher writes in Beyond the Three Seas – Travelers' Tales from Mughal India, that Western travellers found that spoons did not exist in Mughal India.) Whatever the reason, great numbers of people in India even today find themselves uncomfortable with a spoon and unable to manipulate it properly.

I am not discussing the fork and the knife, which some may accept as useful and others may not but the utility of the spoon in matters of eating surely cannot be denied. Yet, if you sit quietly in a common restaurant and watch people using the spoon, you may find that many do not yet know how to manage this simple implement. Some turn it upside down in the air and flip the food expertly into their mouth; others sink their teeth into the metal. Some others are able to reach only about half of the contents of the scoop; yet more fail to lean forward gently when the spoon reaches the mouth – and so on. There is no successful meeting of spoon with mouth, born out of familiarity, grace and habit. Instead the results are clumsy and awkward to see.

This is not to make use of the spoon sound more difficult than it is. If the user agrees that he needs to learn to use the spoon, it surely would bring him a good deal of confidence when he finally properly begins to do so. India is getting quickly urbanized, modernized and, whether we like it or not, Westernized. It will be secretly agreed by all that confidence in using simple, seemingly insignificant articles of cutlery like the spoon cannot but bring enormous self-assurance to the user.

We have looked at some of the direct effects on our people of the presence or absence of simple science and technology. Dr. V. Kurien, pioneer of the Indian cooperative dairy movement, in speaking about the Amul Dairy in Gujarat, demonstrates the indirect effects on our people of modern science and technology:

"450,000 people delivering milk at 900 centers come and stand in 900 queues – irrespective of sex, irrespective of caste. What does it do to a high caste Brahmin to stand behind an 'untouchable' because he came after him and to do so twice a day, everyday of the year. What does it do to the 'untouchable' to stand ahead of the 'high caste Brahmin' because he came earlier. What does it do to both of them to see the milk go into the same can. Their caste system gets submerged in that can of milk! It is not merely an orderly milk collection. Is it not also a blow at the caste system? Our villages are dirty. Our milk collection room is also dirty but it is cleaner than the rest of the village. Someone built a room and put some glazed tiles; another brought some clean water to wash the pots and pans; a third brought insecticides to try to keep the flies away; a fourth sprinkled water to keep the dust down. You may well find this scene in many parts of the country. What do they mean? These are the very first steps in sanitation in that village. How can you talk of clean milk production unless you talk of sanitation.

We have a scheme for veterinary aid for our buffaloes in each district. We employ 75 graduate veterinarians and 900 first aid workers, one in each village and they are employees of the Cooperative, not of the government. We have an elaborate radio telephone communication system and we guarantee that any sick buffalo anywhere in the village, anywhere in the district, will have a veterinarian tend the sick buffalo within four hours of asking for it, day or night, thanks to the communication system.

Now what does it do to a village if a buffalo is sick, suffering from distocia, its uterus is twisted, the calf cannot come out. The buffalo will die and so will the calf. This is normal in the village. It has happened many times in the last hundreds of years. But this time they send for a veterinary. He lies behind the buffalo, puts his hand in, twists the uterus and delivers the calf. What does this display of modern science do to the thinking of our ordinary villager? He will say my son was sick. I sent for a doctor. For four days, no doctor came and my son died. Can't you do something about the health of our children, aren't our children at least as important as our buffaloes? "(3)

technology as cultural influence (re-visit)

How does technology, the child of science, influence the very attitudes and behavior of a people?

In our country, as is well known, we have over the centuries put a great deal of emphasis on asceticism and ascetic habits. We have applauded monks and monkish qualities, we have preached and practiced self-denial; we have approved of mortification of the flesh and in every other way we have favored meditation, self-enlightenment and improvement of man himself as against the material things that surround us. We like to regard ourselves as a spiritual society or as a society given to mysticism and we pride ourselves on being different from the West. Then we observe with surprise the corruption and violence which surrounds us daily in our peaceful country! It perplexes us, we do not know what to make of it and we wonder inwardly whether what we have claimed and what we have believed all along can be true.

Do not think that such a quest for asceticism has not also existed elsewhere. Early Christianity, for example, was engaged in a similar search for the truth. The picture of a sparsely attired, celibate, penurious Christian monk is a commonplace. Like Hinduism, Christianity in Europe also preached that the best things in life were free and that consequently it was necessary to cultivate man himself and his qualities rather than be distracted by the things of this earth.

Petrarch for example, was fond of citing St. Augustine against the medical faculties of Padua, Bologna and Paris. As noted earlier, "he upheld the investigation of the nature of man while condemning the vain search for knowledge about mere things." (4)

In those days, such an argument may have been perfectly sensible. What could possibly carry more weight: a study of all-important man, a study of human beings themselves or a study of mere Nature (mere articles or "mere things") could No one could have foreseen that what was once only the frivolous study of mere things would eventually lead to an enormous movement that became modern science. For science is nothing but observation of mere things and the formulation of conclusions from those observations. Modern science, in turn, led to an ever-growing, pervasive and spreading technology. If St. Augustine were alive today, he would be the first to acknowledge that medical electronics enables us to see the living processes within man without recourse to surgery (that is, non-invasively). It is ironical that a study of mere things should have come full circle and ultimately have led to a study of man himself.

putting it to the people

We now have our twin tools of science and technology. What do we do with them? How do we begin to apply them? How do we begin to convince the people that they require to change, that they must give up myths and beliefs based on blind faith, that they must become more rational in their thinking, that they need to learn to identify and put to use the intellectual and physical skills that are the special contribution of technology and that both of these two strands of science and technology can and should be woven together and employed in the service of their country

How do we signal to the people that mindless pursuit of religion – Hindu, Muslim, Buddhist, Sikh, Jain, Christian, Zoroastrian or other – has simply failed to deliver the goods? In democratic countries, elections are held every four or five years. There is the principle of accountability to the electorate. If the Government has obtained progress for the country, it is rewarded with another term. If it has failed, it is defeated and another Government elected in its place. Even in commerce and industry, good performance is applauded and rewarded and failure automatically calls for a change. Can we not then properly ask ourselves why our culture, of which our religion is the most important component, should have brought us to our present sorry pass?

One way perhaps of not going about our task is by avoiding a frontal attack on religion. There is also really no need for this because many receive spiritual sustenance from their religion and this too is perfectly understandable. As Naipaul has said, religion is a life support system for many people. A person's religion is so intertwined with his life that to make a direct attack upon it or in any other way to deny it to him is to starve him of oxygen or in other words, to incapacitate him.

Is there to be no solution to this age-old problem? There just may be a way. Allow me to take you back to the analogy with which we began this book. We said about the doctor's prescription that it was personal, it was self-administered and that it was quite individual. The treatment was such that it could not be forced on you by anyone.

Like the doctor in our illustration, we have to put it to the Indian people that only modern science and technology will solve our innumerable problems – that our religions, whatever they might be, are neither calculated nor able to solve them. Like the good doctor in our illustration, we need to put it to the people and allow them to decide for themselves. For this, we need simply to change the focus of the argument by not trying to appeal to their minds but instead by trying to appeal to their bodies. I have confidence in the good sense of the people of India to trust them to make the proper choice.

What actually are our basic problems? Let's enumerate. We all need food, we need water, clothing, energy; we need transport, we need houses, we need literacy and education, we need jobs, we need public hygiene and good sanitation, we need medical care. . Not a single one of these basic needs is capable of being provided by any religion. If you happen to be so inclined, religion will certainly bring you mental or spiritual solace but religion absolutely cannot solve any one of your basic material problems. Only science and technology can.

We can go into some of these more closely in order to indicate the general drift of our argument. Take the question of food. We all know that the "green revolution" has not only enabled India to become self-sufficient in food for the first time in practically a century and a half, it has also allowed us to build up reasonable buffer stocks for drought years, floods, earthquakes, possible wartime needs and so on. The green revolution only became possible because of the sciences and technologies of genetics, chemistry, agricultural engineering, electricity, automobile engineering, and botany and so on. Similarly, to provide and ensure clean water, we need knowledge of sciences like meteorology, hydrology, and geology, seismology, and soil mechanics and resources management. Nothing less than this will do. Nothing in its place will do. Repeated yagnas most decidedly will not do. And so it is for all of our other shortages without exception.

TABLE 4

Need	Some essential branches of study
Food	Botany, Chemistry, Agricultural Engineering, Pest Control, Genetics, Food processing and preservation technologies, Physics (Electricity), Automobile Engineering
Water	Water Resources development, Soil and Water conservation, Hydrology, water treatment processes, Meteorology, Geology, Zoology (Fisheries)
Housing	Civil Engineering, Architecture, Design, Structural Engineering, Construction Engineering, Land Betterment, Survey Practices, Urban Planning
Literacy	Audio-Visual technologies, Tutor skills training, problems of Intelligence, Information and Learning, Psychology, Sociology of Mass Schooling, Education of disadvantaged, Printing Technology, Computer Engineering
Education	Sciences / Humanities / Commerce / Law / Information Technologies (computer, video, telecommunications, robotics)
Healthcare	Biology, Physiology, Chemistry, Anatomy, Pharmacology, Pathology, Immunology, Genetics, Medicine/Physiology, Microbiology, Radiology, Epidemiology, Tropical Medicine, Family Planning
Transport	Mechanical, Electrical and Automobile Engineering, Transportation Economics, Traffic Operation and Safety
Energy	Physics, Mechanical/Chemical/Electrical/Nuclear Engineering, Geology, Chemistry, Ecology, Solar/Wind/Other
Clothing/ Textiles	Textile Engineering, Chemistry (textile analysis of dyes, fabrics), synthetic material industry, fashion design

Modern science and technology is a multiple cure for our long-standing illness. We have looked at some of the ways in which science works for a culture, and how irrationality impedes. We have acknowledged the silent services of technology and the need to convince our people that only science and technology can help them. Modern science and technology, therefore, are our twin tools. These are all-purpose, comprehensive tools. They are not restricted to individual problems or even to specifically Indian problems. Science is nothing but a search for the truth and so the scope for its application cannot be anything but comprehensive.

Let's see, therefore, whether we can put science and technology to work in analyzing two issues concerning us at home: the problem of our future national language and the problem of communalism in India.

should we dump English?

This argument has gone on interminably. Language in itself is another power tool. Knowledge of English has conferred an enormous advantage on those who speak and write it. In fact, say its opponents, it has helped to constitute an elite within the country, who then dominate the large majority who cannot handle the language. English has been with us in India for more than 150 years but is still so alien a language to most Indians that less than 10% of the population speak and write it adequately. However, consider the following: In 1835 Macaulay had to choose between English, Sanskrit and Persian. Where would India stand today had he chosen Sanskrit or Persian?

Now, if we mean to get the message of science and technology to the people of India in the shortest possible time, it goes without saying that the message has to be clothed in the language in which the people feel most comfortable. This would mean Hindi as well as several other of the official languages. But do we have the time? We have already spent more than seventy years in debating the matter. We are operating within a limited time framework: our population has already crossed the 1 billion mark and we have, I should think, at best another forty or fifty years in which to translate all knowledge in science and technology (including engineering and medicine, not to mention commerce, law, government, etc.) to the scheduled languages. This seems to me like an impossible task.

Are the people more important than language or is language more important than people? As a poor country with a large population, we are in a desperate position. Our foremost duty is to provide the daily necessities for our people in the shortest possible time. We have absolutely no right to postpone or compromise in this one task. To interrupt the process of development at this time by shifting forces to a new language or languages would be a classic case of changing horse's midstream. There is a strong possibility of being washed away by the current.

The imperative of science and technology promotion requires that we continue the present arrangement and not make any attempt to upset the apple cart, as it were. Once this task has been got underway and time is no longer a serious constraint, fresh attempts should be made to pass the mantle to Hindi and other languages. English is, of course, an international language. There would be no question of our present endeavours having been wasted. Hindi and the other scheduled languages could exist side by side with English in the India of the future, with the former playing the predominant role.

communalism

We come to perhaps the biggest and most enduring problem of all, communalism. In the past, it has felled at least two Prime Ministers (Rajiv Gandhi and V.P. Singh). After the fall of th66eir governments, both went around complaining that the cause was fundamentalism and communalism. This is a matter of public record. It is clear from what they said that they did not have the slightest notion about how what had happened had happened to them.

It is not even only a question of Ram Janmabhoomi vs. Babri Masjid. That is only the culmination of a problem which itself was to be expected. The Punjab problem (Hindu v. Sikh), the Kashmir problem (Muslim v. Hindu), the Sri Lanka problem (Buddhist v. Hindu) as well as the regular outbreaks of communal riots in different parts of our country are all variations on the same theme.

First of all, we must dispose of two stock layperson's arguments purporting to explain the communal problem. Of politicians in general, it is commonly said that:

1) They are only building up a political vote-bank.

2) They are trying to play off one community against the other.

The trouble with these glib rationales is that they serve as alibis and effectively put off any serious discussion of a grave problem. Naturally, both statements are true to a certain extent but they do not and cannot constitute a complete explanation of the communal problem. If they did, how do we explain the fall of not one but two Prime Ministers?

the meaning of secularism

Not long after becoming Prime Minister with an overwhelming majority in 1984, Rajiv Gandhi said that as far as secularism was concerned, he was departing from the dictionary definition of the word.(5) He said that in India it should stand for Sarva Dharma Samabhava, meaning all religions are equal. V.P. Singh said the same thing as Prime Minister in April 1991. He even went on to declare a religious holiday from the Red Fort in his Independence Day speech! Chandrashekar too said more or less the same thing in 1993.

The history of modern science and technology should tell us that you cannot wipe out three hundred and fifty years as easily as that.

Secularism is not all-religious, it is non-religious or anti-religious depending on which particular flavour you favor. It will not suffer a distortion of the meaning of the word. The history of science and technology over the last three or four centuries has shown that religion is in full retreat. How then can any one or all religions be brought back into the picture? Are we then not also postponing the advance of scientific, logical, reasoned thinking and, consequently, are we not preventing the creation, spread and use of technology for our people?

What can be so very wrong with bringing religion into the picture? On the face of it, there may be nothing wrong. After all, religion, all religions, are noble teachings. In essence, in theory, they all ask that you should love your fellow man. But in practice, things work out differently. Religions by definition are either stated dogma or hoary tradition, and each claims that it alone is the revealed truth. Before long, one religion claims that it is superior to the other and the next step is that the respective followers are grappling at each other's throats. This is not just a possible outcome. It is predictable, it was duly predicted and in fact, it is inevitable especially in the poverty-stricken conditions of developing countries like India.

In the film Gandhi, the Mahatma says "I am a Hindu and a Muslim and a Christian and a Jew and so are all of you." This is a touching moment. A point has been reached at which the forces of communalism are gaining ground and threatening the Gandhian philosophy of nonviolence and brotherhood among men. When the Mahatma states that he is a believer in all religions and that every religion constitutes a part of his being, he is, of course, giving expression to a noble sentiment. But when we consider—that religion itself is under serious scrutiny, that a careful study of recent history shows that religion is increasingly on the defensive, that it is unable to solve the acute material problems of the people, should it really surprise us that neither an appeal to the Hindu or the Muslim religion nor even to an amalgam of them, could hope to save the day?

In making his statement, the Mahatma was unfortunately wrong not once or twice but wrong four times over. It proved impossible for him in the end to create a single secular state because he attempted to base its foundation on the running quick sands of religion. Such an outcome was foreseen and foretold at the time. One could say that the failure of the Mahatma's philosophy of sarva dharma samabhava was programmed into the future. (This is not, of course, to dispute or to belittle the highly original weapon of nonviolent noncooperation which he forged and with which he waged his war of independence in our country so successfully. I mean only to say that in the end he was unable to prevent the partition of India on religious lines.)

Secularism does not concern itself only with matters of religion or non-religion. Because it is a product of the thinking which allies itself with modern science and technology, secularism has a bearing on many diverse aspects of life like the humanities, education, administration, the natural and social sciences themselves and so on. Webster's Desk Dictionary's definition is, appropriately, "concern with worldly or non-religious things."

One small illustration. While writing this portion of this book, I happened to be reading a book called Intellectuals, by Paul Johnson. The book is a well-researched account of various thinkers and writers of the last two hundred years, and the list includes Rousseau, Shelley, Ibsen, Marx, Tolstoy, Bertrand Russell, Hemingway, Bertolt Brecht, and Edmund Wilson, among others. The writer makes the point that this category of people, that is, the very breed of "intellectuals," is a comparatively recent phenomenon. In earlier times, society used to be told what it must do, what was right and what was wrong by people like priests, scribes, soothsayers and so on. With the coming of modern science and technology and therefore, the secular approach with it, individuals not representing the Church or other traditional authority were now in a position to and did pontificate to society. It would be difficult even to understand the meaning of the common word "intellectuals" if one were unclear about the enormity of the change wrought in society, and in thinking itself, after the coming of modern science and technology.(6)

Secularism is not, therefore, just an administrative convenience to keep religion separate from matters of state. It does have that effect, but secularism actually reflects the displacement or dethronement of religion from the command position which it occupied earlier. Much difficulty in India arises from the fact that secularism is regarded solely as an antidote to communalism. This restricts its meaning, when the concept demands universal application. It cannot be specially adapted to Indian soil, East Asian soil or any other soil, as people sometimes seek to do. To study and further secularism, it is only necessary to study carefully the history of modern science and to promote what Jawaharlal Nehru in our own country called "the scientific temper." One cannot, therefore, tinker with the true definition of secularism. One is likely not only to lose one's Prime Ministership but the consequences for the country and its people are bound to be calamitous.

It is often said in India, in defence of secularism, that religion must be practiced in the home and not brought out into the public domain. This is correct. But how does one do this? Since the question is not even brought up, there are no attempts made to address it and no possibility of looking for a solution. The State talks increasingly about secularism but the President goes off to visit Tirupati, and an earlier Prime Minister was reported to be a follower of Chandraswami. One Home Minister was a devotee of Saibaba and another Home Minister journeyed before the election at that time in search of the blessings of yet another saint

Secularism may require that religion be practiced only at home but religion is the most important component of culture and culture affects one's activities at every stage, whether the individual is a private citizen or a Government functionary. Where and how does one draw the line? The answer is that one has to go about it in a roundabout way...through the route of science and technology. Material progress brings self-esteem, which brings equality, which, in turn, brings tolerance of other people's religions. Such a solution obviously cannot hapnight. But our understanding that this is the only sure way can make it happen sooner rather than later. Matters of religion and politics are so inextricably linked that it is all but impossible to separate the two by merely ordaining that religion should be confined to the home.

A small, current example of this is to be found in the corporate world. A large industrial company, say TISCO, will not merely speak about the need for fellow-feeling between Hindus and Muslims. It gets both kinds of employees to work together and automatically a sense of fellow-feeling and camaraderie develops. The same thing needs to be done systematically for the nation as a whole.

And of course, this is the way things happened in Europe, as Fukuyama tells us:

"Contrary to those who at the time believed that religion was a necessary and permanent feature of the political landscape, liberalism vanquished religion in Europe...After a centuries-long confrontation with liberalism, religion was taught to be tolerant. In the sixteenth century, it would have seemed strange to most Europeans not to use political power to enforce belief in their particular sectarian faith. Today, the idea that the practice of religions other than one's own should injure one's own faith seems bizarre, even to the most pious churchman. Religion has thus been relegated to the sphere of private life – exiled, it would seem, more or less permanently from European political life except on certain narrow issues like abortion." (7)

acute bewilderment

What can be the reason, one may then ask, why successive Governments seem unable to explain to the people that secularism is not a luxury but a real necessity for the country? The reason is that, like many other people in this country and elsewhere, the Government too suffers from an ailment which I call Acute Bewilderment. The primary symptom is total puzzlement about the true meaning of science while one is surrounded on all sides by the artifacts (and benefits) of science. One of the hopes of this book is that it will act as a bulwark or even as a preventive against this widespread disease.

Mr. L.K. Advani, to give an example, appears to be one of the more prominent victims. The vehicle in which he made his triumphant journey from Somnath to Bihar, where he was arrested, is supposed to have been made in a Japanese Toyota motorcar. Some journalists properly labelled this Toyota Hinduism! Two thousand years of Hinduism did not and could not produce the internal combustion engine. Conversely, if Mr. Advani wished to be true to the precepts of Hinduism, he would really have had to bid goodbye to the benefits of modern science and technology which alone can and did produce such an invention. For the same reasons, travel by an airplane also would not do because that too is a product of Western science and technology. So are the locomotive, the steam-powered ship or diesel-driven ship, the motorcycle, the bicycle and even the tricycle! Mr. Advani would have to settle for a palkhi (palanquin) or choose horseback or a bullock cart. The last mentioned is supposed to have arrived on the scene in India about 2000 years ago. At that time, it constituted a revolutionary form of transport. (8). But then it would take Mr. Advani a long time to get from one part of India to the other. (In another sense, this shows how long it has been since we, in India, can be said to have contributed a new invention to the world of transport.) This does not mean that modern means of transport are not to be allowed to Mr. Advani. What I am saying is that he cannot but fall back on them—he has no choice!

Here's another example of Acute Bewilderment. While I write, I see in a newspaper a photograph of a popular BJP leader addressing a packed meeting in Bombay. (9). The lady is shown wearing a watch and speaking into a microphone. What do these simple gadgets signify? Let's quickly examine how we arrived at the modern wristwatch:

Man began with the sun-dial. However, during nighttime there was no measure of time. No sun, no shadow! How to tell the time? The answer was the water clock, which did not depend on the sun. For the first time, night could be incorporated into the day. Then came the hour glass—but it was inconvenient to keep on turning the glass. The first movement in the direction of a mechanical clock came from the desire of monks and other religious people to say their prayers regularly to God. Boorstin writes that people now thought of time no longer as a flowing stream but as the accumulation of discrete measured moments. "There are few greater revolutions in human experience than this movement from the seasonal or temporary hour to the equal hour. Here was man's declaration of independence from the sun, new proof of the mastery over himself and his surroundings."(10)

Clocke was a Middle Dutch word for "bell." People had to hear the time because there was no mass literacy and they could not "read" the time. This is also the reason why at first there were no dials on clocks. (11) Church towers gradually gave way to bell towers (another example of secularism). Then Galileo introduced the exactness of the pendulum into the clock. The pendulum was later replaced by the spring which made for a small timepiece which made time "portable." Timepieces then made way for wristwatches, and in recent decades we have seen the battery-operated watch followed by the quartz watch and now, by digital watches.

Boorstin describes how the clock was destined to be the mother of machines because clockmakers were the first to consciously apply the theories of mechanics and physics to the making of machines: As early as 1763, master watchmaker Ferdinand Berthoud could list sixteen different sorts of workmen involved in producing clocks and twenty-one making watches. These were makers of the movement; finishers; borers; makers of springs; engravers of brass needles; pendulum makers; engravers of dials; polishers of brass parts; enamellers of dials; silverers of brass dials; engravers of cases; bronze gilders; painters to imitate gilding in colours; founders of wheels; turners and polishers of bells.

"The clock enticed man across boundaries of religion, language and politics. Even before the vast colonial migrations and the settlement of the New World, the movements of skilled craftsmen exerted an influence far out of proportion to their numbers. Before power-driven transportation, before the rise of mass production, it was often the craftsmen themselves rather than their product that travelled."(12)

If, therefore, a prominent political person sports a watch but is not aware of the historical development of the clock industry and all that it represents, the position is clearly no different from the tulsi plant and its ritual maintenance that we discussed earlier.

Also, does not all this once again represent an anxious search for truth? Hinduism or Islam could not and did not bring about this kind of progress in horology. Nor is this contradiction limited only to us Hindus in India. If you have read in the press that Saudi Arabian women were (until 2018) prohibited from driving motorcars or that truck drivers in Pakistan went on a nationwide strike (1990) rather than pay blood money, these are only different aspects of the same basic contradiction.

India could have chosen to become a theocratic state in 1947. If Pakistan was brought into being for the Muslims, what was to prevent the remainder of the country from being set up for Hindus? Why did it not happen? Because the entire struggle for independence waged by the Congress Party over 25 long years had been based on the premise of a secular state: sarwa dharma samabhava, as Mahatma Gandhi saw it, or a non-religious state, as Pandit Nehru interpreted it. It was also because of the very strong view held by Nehru that only a secular state could deliver the goods, enabling the country first to survive and then to rescue Indians, both Hindus and Muslims, from poverty.

Our neighbour, Nepal, is a Hindu state. Predictably, it is even poorer than we are. (13) In fact, Nepal is the poorest country in the subcontinent. However, so subtle is the role played by modern science and technology, so hidden from the common view that even Western observers whose very society is based on that platform sometimes fail to perceive this fact. The question arises: the Hindu state may have been a sufficiency for the past (a glorious civilization arose!) but can it at all be a path for the future?

RJ v. BM

Whatever else the Ram Janmabhoomi / Babri Masjid dispute may have left unsettled, two things are clear beyond reasonable doubt. The first is that large masses of the Indian people have absolutely no use for or understanding of archaeology. Otherwise, considerations of religion apart, who in his right mind would want to totally destroy a beautiful mosque constructed as long ago as 1520 and put up something else in its place? What would the people of the USA or Europe not give to have a similar, additional historically valuable building on the soil of their countries?

The second thing that this episode brings out clearly once again is that many of our leaders also have no sense of history. Surely, together with Buddha, Ashoka, the two Chandragupta's, Kanishka and Harsha, the Moghul dynasty proper which began with Babar and ended with Aurangzeb is also part of India's rich history—an exciting, vibrant part. The word Moghul has even become part of the English language. Yet our inclination seems to be steadily towards mythology.

applying MoST to communalism

In looking at the matter of Hindus v. Muslims in India, first, let's view it from the side of the Hindus, the majority community. If we show that it is impracticable to dictate to the Muslim minority, then it follows that it would be equally difficult—if not more so, because of numbers—for Muslims to dictate to the Hindus in this country. If we show that it is not possible to end the problem, then it becomes easier to accept the solution of alleviation; that is, the need for both communities to reach an agreement to live together amicably.

The Muslim community in India already numbers about 200 million. Regardless of what extreme rightist Hindu organizations might say, it is not possible to cow down such a large minority. If violence, God forbid, were to break out in a large way, thousands upon thousands of Hindus (yes Hindus, as well as Muslims) would be slain. Such a solution, if indeed it can be called a solution, is simply insane. Similarly, if Muslims were to attempt to assault the Hindu majority, it would be a horrendous outcome for both communities. Given, therefore, the size of the two communities in India, it is impossible to think of any viable solution except one which would allow both communities to live together, to adapt to each other and, if one can venture to voice such a hope, to prosper together.

Because both communities have remained hopelessly backward, the problem has got intensified. If we can show how backwardness came about, how it overtook both communities and how now both communities can progress together, the communal problem, which seems so intractable at present, will automatically fade away or at least be considerably attenuated. Does this seem so difficult to achieve?

Let us take an actual example. Theoretically, there can be only four possible solutions to the problem of Ram Janmabhoomi vs Babri Masjid. It could be any one of the following:

1) the Hindus are right

2) the Muslims are right

3) both are right; or

4) both are wrong!

Alternatives (1) and (2) lead to an obvious conclusion: we simply end up destroying ourselves. These alternatives, therefore cannot be considered and must be discarded. Alternative (3) is what the Government has been pushing as the solution for the last sixty years. This is a very noble concept but it isn't working! Sarva Dharma

Samabhava. They also say that this is what secularism is. Nothing could be further from the truth! As we have already said, secularism is not all-religious, it is non-religious, even anti-religious in the sense that it is headed in a direction which is the opposite of religion. If you proceed to foist the wrong solution on the problem, then the problem not only remains unresolved, it is aggravated—and this is what has been happening.

No one appears to have considered alternative 4. Both religions are wrong! If this were not so, would both communities be in the hapless position in which they find themselves today? Neither religion is capable of fulfilling the basic economic needs of the community. Both have lost out to modern science and technology. Hindu and Muslim cultures, based on their respective religions, have become stationary and stagnant and are incapable of begetting progress. In their poverty-stricken condition, it is no wonder that they are quarrelling and even attacking each other? If it were possible to show them that they are deluding themselves and that, if they need to progress, they must grasp the twin tools of science and technology and therefore, confine religion to their homes, then it might be possible to find a way out of the present terrible morass.

(Note: This was written well before the Supreme Court decision of 2019 – after deliberations extending to nearly a quarter century!)

thinking locally, acting globally

In a country as large and diverse as India, there are bound to be differences between regions. Differences of exact ethnic stock, of language and literature, of dress, of food, of social customs, sometimes of religion and so on. It is necessary that we boldly acknowledge the existence of these outward differences. Behind and beneath these differences, however, run strong, invisible bonds represented by a common market, a common currency, a common national language, a common judicial system, common transportation systems like airlines, railways and bus routes, a common manufacturing system, national movements of labour and so on. All of these commonalities or bonds are dependent, in one way or another, on the forces of science and technology and can only be furthered by and deepened by the common goal of secularism.

By reason of advancing economic development, we are proceeding towards that destination anyway but our journey can be made more swift, our similarities emphasized, and our problems minimized or more easily solved, if we realize that secularism (the whole-hearted acceptance and practice of the forces of science and technology) is to be our common goal. Development itself can flow the more easily between state borders if this common platform is acknowledged and accepted by all. A balance can be struck between encouragement and promotion of legitimate state differences and the paramount need for the federal state to exist. Mental boundaries which were formerly vague and inchoate now become more real and tangible. The question of viability, economic or otherwise, is brought to the surface. Regionalism and secessionism are seen to be the artificial, disruptive, breakaway forces that they are. If religion cannot be the basis for the existence of a political state, when it is seen that whole nations elsewhere are grouping together with economic pacts and when it is obvious that the entire world is moving towards one global economy, the need for small, different, intransigent areas to want to break away begins to appear more and more like an exercise in futility.

Arab Muslim civilization

If we are going to consider Babar, his generals, the Babri Masjid and India's Muslim population, it is imperative that we also consider the role played by Arab civilization in the history of the world. The average person in India, more particularly the average Hindu, remains unaware of the considerable achievements of Arab Muslim civilization. In fields like astronomy, biology, medicine, chemistry, natural history, agriculture and more, Arab achievements from the eighth century to the twelfth century remained unrivalled in the world.

Of course, there had been similar civilizations before, including in India itself, but Arab civilization was the very latest in history before the advent in the Western world of modern science and technology. In fact, Arab civilization acted as a bridge between ancient Greek learning and Western civilization. During the time of the Dark Ages in Europe, many valuable works in Greek and Hebrew were first translated into Arabic before being translated again into Latin. If not for Arab scholarship in this regard at that critical time, many works might have been irretrievably lost to the Western world. (14)

Had it maintained its exceptional lead, Arab civilization, not the West, might well have become the birthplace and then the cradle of modern science and technology. But that was not to be. Why? How did it lose the head-on advantage it had already secured over Europe?

Various reasons have been given. There was no philosophical questioning of the sort that leads to scientific discovery. The theistic view of life defeated the doctrine of qadr, or free will. The Koran was assembled in the Arabic language, it represented the absolute authority of Islam and it was forbidden to change it. As mentioned earlier, in the tenth century a scholastic battle broke out among Arab philosophers as to what was more important: the Islamic scriptures, or the findings of natural scientists. The battle was won by Al Ghazzali, who was on the side of the scriptures. All of Islam's discoveries and the guiding principles which governed these discoveries were made to conform to what had been set out in the religious books. In this way, a glorious advantage was lost. Arab civilization and the Muslim peoples who constituted it have never recovered from the blow. A couple of centuries later, when the nascent Western civilization came to the same crossroads in the course of its own history, it boldly and confidently negotiated the turn. At this point was born modern science and technology.

At its peak, the Muslim world stretched from Spain and Portugal in the West to Indonesia in the East. By way of contrast, Hindu civilization reached its zenith as long ago as 600 AD. After the Golden Age characterized by the Gupta period, the story is one of almost continuous decline (except for certain small civilizations in the South) until the battle of Talikota in 1565 and the resultant fall of the Vijayanagar kingdom brought about an end to Hindu aspirations. Furthermore, the reach of Hindu civilization, although certainly to South East Asia, has not been able to equal the enormous spread of Muslim civilization because, apart from India itself, the only Hindu country in the world today is neighbouring, tiny Nepal. During different periods in history, therefore, both the Hindus and the Muslims lost out, but the fall of the Muslims is much more dramatic because it came so very close to the beginnings of modern science and technology.

The victor, the all-vanquishing conqueror is, as you will have guessed, the Western world because it possessed the two tools of modern science and technology. Is it not time, therefore, that we pause to consider our own kind of perestroika movement for India? Not only do Hindus and Muslims in our country remain some of the poorest people in the world, they are also now properly set against each other because of a supposed conflict between followers of mandir and mosque. It is rather like witnessing a vigorous wrestling match between two heavy, foolhardy contestants in a boat which is leaking heavily and even likely to sink unless we are more careful.

Conclusion

I remain convinced that science and technology are the key to our future. If we define secularism arbitrarily or wrongly, or even if we fail to realize the full implications of the word, we will be wantonly throwing away our only passport to the future. We might as well hope to cross the oceans without benefit of compass and rudder to our ship-of-state. A proper understanding of secularism can define an approach to our social, economic, political and cultural problems in a future that is getting more and more complex to understand. It can constitute an answer to our problems of communalism, casteism, regionalism and secessionism and can help us as a nation to march to the future with a proper sense of our destiny.

Part 2

(intellectual journey)

Chapter 4
WHAT IS SCIENCE? companion, from the cradle to the grave

A belief is not merely an idea the mind possesses; it is an idea that possesses the mind – Robert Bolton

Circular reality is the type of reality that is involved in beliefs. There is a way of looking at the world which gives a world-view which reinforces the way of looking at the world. There is a perceptional lock-in. - Edward de Bono, Conflicts

The logic of modern science can explain a great deal about our world: why we residents of developed democracies are office workers rather than peasants eking out a living on the land, why we are members of labor unions and professional organizations rather than tribes or clans, why we obey the authority of a bureaucratic superior rather than a priest, why we are literate and speak a common national language. - Francis Fukuyama, The End of History and the Last Man

• **overcoming science anxiety** • **what is science?** • **science and nature** • **unravelling the knot** • **what science is not** • **onion-skin dissection** • **extrapolations** • **OTEST**

overcoming science anxiety

Why is there a barrier to science? If science and technology is the missing element and the one that needs to be supplied for the construction of a cure and indeed when there is so much of science and technology in front of us and surrounding us, why in truth is there so much resistance to science, especially to an effort to understand science?

One possible answer is that there is perhaps too much science around! Where once, in Michael Faraday's time, there were lecture-table experiments and public lectures to go with them by way of explanation, we now have science and its products pouring out of our ears. Every day there is an announcement of some new discovery or the other. There is no longer the same wonderment with science as once there used to be.

Further, science has become too complex leading to science anxiety. For those who hitherto have paid little or no attention to science, some may feel the need to start with science but for many even among such people, this becomes a somewhat wrenching experience. Some agree that India has been slow in accepting modern science and technology but feel that any historical account is likely to be a dreary affair. Others refuse to admit that our culture has been a laggard but do not provide any independent explanation for the fact that India still remains one of the poorest countries in the world. Finally, there are those who are reluctant to change their ways anyway.

Everyone has heard of STEM—that is, science, technology, engineering and mathematics. As an expression of college or university curricula, this is perfectly in order. Different students might want to study one or more of any of these subjects. But, as an introduction to science, my view is that this acronym can be misleading. After all, engineering is a combination of science and technology, so perhaps there is a certain repetition or redundancy there and therefore, an avoidable confusion in understanding, especially to an initiate.

I also feel that mathematics should not be bracketed with science. Mathematics is often necessary for confirmation of various propositions in science but it is entirely possible to become enchanted with science without necessarily being proficient in maths. For many, "maths" evokes an even greater dread than "science," keeping large numbers of people, young and old, from experiencing the excitement of science.

My own preference is for MoST. MoST stands for "modern science and technology." Every letter counts. For example, science has always been with man but the modern world is taken to have begun with the coming of modern science—usually associated with the period corresponding to the life of Galileo Galilei (1564-1642). Technology is given equal importance because, as sought to be explained elsewhere in this book, technology transforms culture. So, study science we must and therefore, we now begin our examination of this branch of knowledge which quite literally has changed the face of the world and which we needst must employ if we are to promote and secure growth in India.

what is science?

What is this mysterious thing called Science? We have claimed that the proper presence in any country of its latter-day equivalent, modern science, has brought unprecedented prosperity to that country. Equally we have claimed that its lack has brought about stagnation and destitution. What does "science" mean? What does it stand for? How do we isolate and understand this slippery thing which is all around us and still eludes our grasp?

Some years ago, in a programme on Bombay Doordarshan called "What's the Good Word," this question was asked: What's the word which we come across every day in school and college which stands for the Latin expression "to know" ? As far as my memory goes, no one on the panel was able to answer! Neither was anybody in the audience. The word is, of course, Science. Science is a relentless search for knowledge, that's all—and everything—that it is.

Most of us in India have hardly paused to really consider the meaning of the word. If we do, possibly the very first occasion is when it comes to be time to finish school and to enter college. To begin a career, we now need to choose one of three streams. Which is it to be? Arts, Science or Commerce? A large number of those choosing Science do so because of "better job prospects". Engineering or Medicine (and now Computers)? These are the prestigious careers, the most lucrative and therefore these attract the most ambitious candidates. On the other hand, while opportunities for students in the arts and commerce streams have expanded in recent years, there was a time not so long ago when at least to choose Arts for a career amounted to taking one's place in "a waiting room for ladies until they got married!" There was also possibly on all hands a secret dread of the word "science". To many, it conjured up visions of complicated tables in mathematics, obscure equations in algebra, dreadful experiments in biology laboratories... It was much easier to tackle narrative subjects like history, literature, philosophy, economics, or sociology.

"Science" is such a common word that no one really stops to think about it. But science, or at least general science, can be inviting and among the most user-friendly of subjects. It requires no special knowledge of mathematics nor does it take any practical skills. It does not call for any special aptitude of any kind except perhaps curiosity and, in the case of this book, a love for reading. Armed with this one fondness alone, it can lead directly and inexorably to a fascinating search for truth.

How do we define Science? The Random House (College Edition) Dictionary calls it:

1. a branch of knowledge or study dealing with a body of facts or truths systematically arranged and showing the operation of general laws
2. systematic knowledge of the physical or material world
3. systematized knowledge of any kind
4. any skill that reflects a precise application of facts or principles

Chamber's Twentieth Century Dictionary puts it like this: Science, knowledge: knowledge ascertained by observation and experiment, critically tested, systematized and brought under general principles; a department or branch of such knowledge or study; a skilled craft.

Both may serve us as definitions but aren't they somewhat tiresome descriptions? This is usually the trouble with definitions. They need to be precise and in the process they fail to bring out the true flavour of the subject they are defining. So, consider the following definition by our own Prof. S.K. Ookerjee of Mumbai. His definition is disarmingly simple. True, it is about scientific temper but that is what we are really talking about, isn't it? Prof. Ookerjee was writing to the Times of India:

" By 'scientific temper' is meant an unprejudiced mind, ready and able to make a disinterested study of any subject, unswayed by passions, guided by reason, free of superstition and unafraid to accept conclusions – however unpalatable – when the available evidence logically leads to them. It is the temper which, according to Socrates, goes where the argument leads". (1)

How much more simple, practical and exciting this is! We said "disarmingly simple," and this is so. But a closer look at this definition will also show that science is quite rigorous in its demands. To go where the argument leads, to discard or to push aside ruthlessly whatever might stand in the way, may not be quite as easy as it looks. But this is precisely what science calls for. Tradition, custom, ritual, ways of thinking, entire religions can and have been challenged, even overturned, by this simple definition and as a consequence, a world (scientific) revolution created and set in motion.

Prof. Ookerjee's other point in writing his letter was that a scientific temper doesn't necessarily require a science education. It can equally well be developed through other disciplines like history, economics and philosophy. This also is true but think of it. How many people in India today even with a science education go about exercising scientific temper? Precious few! So that's what we have to first address ourselves to. How to develop science knowledge into simple, logical, rational, scientific thinking. Once started and got going, it is bound to also affect non-science subjects like economics, history and philosophy and we should be patient while encouraging this to happen.

Science is both comprehensive and incremental. We have now had modern science with us for nearly 350 years. From early developments in astronomy and physics, impressive bodies of knowledge have been accumulated in disciplines like physics, chemistry, metallurgy, geology, biology, zoology, botany and more. The broad principles of each of these subjects intersect with the principles of every other and together they constitute one giant edifice of knowledge and progress. It is important to understand this principle of inter-connection between the different sciences. Each bit of information or knowledge is tried and tested and generally fits into the principles of the other sciences. If any one of the main principles was to be proved false, it would endanger and bring about the fall of the entire edifice.

On the one hand, therefore, this large, differentiated body of knowledge exists while at the same time it is constantly being added to by contributions from researchers and scientists all over the world.

Dr. Lewis Thomas describes the process in this way:

"It sometimes looks like a lonely activity but it is as much the opposite of lonely as human behavior can be. There is nothing so social, so communal, and so interdependent. An active field of science is like an immense intellectual anthill... There is nothing to touch the spectacle. In the midst of what seems a collective derangement of minds in total disorder, with bits of information being scattered about, torn to shreds, disintegrated, reconstituted, engulfed, in a kind of activity that seems as random and agitated as that of bees in a disturbed part of the hive, there suddenly emerges, with the purity of a slow phrase of music, a single new piece of truth about nature". (2)

science and nature

What is the objective of Science? Is it conquest of Nature? Does it involve the subjugation of Nature or does it seek harmony with Nature? Many people harbour in their minds the unspoken thought that science is somehow antagonistic to Nature. Nothing could be further from the truth. Science seeks only an understanding of Nature but it will not put even Nature on such a high pedestal that it will accept unquestioningly all that Nature does or everything that is done in the name of Nature.

For example, smallpox was a completely natural happening. Even in the USA, some two hundred years ago, Thomas Jefferson had to defend and promote the introduction of inoculation for smallpox against the strongly held views of clergymen and senior political leaders, who said that it was against Nature and against the will of God. We in India said that it spoke of warmth or heat in the body and to counter the illness we even gave a name to the goddess of smallpox: Sheetaladevi, a goddess who brings coolness. By doing this, we condemned thousands to suffer a horrible death and still more thousands carried and still carry the terrible marks of smallpox on them all their lives.

On a visit to Teheran in 1974 or 1975, I was waiting for the lift in the lobby of an impressive high-rise building. When the lift arrived on the ground floor and the door opened, I saw for the first time in my life a white man (many Iranians are very fair) with deep smallpox marks on his face. I was taken aback although, of course, I tried not to show it. So accustomed was I to seeing the scars of this dreadful disease on only coloured Indian faces that I had never realised that European man had been rid of this disfigurement problem for at least several generations. Iran is, of course, an intermediate country where the complexion of many people is fair but where the disease, Iran being a developing country still, had not entirely been stamped out. At that moment, I also became aware for the first time of the possibilities of the interesting subject of epidemiology and the geography of disease! I also remembered briefly the case of the pump-handle at Broad Street.

The German physician Paracelsus argued in the 1530s that "God desires that we do not simply accept an object as an object but investigate why it has been created. Then we can...cook raw food so that it tastes good in the mouth and build for ourselves winter apartments and roofs against the rains!"(3)

We in India are so little aware of science and speak so misguidedly about harmony with nature at all times, this idea being one of our great legacies from the past, that often there is a flat contradiction between the two and it does not even occur to us. Some thirty years ago, India's first air-conditioned temple was built in Jaipur. (One might properly ask why more temples need to be put up when there is already a surfeit of temples in this country and then why further money has to be spent on air-conditioning them.) In the presence of a number of eminent people who had arrived from different parts of the country, Swami Ragananda declared that true worship meant seeing God in man and Nature. None of the eminent visitors had walked to the venue. They had needed to take a plane or train or to arrive by car. It also never occurred to any of these worthy gentlemen that nothing could be more natural than the weather! If one is going to benefit by climate control, and in a tropical country such as ours there are many benefits, one should at least cease extolling the undying virtues of Nature. (4)

As we said, when science first developed, it did so because of our need to understand Nature. In earlier years, science was called natural philosophy. There never was any intention of dominating Nature. This became necessary only later when we were confronted with a choice between benefiting man or remaining in harmony with Nature. Western society did not flinch from making this decision, accounting today for the great body of science which they have built up and consequently, the prosperity that they have attained for their peoples. Chinese and Indian civilizations, despite a head-start, kept paying tribute to harmony with Nature, suffered from a lack of nerve, never made the crucial decision, were unable to make the transition to modern science and therefore, remain developing societies to this day.

unravelling the knot

Science can be a way of unravelling the knot. It can lead you to, say, and study of the night sky or, if you are so inclined, the study of plants. It can teach you why a museum is an exciting experience because it can take you to history and to archaeology. You need to know why they call Jaisalmer or Bhopal a beautiful city? Science can tell you. How? It can lead you to archaeology and from there to architecture and history or the other way round. You notice the paws of a dog or a cat as it goes by—it can spur an interest in zoology. Did you need to know, before the first Gulf War, why Saddam Hussein was on the wrong side of history? An account of the sad decline of Arab science could have led you to the answer. Science is, therefore, as large as life itself. It is a continuous search to draw truth from confusion or obfuscation, downright ignorance, or automatic attribution to God. During the ten thousand years or so of recorded human civilization, there have been countless instances of total ignorance or inadvertent avoidance or even deliberate suppression of the truth that affected our cultures, both Eastern and Western. These have not usually been passing episodes but have continued for centuries together until the truth was discovered, asserted and finally made known. Whole branches of science like biology, zoology, botany, geography, astronomy have all had to go through this kind of trial.(5)

It is customary to divide knowledge into two large parts –science and the humanities. A legacy of my schooldays was, I discovered, a dread of science in general. A background of economics and later in college, law, took me even further away from science.

Having stumbled upon general science at thirty-seven, I finally began to see, at least in my opinion, the clear advantages of science as an entry point to knowledge. For example, I think that, even if the subjects are properly taught, one would have to be at least in one's teens before one got even a feel for the classics or the humanities. On the other hand, when a parent or a friend holds a child by his hand, takes him to a garden and explains the various things to be seen there, one could say that the child's initial lessons in botany or zoology or geology have already begun. If the visit happened to be at night, he/she could be introduced to the wonders of the night-sky. This comes on top of the child's own irrepressible urge for knowledge at that age. Additionally, it has only recently been established that the period from one to six years is critically important because apparently children's brains develop fastest at that age – and that itself appears to be no coincidence..

When the approach is through the humanities, the influence is on one individual person to begin with. An object or artifact of science, on the other hand, say for example a smart phone or a tape recorder or an airplane, would affect large numbers of people at the same time and even successively.

Finally and most importantly, the humanities by themselves do not create jobs, at least jobs in large numbers. Science is the most direct and most immediate route to a multiplicity of jobs in commerce and industry. The lives and well being of whole nations depend on it.

To go where the argument leads, as is stated in the professor's definition, may seem like a simple matter but, in reality, it took a great deal of intellectual conviction, of resolution, of courage and effort before the light was permitted to be seen, the required paths followed and the real truth allowed to become known.

Before I conclude this section, I feel obliged to show, especially for Indian audiences, how Yukichi Fukuzawa dealt with his own childhood fears... As we said earlier (Chap. 2), Japan is the only Asian country which realized early on that it lacked something that Europe possessed. A good amount of the credit for this must go to Fukuzawa. He lived from 1834 to 1901 and his autobiography makes extremely interesting reading, particularly because of the striking parallels with the India of our own times. The following is a lengthy extract from the book:

"One day when I was twelve or thirteen years old, I ran through the room in one of my mischievous moments and stepped on some papers which my brother was arranging on the floor. Suddenly he broke out in disgust: "Stop, you dunce!" Then he began to speak solemnly. "Do you not see what is written here? He said "Is this not Okudaira Taizen – no Tayu – your Lord's name?" "I did not know it" I hastily apologized. "I am sorry" "You say you did not know" he replied indignantly. "But if you have eyes, you should see. What do you think of trampling your lord's name under foot? The sacred code of lord and vassal is..."

Here my brother was beginning to recite the samurai rules of duty. There was nothing for me to do but bow my head to the floor and plead: "I was very careless, please forgive me". But in my heart there was no apology. All the time I was thinking: "Why scold about it? Did I step on my lord's head? What is wrong with stepping on a piece of paper?"

Then I went on, reasoning in my childish mind that if it was so wicked to step on a man's name, it would be very much more wicked to step on a god's name and I determined to test the truth. So I stole one of the charms, the thin paper slips, bearing sacred names, which are kept in many households for avoiding bad luck. And I deliberately trampled on it when nobody was looking. But no heavenly vengeance came.

"It is just as I thought!" I said to myself. "What right did my brother have to scold me?"

I felt that I had made a great discovery! But this I could not tell anybody, not even my mother or sisters"

When he grew older, Fukuzawa became more reckless and decided that talk about divine punishment was a lie. He thought of finding out what the "god of Inari" really was.

"There was an Inari shrine in the corner of my uncle's garden, as in many other households. I opened the shrine and found only a stone there. I threw it away and put in another stone which I picked up on the road. Then I went on to explore the Inari shrine of our neighbor, Shimomura. Here the token of the god was a wooden tablet. I threw it away too and waited for what might happen. When the season of the Inari festival came, may people gathered to put up flags, beat drums and make offerings of the sacred rice-wine. During all the round of festival services, I was chuckling to myself: "There they are – worshipping my stones, the fools!" Thus from childhood I have never had any fear of gods or Buddha. Nor have I ever had any faith in augury and magic, or in the fox and badger which, people say, have power to deceive men. I was a happy child, and my mind was never clouded by unreasonable fears." (6)

what science is not

What is science not? Science is not technology. The two are separate and need to be understood separately. Science concerns itself with the mind. It is an approach, an attitude, a simple sense of curiosity, born from a desire to discover the truth. Science requires elements like hypotheses and evidence—this makes it a cerebral thing. Technology, on the other hand, is an application of science. It represents a practical application of science and scientific truths to the everyday requirements of the world.

Naturally, science and technology go hand in hand. These days, the interval between the discovery and enunciation of scientific propositions and their conversion into industrial or commercial opportunities is becoming smaller and smaller. Yet sometimes, technology can, in reverse order, also contribute to progress in science. For example, had we not known of the concept of the water-pump, it would have probably have taken us much longer to understand, in biology, the workings of the human heart. (7) After the coming of printing, there may have been a visible, intuitive connection between the display in books of mechanical piping and plumbing and the understanding of the human venous or arterial systems.(8)

When it comes to science, therefore, most people will agree that we have a great deal to be thankful for. Earlier, we have tried to show how entire nations were made really prosperous for the first time in their history by the methods and the tools of science. We need to clearly understand this in India. It is only science which will enable us to be lifted up from poverty. Yet there is a great deal of careless criticism these days about the role and usefulness of science. Of course, every one of these critics benefits from the innumerable products of science. The nuclear holocaust, when it comes, is supposed to be the culmination of science; so is the complaint that our land, air and waters have been contaminated by the excessive use of science. This is unfair criticism of science. Science is only an attempt to arrive at the truth and the truth certainly does not require the destruction of the world or the despoliation of its resources

.Science is not only not neutral in these matters, it is actually partial towards the welfare and well-being of man. If this were not so, there would be no use for science. Science has already benefited mankind in countless ways: the evidence is there for all to see. If science is sometimes pressed into products or uses which are patently wrong, then the fault is not, cannot be, that of science but of ourselves for being unattentive or having allowed our judgment to become warped and for choosing that use. In other words, science pressed into the wrong technology.

Anyway, it is no longer possible to disinvent science and technology. Both are here to stay. Therefore, the only thing for us to do is to make certain, individually as well as by public policies and other Government action, that our resources are not employed for misguided or wrongful uses of science. Fire has been a boon for mankind. Without it, cooked meals might not have been possible nor much chemistry or metallurgy. But this does not mean that the act of the arsonist is justified. Similarly, a knife can be used both to cut up vegetables in the kitchen or by the surgeon in the operating room—but this does not mean that stabbings in communal riots should be acceptable. It all depends on the use to which you put science—whether it serves the cause of man or goes against it. That must be the final test.

onion-skin dissection

Many people are unsure in their minds as to how any product of science could possibly be opposed to the concepts of religion. The two are seen as distinct and unrelated to each other. The question of opposition is never seen to arise. The two have existed side by side for so long that it seems difficult for the common person to understand any question of opposition or contrariness. However, as we shall explain, this is not the case.

Take any product of science, say, a motorcar and let's do a cross-section on it. We call this type of dissection a PSSP. It would show four onion-skin types of layers. Thus:

PSSP

Motor car

Product

Systems

Engine, battery, electrical systems, tyres and
tubes, steel frame and chassis, petrol etc.

Sciences

Physics, Mechanics, Hydraulics,
Electronics, Chemistry, Metallurgy,
Petroleum technology, Geology etc

**Philosophy
Of Science**

Principles of Science

Each product is dependent on its constituent systems, the systems are themselves dependent on the different sciences and finally, each science comes to life because of the philosophy of science, which we have explained, is nothing but a search for the truth. Once dissected in this fashion, it will be seen that each product of science and technology is finally dependent for its existence on a reasoning or philosophy which began from small beginnings, from elementary positions, from local rather than general principles, from immediate rather than long term considerations and one could even say, quite often, from unguided rather than guided or planned objectives.

Now, if one looks up the history of any of the sciences on which this philosophy is based, sciences such as physics, chemistry, electronics, metallurgy, geology etc., it is possible to zero in on how religion was not only not a help but how, instead, it came to obstruct progress, how it tried to head off things in a different direction and how, therefore, it could not have thrown up a product like the motorcar, although it i.e. religion, had existed for much longer than modern science itself.

This is not the place to give a long historical account of the sciences or religion but let us briefly illustrate a few points to show where opposition and conflict arose:

Astronomy: When Galileo looked up the stars in his telescope, the Church refused to admit reality!

Physics: When Newton worked out quantitatively the movement of the planets and other heavenly bodies, the Church was opposed to it.

Chemistry: Claims that everything on earth, in the sun, the moon, the planets, the stars, the galaxies, the entire cosmos is made up of one or more chemical elements but the Church was opposed to finiteness of this kind.

Geology: The Greeks believed that matter comprised five elements such as earth, air, fire, water and ether - and this was implicitly accepted by the Church for centuries together.

Physiology: Dissection of dead bodies was not allowed by several religions.

Philosophy: prescribed abstinence, denial, mortification of the flesh.

Luther's disciple, Melanchthon, said a few years after Luther's death:"It is part of a good mind to adopt the truth as revealed by God and to acquiesce in it." (9)

Geography: It was forbidden to travel overseas (India, China and Japan).

Zoology: For example, the Hindu concept of the holy cow and the Muslim and Jewish proscription of the pig.

Literature: The Koran was not permitted to be translated from the Arabic. It was to be committed to memory i.e. reliance on memory. Fear of blasphemy kept the printing press out of the Muslim world for centuries – although, as we have seen, it was the Arabs who had brought the Chinese invention of paper to Europe!

If religion was positioned away from the various sciences in this manner, it follows that it could not have resulted in the different steps that came attempted to be taken, directly and indirectly, which led to the motorcar. Although, therefore, religion has existed from almost the beginnings of man and modern science is of much later vintage, it will be seen how the latter upstaged the former in delivering to man the numerous material objects on which he is so dependent today.

Our second example of a PSSP dissection is that of the loudspeaker and microphones. For the loudspeaker and the microphone to be invented, it was necessary for modern science to analyze or break down the elements of sound and then to synthesize or put them all back together again. Thus:

Product

Loudspeaker +
Microphone

Systems

Transducers to convert sound to electrical
signals and further devices to convert these

Sciences

Chemistry, Physics, Electricity,
principles of Sound, Metallurgy etc.

**Philosophy
Of Science**

Principles of Science

PSSP

It is this foundation which is the bedrock of all science. It involves an unceasing search for reality and for the truth. At every step of the way, this quest has to be kept uppermost in mind. At every stage, each step has to mesh with other steps already taken in other sciences; else the entire structure is likely to be jeopardized. It is this underlying philosophy which is opposed to the blind faith implicit in religion.

extrapolations

We have been discussing dissection by PSSP. There are benefits of other kinds in such dissection. Let us extrapolate these elements or onion-layers which make up our industrial product and see what we come up with:

(1) Many students complain that their studies are dry, devoid of interest to them and unrelated to everyday life. If teachers kept PSSP in mind and explained the onion-type layers that make up each product and how they are interrelated and dependent on each other, the connection with everyday life would quickly be seen. Lectures in schools, colleges and universities which brought out the richness and excitement of this type of connection - not difficult to do - would make academic life deeply interesting to students and might lead - who knows! - to a movement away from the proverbial college canteen and back to the classroom!

(2) Vocational guidance becomes easier and more intelligible to the aspiring student. Hitherto, such guidance has meant only an enumeration of the different courses of studies available, the job opportunities likely to be available but very rarely the precise nature of the dependence of the career or vocation on those sciences, the interconnections between those sciences themselves, the state of development of those sciences, their future in agriculture, industry,

commerce and so on. With PSSP as a guide, all this would become automatically available to counsellor as well as student.

(3) Explanation of cross-skills and inter-disciplines becomes easier. Many courses in academic life and many job specifications today call for proficiency in more than one discipline and in fields that lie midway between two disciplines e.g. astro-physics, bio-chemistry, medical electronics , geo-informatics (geography and information technology) and so on.

(4) the nature of mathematics, which seeks to express these relationships in precise or quantitative language becomes clear.

(5) the role of engineering which brings all the factors together and puts them into application becomes clear

(6) it becomes possible to understand that each science can have its own history. For example, the history of the telescope really amounts to a history of astronomy and how man has viewed the heavens - the sun, the moon, the planets, the stars, the galaxies etc. - from the very beginning. Man began by observing with the naked eye, then with the telescope, then by optical astronomy and now through the electro-magnetic spectrum and radio-telescopy. Similarly, one can study the development of chemistry from early man, then called alchemy, right up to the present time in a history of chemistry. No longer need history be tied down to merely an account of wars, of kings, of political and economic developments. We have already spoken of the geography of disease (see pg 141) It now becomes possible to have a history of geography which would explain how geography at first often consisted of mere speculation or surmise, how cartography (or map-making) changed the history of the world and so on. (I refer to this topic again, in a slightly different context, in Chapter 8)

Au contraire, can one also conclude from all this, therefore, that religion is unable to provide the overall experience and background in various sciences enabling us to solve our immediate material problems? If we need houses, no amount of prayer is likely to provide houses. We need civil engineers equipped with knowledge of various sciences to be able to build houses. If we need clothing, we need both the organized mill sector and power looms for the purpose, especially if you consider the quantity of cloth required and the synthetic varieties which are so much in demand in India because of relatively easy upkeep. If it was not for modern science, synthetic cloth, an offshoot of petroleum technology, could not have been invented. If we need better transport, we have to look for engineers to build our roads and other engineers to build our planes, motorcars, buses, trains, trams, motorcycles and so on. If we need water, no amount of yagnas or importuning to God will provide water. We need study of meteorology, hydrology, geology, chemistry, engineering for dams, botany for trees and so on.

This was how the modern mindset was obtained. It happened over a certain course of time and in a number of different ways. The thinking of a whole people cannot be changed abruptly. It began with a basic structural alteration in the direction of thinking, away from a direction which always looked for explanation towards God or Providence to a direction which looked to man himself for answers to his myriad questions.

Arthur Koestler says in "The Sleepwalkers":

"The main achievement of the first part of the scientific revolution was done chiefly by three men: Copernicus, Kepler and Galileo. After that, the road was open to the Newtonian synthesis; from there on the journey led with rapidly gathering speed to the atomic age. It was the most important turning point in man's history; and it caused a more radical change in his mode of existence than the acquisition of a third eye or some other biological mutation could have achieved." (10) We in India also actually visualized a third eye on Shiva's forehead but alas we stopped there and went no further.

OTEST

I thought that I would conclude this chapter on a lofty note. But then I realized that I had still not properly accounted for certain characteristics of science which I felt I had discovered in it, qualities which had existed all along of course but which I had not yet clearly identified, categorized and labelled in my own mind—and this needed to be done, for my own benefit and, I hope, for the benefit of my readers. Again, this realization was a moment of epiphany for me. And it is probably best described by the simple statement that science can be likened to a Swiss knife, science is multifunctional. I made up the acronym OTEST to indicate these qualities.

Organization of knowledge:

Knowledge and information is coming at you all the time and from every direction. You need to classify this information and put it into separate categories: Physics, Chemistry, Biology, Zoology, Botany, Metallurgy, History, Geography, all done, of course, with the help of the science of classification itself which is taxonomy. (the word often used and here used in a wider or general sense.}. Think of these as coat hooks on which you would hang a new piece of knowledge, in the same way as you would throw your coat in the hall. When you do this, you are in box mode or silo mode or whatever you wish to call it. Instead of one large, amorphous body, your knowledge is now compartmentalized, easy to remember and ready to use. Just sorting out matters in this way in the mind gives an enormous sense of mental satisfaction. Being in box or silo mode helps to intensify information but, because this imparts confidence, I also think of it as the first critical step towards innovation.

Transformation of society:

Who can deny that products of science have transformed society? The printing machine, the internal combustion engine, the cell phone, the birth control pill, the airplane, etc. In his well-known book, "The Railway Journey", German historian of cultural studies, Wolfgang Schivelbusch, shows how our very perceptions of distance, time, speed and risk were altered by simple railway travel (11). On the other hand, when science is not given full rein, a bitter price is usually paid by society.

Engine of Growth:

All "developed" countries are based on modern science and technology. Without MoST, they wouldn't be developed. All "developing" countries are aspiring to get there although, astonishingly, many still seem to be unclear that modern science and technology is the prime engine of growth and everything else has either to be adapted to it or summarily removed from obstructing its path.

Straddle Mode:

In the earlier box mode or silo mode, you are placing information into separate boxes. In straddle mode, you are encouraging your mind to straddle boxes or subjects. You discover that every subject is connected somehow with every other and you actively encourage your mind (or actually, follow your bounding mind) to cruise or transit among them. Cross skills, multi-disciplines, inter-disciplines are the result. You are not bound to any one subject or one topic; instead you are in command of all and can view and review the whole picture.

Transformation of the Individual:

Science and (especially) technology give you, the individual, self-confidence and therefore, self-esteem; these qualities spur creativity and provide drive. Each individual in a country is changed and all such societies and every such nation is transformed.

As we have seen, India was somehow left behind in the advance of modern science and technology. It is essential that we make up for lost time. We no longer have the luxury of looking at science as merely an interesting repository of knowledge or as a mere assemblage of information just allowed to sit there. It needs to be got out and pressed into service: Think of a car-carrier—the kind commonly to be seen on the roads transporting a dozen or so cars from factory to showroom. In place of cars, think of several, intractable Indian problems (communalism, reservations, shortage of jobs, transportation itself, etc.) each represented by a large, rectangular metal shipping container, all being transported on this imaginary car-carrier to a given destination. Think of the car-carrier's engine providing the thrust as science, now unbound—as a force moving all that weight forward. Imagine all those multifarious social problems, now subjected to examination by modern science and technology, emerging all the better for it and often ending in solutions to these intractable problems. When you apply the logic of modern science and technology to a nation's problems, they often dissolve rapidly into unexpected solutions. They speak about the platform effects enjoyed by companies like Apple, Microsoft, Google and FaceBook. Think about the limitless platform effects of science!

Chapter 5

THE ABC OF SCIENCE

or Astronomy, Biology and Chemistry - a science primer

Who indeed could afford to ignore science today? At every turn we have to seek its aid.... The future belongs to science and those who make friends with science.— Jawaharlal Nehru

I have proceeded on the theory that few persons want to become botanists, but that many would be interested in knowing more of the living world about them. There is the fact, for example, that every green leaf that turns its face to the sun is a sugar factory busily at work. All growth in this world, animal or vegetable, is based on the leaf that makes sugar in the sun. It is one of the world's great fundamental facts, but it is quite unknown to all save a chosen few. – William Atherton Dupuy's Our Plant Friends and Foes

• from black boxes to PSSP • the philosophy of science • raising the curtain • why astronomy? • to physics and mathematics • why astronomy(contd) • introduction to chemistry • from chemistry to biology • ...and to botany and zoology • the three tables

An introduction to science is too important to be just a chance acquaintance or a hit-or-miss affair. In this chapter, we will suggest ways in which such an introduction can be attempted. As far as I am aware, no serious effort has been made in our country thus far for the excitement and thrill of science to be grafted on to individuals. My feeling is that once the seeds have been properly planted, growth is generally assured. Of course, everything depends on the individual himself or herself but it cannot be emphasized enough that all that is truly required—literally all—is a curious, questing mind and a fondness for reading. (I would have liked to say passionate desire for reading but in most cases, this itself will come as a direct result of having made a beginning.) No previous knowledge of science is required, no mathematical inclinations, no superior intellect - nothing! It's as easy as ABC—or, if you prefer, Astronomy, Biology and Chemistry

from black boxes to PSSP

We are surrounded on every side by the products of modern science and technology. We use the telephone, the motorcar, the lift or elevator, electricity, the camera, television, the computer, the watch practically all the time. Most of these modern conveniences are now such improved versions of the original models that they constitute what is known as black boxes to most of us. That is to say, we no longer understand the intricate principles involved in their working—all we know and need to know is how to use them. This still remains the case. Products will become more complex and increasingly more difficult for the lay person to understand in detail. But these difficulties belong to the category which, as you will remember, we have called Systems in our earlier, cross-sectional analysis of products (PSSP). We give below a pictorial representation of PSSP:

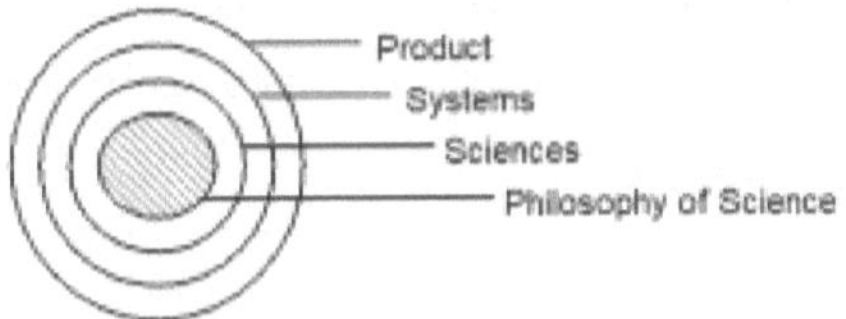

We begin with the philosophy of science, the innermost plank or kernel of that cross-section; the fourth layer of the onion, counting from the surface. Once we have understood the general philosophy of science, it is possible to easily move on to the category of the different sciences themselves. Otherwise, this usually remains a blur in the minds of many people. At this point, if one desires, one can pause a little to consider one or more of the sciences themselves. Study of these sciences can lead to an understanding of the various systems used in the product and thus lead to an understanding of how the product was put together and therefore an understanding of the product itself.

Split up in this manner, it is much easier to understand the composition of our black boxes. For most people, this approach is likely to create better understanding of technology and perhaps, therefore, a better sense of satisfaction about their own place in this complex world. In the long run, it can spark off creativity and innovation—that is, the development of further ideas for the improvement of life, including, most importantly, the simple ideas that are so necessary for the solutions to the myriad little problems that bedevil life in developing countries today.

Of course, experts or professionals, those employed in a given field or those fond of tinkering with products can take a shortcut and deal only with systems or products but even in their cases a knowledge of the philosophy of science, which frequently is not even thought of, will help in fixing the product and themselves in the total scheme of things.

the philosophy of science

The biggest advantage of a philosophy of science is that, being the most fundamental stage, it is the easiest to understand and the most exciting to read and learn about. For example, many accountants may be unaware that it was during the run-up to the Renaissance that double-entry bookkeeping was invented by Luca Pacioli (1496) in Italy. Fernand Braudel quotes historian Werner Sombart as saying that "it is simply impossible to imagine capitalism without double-entry bookkeeping; they are like form and content. Double-entry bookkeeping was born of the same spirit as the systems of Galileo and Newton and the modern schools of physics and chemistry".(1)

Similarly, lawyers do require to study Roman law but in order to understand life and times in the Roman era, one needs some awareness of the classical Greek and Roman periods as well as of life in medieval times so that one is better able to distinguish these periods from our own times. A study of the history of general science quickly shows up the differences.

The economist or sociologist, which earlier were narrative subjects, may not have stopped to ponder why his discipline was called a " social science" in the first place. In his book on history, E.H. Carr explains how, when the physical sciences had begun to make great strides in the 17th and 18th centuries, man began to consider why the same principles should not also be applied to his knowledge of society, hence 'social science'. Carr then goes on to say:

The word law came down trailing clouds of glory from Galileo and Newton.... .(thus) Gresham's law, Adam Smith's law of the market, Malthus' law of population, Lassalle's iron law of wages and Marx in the preface to Capital discovering the " economic law of motion of modern society. (2)

In respect of economics, Bronowski and Mazlish say this about Adam Smith:

...he introduced science into the study of economics. Although he talked much about 'the invisible hand and the 'natural course of things', Smith really freed man from the tyranny of chance by forming for him the analytical tools with which he might learn to control his economic activities.(3)

We have seen how the coming of science and technology tended to take power away from the rulers, the Church and the nobility and to invest it in the common people. On his part, the ruler realized that from now on it would be profitable to expropriate with indemnification rather than confiscation, to take by law or judicial proceedings rather than by seizure and above all, to come to rely on regular taxes at stipulated rates rather than emergency exactions of an indefinite amount.(4) It becomes a lot easier to absorb the full flavour of all these types of change if one is also acquainted with the history of science.

raising the curtain

How then do we start? Which subject, which part, do we choose which will ensure that the giant world of science is opened up to us? The subject we choose should itself lead to other subjects; in other words, it must have a kind of looping effect, preferably bringing us back to the original subject or subjects with re-doubled vigour.

Fortunately, there is such a subject, and we will let it work for us as a very convenient entry-point.

The history of science as it has unfolded over the past three or four centuries is filled with a number of curious prejudices and reactions. One of these, as mentioned earlier, is our dread of the word "science" itself. Another is the fear which seizes most people when we mention the word astronomy. And yet, the act of looking up at the sky at night and wondering about the moon and the stars is common to all humans. Even during the day, we are only dimly aware of the presence of the sun in the skies as it makes its journey daily from east to west. We complain constantly about the heat but if we turn our face slightly to the sun and feel its presence on our cheek, we rarely marvel at the distance of 93 million miles that those rays, a few among many rays which were at a temperature of 15,000,000 degrees Centigrade when they commenced their journey, will have travelled before they reach us.

One reason for the lack of present-day interest in the night-sky is the fact of the presence of night-light. This is the pale light thrown out to the sky by millions of light bulbs and street lamps. This canopy of electric light envelops us all in modern towns and cities after the sun has set. It is no longer natural to look up. In addition to night-light, there are also plenty of distractions at eye-level itself, all adding up to an increased lack of interest in the night-sky. This is unfortunate for us in India because conditions in most parts of the country during most of the year are very conducive to star-gazing.

why astronomy?

Why then astronomy, and why begin with astronomy? The answer to the first question is that while mathematical astronomy may be a complex subject, simple star-gazing is decidedly not so and can, in fact, be quite fascinating. One starts to learn that the stars that we see in the sky at night are very much like our own sun, enough to make us marvel at these wondrous objects of nature but not so as to overwhelm us, leading to blind worship of the sun. We learn that many of these stars are much larger than the sun but that they seem faint to us because they are at a greater distance from us than our sun. We are told about the difference between stars, which are huge balls of fire emitting energy in the form of heat and light, and planets, which merely reflect the light from the stars. We begin to recognize groups of stars in the form of constellations and watch their progress from east to west (in exactly the same way as the sun) as the night grows older. We read that the moon is only a planet reflecting the light of the sun(our star), that it is much smaller than our earth and that it is only a fraction of the distance from us than is the sun.

The night-sky becomes so familiar to us that the stars become our friends. One gets off a bus or train or plane at a distant destination at a late hour and the first impulse is to look up at the sky to spot one's friends, unfailingly there ahead of our arrival and waiting to welcome us.

One learns that the very existence of night and day, their very meaning, is not possible without an understanding of the sun. One learns that perhaps life on earth became possible not necessarily because of some superior Providence but because the earth, a planet, happened to be just the right distance from the sun. If we had been nearer, we would have been vapourized and if we had been more distant, we would have been frozen. Life on our earth in all its myriad manifestations, now becomes possible only because of the fortuitous fact of our being the right distance from the sun! Is this not rather different from what was passed on to us by our forbears, namely, that the sun was an automatic, indisputable every day manifestation of God and that we needed to worship it every morning while we circumambulated possibly a tulsi plant ?

One needs to know about astronomy if one needs an understanding of what day is and what night is, (as already noted), why the days of the week are called as they are, why the week was chosen as man's own cluster and dictated by the visible forces of Nature (for the planetary forces were invisible), (5) why the seasons are different from each other, why the calendar was important to man and what twists and turns there were to be before much of the world decided on the Gregorian calendar. One needs to know about astronomy if one wishes to understand why the sky appears blue, why we cannot look at the sun for long without risk of permanent damage to our eyes, why the moon goes through its phases which are still so important to some religions and why the tides behave as they do.

Astronomy, or star-gazing in our case, is tied up with so many different aspects of life that not to undertake its study is actually to condemn oneself to a lifetime of ignorance. Because it is so fundamental and because it deals with objects of such awe-inspiring size and history, it is probably the most dazzling science of all. Among its "big names" have been people who, earlier, in their ordinary lives, were music teacher, optician, accountant, peer, brewer, watchmaker, pharmacist, portrait painter and even donkey driver . (6)

Hence, I believe it is a serious mistake to restrict topics concerning astronomy to just a few chapters in a geography book as used to be the standard practice in so many Indian schools. We need teachers who have experienced the thrill and the excitement of astronomy and are prepared, for example, to take their young students, from an early age, on a voyage of discovery of the stars. Night-school could also begin to mean the beginnings of a lifetime of intellectual excitement and pleasure rather than just a dreary term for adult education.

In school, we were told again and again how the mast was seen before the hull as the ship came in from the horizon. We were told that this was proof that the earth was round. It was never explained why it mattered at all whether the earth was round(with an equatorial bulge) or flat or square or of an oblong shape. It does. No one cared to explain how man had always considered himself and his earth as the centre of the universe (geocentrism) and how it came as a great shock to him to learn that his earth was only a speck of sand in a giant solar system with the sun as centre(heliocentrism) which system itself constituted just a dot in his enormous galaxy, the Milky Way, and how there were billions and billions of such galaxies in the observable universe!

Unless the foundation is planned and built right the resulting structure is bound to go wrong. By not giving pride of place to astronomy in our education, we are ensuring for our students a lifetime of dullness, disinterest and sharp removal from reality. Later in this chapter, the connections that astronomy has with physics, chemistry, biology and so on become clearer and we see how this science of stars concerns all of life itself and how, therefore, to neglect or reject astronomy is to, at least in my opinion, set one's face against easy advancement in learning.

why astronomy? (contd.)

Why begin with astronomy? Aside from what we discussed earlier, it turns out that this is also the historical position. Early man looked up at the heavens, saw the sun, the moon, the stars and the planets and wondered what his own place was in relation to these heavenly bodies. Who was he? What was life? What was death? What did it all mean? Were these heavenly bodies manifestations of an omnipresent, all-powerful God? His very early livelihood, including his agriculture, seemed to depend upon the wishes of the gods. He saw himself as a small, insignificant object compared to the mighty forces of Nature. These practical, philosophical questions were intimately tied up with early man's observation and study of the skies.

The Babylonians, the Egyptians, the Greeks, the Romans, we in India, the Arabs and the Europeans—all peoples were deeply interested in astronomy. It led to the keeping of records of sunrise, sunset, moonrise, moonset, eclipses, comets and so on. This was computational astronomy or statistical astronomy. The Chinese have certain astronomical records dating back to 1361 BC and recourse is made to these records by modern astronomers even to this day.(7) As regards India, it is not clear whether there were very few written records or whether those records, although written, have somehow been destroyed.

However, of all the civilizations of the past, the Greeks were probably the only ones who tried to draw out or reason out the meaning of these astronomical happenings. They agreed that astronomical events such as these marked the efflux of time but why were things happening as they were? Was there a hidden meaning to it all or were they simply random events?

to physics and mathematics

By its very nature, astronomy was bound to be closely associated with physics and mathematics. If planets were to move in circles, if the sun and moon were to remain suspended in the skies, if the stars were to be pinpoints of light from another world, laws in physics would have to be worked out to explain these occurrences. For purposes of exactness, they would have to be put in mathematical terms. Heat, light, motion, sound, gravity, mechanics, hydraulics, optics all came into play and were fully joined with astronomy as a mother science. Therefore, however one looks at it, whether historically, philosophically or analytically, astronomy is the science to begin with. It leads inevitably to all the other sciences as we have tried to show.

It is not, of course, required that every person begin with astronomy. If you are already into star-gazing or you are studying physics or any other branch of science, it is equally possible to understand all that is here involved. It is possible to go back cheerfully from physics to astronomy just as it is possible to go from astronomy to physics. My recommendation of astronomy or simple star-gazing is for people who, surrounded as they are by science on all sides, with ever increasing quantities heaped on them each day, suffer from a sense of total bewilderment as they try desperately to organize all this mass of information in their heads and endeavour to make sense of it all.

Thus, astronomy may seem to be a daunting proposition but star-gazing quickly brings it within the reach of a lay person. Physics and chemistry may at times sound dull and dreary but if one is told that they are , in fact, opposite sides of the same coin, that one is energy and that the other is matter, it does begin to make sense and therefore, makes it a whole lot more interesting.

The Worlds Around Us

It was by accident that I came across Patrick Moore's The Worlds Around Us in a Pune bookshop some fifty years ago. Man had landed on the moon and, of course, there had been many journeys into space before that. Wanting to try and understand what it all meant, I bought and began to read Moore's slim little book. I had no idea then that he was well known to British radio and TV audiences and that he had converted thousands and thousands of listeners and viewers to the wonders of astronomy.* In my ignorance, I had always associated any accounts of the sun, moon, stars etc. with the subject of geography. I was aware of the existence of astronomy as a discipline but I took it to be an esoteric, mathematical subject far removed from lay people like myself. In my wildest dreams, I never would have imagined that astronomy would be instrumental in opening up for me a whole new world of knowledge. Today, I am convinced that there is probably no easier way to assail the fortress of knowledge than by starting with astronomy but this was not known to me at the time.

(*Sir Patrick Moore died in 2013)

Many of the facts that Moore pointed out in his book I had, in fact, learned at some vague occasion in school before but they were never explained in quite the same way. I discovered that the sun was only an average-sized star, that our Earth itself was a little satellite and the moon a satellite of Earth. I understood that the fact that the sun was about 93 million miles away from us caused its light to take about 8 minutes to reach us whereas in the case of some other stars we could see quite clearly in the night-sky, the distance was so great that it took many light-years to reach us. These facts and many more. It may have been the way the facts were set out in this book or it may been my anxiousness to learn but I now see clearly how this slender book caused the beginning of my wonderment with nature, our earth, the constellations, the entire universe.

Earlier, I had attempted to run away from Science. Now I was eager to know all about general science. I reasoned that we lived in a scientific age and it was necessary that I at least make the effort to know more. Summoning some courage, I chose next a Pelican book by Alan Isaacs, An Introduction to Science. This book was divided into 3 parts. I was utterly unprepared for the fact that the first part (17 pages) was about The Universe—another interesting account of what I had just read earlier in Moore! I felt happy and emboldened, confident that I was going in the right direction, doing things the right way. The second and third parts of the book were about Matter and Energy (Chemistry and Physics). I had never had them referred to in that way. It seemed so much more interesting to a novice like me attempting a preview of the subject on his own for the first time. Well, these two parts were also divided into different chapters. All I can say is that far from proving an intimidating experience, Alan Isaacs' book led from one chapter to another as painlessly and as absorbingly as a newcomer, an initiate like me, could possibly have hoped for.

introduction to chemistry

The next step was quite obvious. After a gap of a few months, I picked up Chemistry, another Pelican book, this time by Kenneth Hutton. Fascinating book, engrossing subject! I remembered the time—only perhaps a year earlier—when I would not have been caught dead with a book on Chemistry! Today, I am convinced that no educated person, whether one has a background in the arts or in the sciences, can afford to be without at least a rudimentary idea of chemistry.

Find this difficult to accept? Extravagant statement to make? Well, let me ask you: If you were required to name the elements which went into the making up of objects surrounding you at this very moment, would you be able to answer? If you are seated in your living room, can you tell the rough composition of the fabric on the sofa, the telephone, the window, the pencil and so on? If you find yourself unable to answer in even a general way, how then are you going to be able to approach the subjects of the cosmos or the universe? (this was the anxious concern of a young female relative who happened to be discussing this matter with me.)

I had now learned that chemistry begins with the elements that make up all the things that we find on this earth and in our universe. Chemistry tells us that everything in this universe is either an element or a combination of different elements, which we call alloys. Chemistry is nothing but an alphabet of the universe! Just as without the letters of the alphabet, you cannot make words and without words, you cannot make sentences and without sentences you cannot write books and therefore, make known your thoughts, so also without chemistry you cannot make sense of any of the various things that surround you. Naturally, chemistry does not stop only at this. It deals with other things as well. What I am trying to express here with regard to chemistry, astronomy and physics is that:

- they show up at every stage in our life

- it is necessary to have at least an elementary idea of these sciences

- simple books for instruction in these sciences exist today

- knowledge of these sciences is simple and can be highly interesting;

- and finally they constitute, in my opinion, the foundation on which can be built an acquaintance with other related sciences and therefore, also with the humanities.

from chemistry to biology...

One of the elements in the Periodic Table in chemistry is Iron. Therefore, everything connected with Iron becomes ferrous chemistry (or ferrous metallurgy) and all the rest becomes non-ferrous chemistry (or non-ferrous metallurgy). Another of the elements in the Periodic Table is Carbon. It turns out that this is the most versatile element of all. It is said that there are probably more than a million compounds of carbon. Therefore, there are 2 separate divisions in chemistry: one division comprising all the materials that contain carbon (organic chemistry) and the other consisting of all the materials which contain elements other than carbon (inorganic chemistry). It happens that the living human being is also a compound of carbon.

We are now transported into the subject of Biology which is, of course, the science of all living things. Biology leads directly to Physiology and Medicine. Medicine consists of the study of the human body in ease and dis-ease. Botany becomes the science of plants and Zoology is the science of animals. Do you see how one topic leads gently on to the other This also is another way of illustrating inter-discipline, multi-discipline and cross-skills, words we so often hear in the academic world. The problem is that often we are told all this, and even experience it without being aware, but as students were never shown how it worked in practice.

This must have been also around the time I picked up from the Mumbai Santacruz airport bookshop Isaac Asimov's "The Intelligent Man's Guide to the Biological Sciences". My first concern, believe it or not, was to hide the title of the book from other prying travellers. I was a mere beginner and absolutely did not want to be mistaken for an intelligent man. The book was so engrossing that I devoured the whole thing in one month flat. It was a fantastic guide and the very next month I proceeded to buy and thoroughly enjoy Asimov's companion volume, "The Intelligent Man's Guide to the Physical Sciences". Now there was no looking back. I had not only got over my instinctive dread of science but was beginning to really enjoy reading about it.

Only the other day, however, I somehow thought of looking up a list of all the books Isaac Asimov had written. The list extended to over 44 pages on the internet. Asimov was a prolific writer. He wrote science fiction, mysteries, comics, plays, poems, non-fiction and even limericks, lecherous and non-lecherous! After reading the above two volumes, I personally came close to recognising for myself, as has been said , " through science, the interdependence of all living systems".

After Asimov died, someone wrote that his statue deserved to be erected in every city in the world - for having made science so accessible to everyone.

A tribute which, although seemingly so extravagant in itself, I, nevertheless, most heartily endorse.

...and to botany and zoology

1) We speak about dwindling forest cover in India. This is one of our big ecological problems. However, it is not generally appreciated that nearly 67% of the wood cut down in developing countries including India is for purposes of fuel. (Of this, it is calculated that only about 30% heat actually goes into the cooking pot, so it is an extremely inefficient form of heating.) Therefore, while we can do our best to see that trees are cut down if absolutely necessary, only the science of botany will show how more trees can be grown. Botany can tell us all about how to grow trees, what trees to grow and where to grow them. For every tree cut down, botany can show how ten more can be grown in its place. Botany can also teach us when certain trees need to be pruned or even to be cut down!

I remember a glowing account of a recent Sunderlal Bahuguna visit to the city in one of the Bombay newspapers several years ago. Bahuguna spoke about the Chipko (embrace trees) movement, how our savants, sages and rishis of old had spoken of the need to love trees and to protect them. This all sounded very well but as I read, I dimly remembered another story in the same newspaper a few weeks earlier. A house had collapsed in the Girgaum area of Bombay. Some people had died in the collapse. When the newspaper's reporter interviewed a few of the survivors, an elderly Goan couple told him bitterly that they had repeatedly warned the other residents that something ought to be done about the banyan (vad) tree which had grown from one of the upper storeys of the lavatory block. Their warning had fallen on deaf ears. Now it had brought about collapse of the whole building. There are times when trees must be pruned or cut down just as there are times when trees must be protected and more grown!

2) India's holy cow has become an international byword for something precious and not easily to be touched. Yet what is the state of the cow in India? As is well known, India has the largest cattle population in the whole world and one of the lowest yields of milk per cow ! With cross-breeding and cross-fertilisation, this yield, which is approximately l litre of milk per day can be got up to 8 litres or even 10 to 15 litres per day or more! Only the science of Zoology is in a position to help to do this. Mere incantation of the statement that the cow is holy will get us nowhere. Nehru once angrily said that the cow was no more holy to him than the horse! The anatomy of the cow is different from that of man. Man is unable to assimilate grass. If he ate it, he would eject it more or less exactly as eaten. The cow has a four-chambered stomach which is designed to ingest grass, its principal form of sustenance. Only Zoology studies the anatomy of the cow (as it does of all other animals) and only Zoology is capable

of transforming the large cattle population of India into one of the world's great dairy industries.

the three tables

I cannot end this chapter without mention of the Three Tables. I will not describe their contents in detail just as I have refrained from going into the sciences themselves in detail but only hinted at the pleasure to be got from studying them (and the futility of trying to lead one's life without them).

The three tables are:

In Astronomy/ Physics, **the electromagnetic spectrum**. You simply have to know about the excitement of the electromagnetic spectrum if you are to know all about rays, say, cosmic rays, X rays, infra-red rays, ultra-violet rays, radio waves, TV waves, microwaves and even sunlight and what is called the visible window.

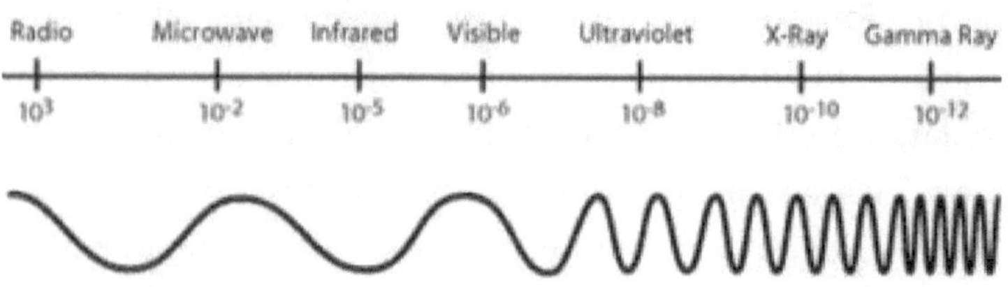

In Chemistry, the **Periodic Table**. You really must read about Mendeleev's Periodic Table to know the thrill and excitement that must have attended it all as vacancy after vacancy in the elements began   to   be   filled,   exactly   as

PERIODIC TABLE OF ELEMENTS

1A																	8A
H	2A											3A	4A	5A	6A	7A	He
Li	Be											B	C	N	O	F	Ne
Na	Mg	3B	4B	5B	6B	7B		8B		1B	2B	Al	Si	P	S	Cl	Ar
K	Ca	Sc	Ti	V	Cr	Mn	Fe	Co	Ni	Cu	Zn	Ga	Ge	As	Se	Br	Kr
Rb	Sr	Y	Zr	Nb	Mo	Tc	Ru	Rh	Pd	Ag	Cd	In	Sn	Sb	Te	I	Xe
Cs	Ba	57-71	Hf	Ta	W	Re	Os	Ir	Pt	Au	Hg	Tl	Pb	Bi	Po	At	Rn
Fr	Ra	89-103	Rf	Db	Sg	Bh	Hs	Mt	Ds	Rg	Cn	Uut	Fl	Uup	Lv	Uus	Uuo

Lanthanides	La	Ce	Pr	Nd	Pm	Sm	Eu	Gd	Tb	Dy	Ho	Er	Tm	Yb	Lu
Actinides	Ac	Th	Pa	U	Np	Pu	Am	Cm	Bk	Cf	Es	Fm	Md	No	Lr

predicted. In Evolution and Biology, the **Geological Table** which tells you about the different ages of man on earth. This will enable you to get a good handle on History and Archaeology as well as on Paleontology. No better method exists of providing a broader background against which to judge historical, geographical and geological happenings.

Do you realize that you have now also actually discovered a tool for approaching all knowledge? The sheer volume of knowledge and the intricacies of its various departments earlier made it seem unapproachable. Now you yourself want to separate out each of these subjects in your mind and to compartmentalize, as well as connect, them. It makes things that much easier to remember. It also makes it easier to add subsequent bits of information to these compartments as they become known to you from your reading. We earlier called this   being   in   *box*   *mode*   *or*   *silo*   *mode.*

GEOLOGIC TIME SCALE

Time Units of the Geologic Time Scale				Development of Plants and Animals
Eon	Era	Period	Epoch	
Phanerozoic	Cenozoic	Quaternary	Holocene —0.01—	Earliest *Homo sapiens*
			Pleistocene —1.6—	
		Tertiary	Pliocene —5.3—	Earliest hominids
			Miocene —23.8—	
			Oligocene —33.7—	"Age of Mammals"
			Eocene —55—	
			Palaeocene —65—	Extinction of dinosaurs and many other species
	Mesozoic	Cretaceous —145—	"Age of Reptiles"	First flowering plants
		Jurassic —200—		First birds
				Dinosaurs dominant
		Triassic —248—		First mammals
	Palaeozoic	Permian —286—	"Age of Amphibians"	Extinction of trilobites and many other marine animals
		Carboniferous — Pennsylvanian —320—		First reptiles
				Large coal swamps
		Carboniferous — Mississippian —360—		Amphibians abundant
		Devonian —410—	"Age of Fishes"	First amphibians
				First insect fossils
		Silurian —438—		Fishes dominant
		Ordovician —505—	"Age of Invertebrates"	First land plants
				First fishes
		Cambrian —545—		Trilobites dominant
				First organisms with shells
		Vendian —650—	"Soft-bodied faunas"	Abundant Ediacaran faunas
Proterozoic				First multicelled organisms
	Archaean — 2500	Collectively called Precambrian comprises about 87% of the geological time scale		
	3800			First one-celled organisms
				Age of oldest rocks
Hadean	4600 Ma			Origin of the earth

...and that leaves one other matter still to be tackled. This I have called "spillover mode" or "straddle mode". I have said that knowledge of science even helped with an understanding of the humanities. I want to show how you can skip gaily and even daily, if required, between one and the other. In the next chapter, therefore, we attempt to trace out the connections, the relationships which science has and must have with not only all other sciences but in fact, with every other department of knowledge.

Looking back on all this , would I ever have dreamed of my undertaking such a project for myself? Hardly! Somehow, I needed to acknowledge my eternal debt to this small bookshop from whence my journey had begun. I don't mind telling you, therefore, that on subsequent trips to Pune, when passing the Deccan Gymkhana area, I would carefully park the car alongside the pavement in this busy area and, to the consternation of my family in the car, now clamouring for me to come back in and not make a spectacle of myself, I would exit the car for a few moments, stand at attention, solemnly salute the shop from a distance and then quickly get back in! People from the market would rush to ask me anxiously: "Kya ho gaya sahib?" (what has happened, sir?)" but from my impish smile, somehow sensing that it must be something happy and pleasurable. It left us all each time, most of all me, with a glowing feeling.

Chapter 6

STRADDLING FENCES : FROM SCIENCE TO THE HUMANITIES AND BACK!

I see the Tao of learning as letting the knowledge of any one thing spread to your knowledge of all things –Steven J. Bennett (quoting imaginary philosopher sage Master Hui), Playing Hardball with Soft Skills

Science and technology revolutionize our lives but memory, tradition and myth frame our response. - Arthur M Schlesinger

• from science to the humanities • how knowledge spreads • Greece and the Renaissance • the social sciences • dynamics: why Australia? • prosperity bypasses India • from backward to forward • West Indians, East Indians • Yes, you can! • American Indians, Indian Indians • the woodcarvers of Nagina • colours from the paintbox • how botany and zoology translates into flora and fauna

from science to the humanities

Those of us who are "non-science" people for too long have been fighting shy of science. Let's remember that science is rooted in scire, the Latin word for "to know" or "to understand" and that it is nothing but an unceasing search for the truth. If one were asked to make a rough division of all the knowledge that exists, one way of doing it would be to say that approximately one-half of it is the sciences and the other half comprises the arts and humanities.

Science   Humanities

Because of the technical nature of many sciences, knowledge in the humanities will not always lead automatically or easily to understanding in the sciences. But it is certainly possible to claim and I will try to show that knowledge of science can lead to a better understanding of the humanities. Even a knowledge of the history of science will do. Once the initial journey is made, from one to the other in either direction, it is possible to go back and forth at will.

Let's begin with Architecture. One way of looking at architecture is as an amalgam of both technology and aesthetics. Architecture changes over time and these changes are bound to reflect the technology of the time. Here is one illustration: V. Shantaram, the film director, chose to superimpose Sanchi on the Plaza Cinema at Dadar (Mumbai) but instead of proving attractive, this artificial throwback in time becomes an eyesore. Why? Can the reasons be that materials have changed, techniques have changed, environmental conditions have changed, tastes have changed and people have changed? Knowledge of all these components alone can ensure that, as American architect Louis Sullivan said, form follows function. Therefore, an acquaintance with the technology involved is not just helpful but essential for the aesthetic required.

We often hear the complaint that Indians do not have a sense of history and therefore, do not have understanding or liking for archaeology. They tend to confuse history with mythology. (1) Is there a way out? We have a priceless collection of sculpture, architecture and other art objects in our country. We have an exciting, vibrant history to go with it. On the other hand, we have millions of people who have absolutely no use for history and archaeology. Can science point the way? Let's see.

An exploration of astronomy (night sky watching) can result in a sense of awe and wonderment. This can lead to a concern for history, an attempt to understand what transpired because of the passage of time (or during a particular time). A study of Indian history could lead to a sense of curiosity about the Moghul period and, to go with it, Moghul architecture. Once into Moghul architecture, you are drawn to a study of Hindu, Jain and Buddhist architecture. Which could lead to a study of British architecture in India, which again could lead to a study of Western architecture in Europe. And so on. Each topic is exciting in itself and automatically leads to the next one. It is capable of bringing in its wake an enduring interest in history and archaeology, both Indian and Western.

As regards the late start of our interest in these subjects, George Kubler, on the subject of archaeology itself, says "the systematic study of things is less than five hundred years old beginning with the description of works of art in the artists' biographies of the Italian Renaissance. The method was extended to the description of all kinds of things only after 1750" (2) So, interest in archaelogy also began in Europe only about 250 years ago. It could only come about, in my opinion, as a result of the developments in science and technology and the consequences of these developments on European man.

how knowledge spreads

"The Greek god of the sky was Ouranos. The Romans later called him Uranus. In the eighteenth century, an astronomer named a new planet after this mighty deity. A chemist named a newly discovered metal after the planet and called it uranium." Thus, points out writer Isaac Asimov, the oldest of the Greek gods lives on in a word connected with the newest and most dreadful of scientific weapons. (3) In one leap and with one name, therefore, we pass from mythology to history to astronomy to metallurgy or chemistry and of course ,in passing, to the science of the derivation of words itself, etymology.

See what I mean? Talking about history, unfortunately many of us (including myself, at one point) are unclear about even the Greek or Roman contributions to culture. Even the Olympic Games' people seem not have been clear. Olympic gold medals with the Roman Colloseum (a famous ancient site in Rome) as background were regularly issued until a correction was finally made in 2004. The Greek period is thought to have been from approximately 500 BC to 150 AD and the Roman period extended from approximately 27BC to 400 AD. Knowledge of the Greeks and the Romans in classical times is vital for a study of the history of science. Thus, a basic knowledge of history becomes necessary in order to understand science. In the same way, knowledge of science or the history of science becomes necessary for an understanding of history. If you were vaguely familiar with how astronomy began and if you also knew a rough outline of the history of metallurgy or chemistry, then can you imagine the four-fold, mutually reinforcing effect of the simple name, Ouranos on you?

It is said that when Albert Einstein was a youth, he would see a star and allow his mind to travel back on its beam of light into history.

If the light comes from Rigel, for instance, we know that the light that reaches our eyes today started its journey about 1500 years ago. We are moved to think of what life might have been like back then. We may consider, then later read about and perhaps use that period (say, the Roman period, 400 AD) as a benchmark. So, whether we like it or not, we are launched into history. And so it is with all of science. Each discipline is connected with every other discipline and it is possible cheerfully to pass from one to the other.

When we see the sun, it is for no more than a few seconds. If we look at it any longer, it could seriously affect our eyes. If we continued to look, we could become blind and lose our eyesight altogether. The sun is nearly 93 million miles away from us but the energy generated within it is so intense that we cannot afford to see it with the naked eye for more than just a few seconds.

How does the sun generate such energy? We learn that element No. 1 in Chemistry (hydrogen) is converted to element No. 2 (helium) at such a fast rate that more than 4 million tons of mass are being lost from the sun every second. The light and the heat generated by such radioactive transformation reaches us on earth and makes possible all life. Thus, astronomy points to chemistry through understanding of physics (radioactive transformation), which leads to biology, including botany and zoology. Knowledge of astronomy is necessary to understand cosmology (properties of the universe as a whole), cosmogony. (origin and evolution of the universe) and philosophy. We know that another name for philosophy is metaphysics (from the Greek word for "after": meta) suggesting something over and above and beyond mere physics. Physics itself, as we will learn, is the opposite of chemistry, the one being matter and the other, energy. Einstein demonstrated how matter is convertible into energy and it is possible, theoretically and technically, to show that energy can be converted back into matter. The following has been accessed from the Internet:

Energy is converted to matter in nature but on an atomic level. When a naturally occurring radioactive atom eg K-40 decays and produces a gamma ray more energetic than 1.022 MeV(Million Electron Volts), there is a possibility that it will pass by the nucleus of an atom and undergo pair production The gamma will disappear to produce an electron and a positron. This is a conversion of energy to matter. It happens all the time. (Stephen Frantz, former Director, Reed Nuclear Reactor).

To know and study physics is to learn about mechanics, hydraulics, the subjects of heat, motion, sound, gravity, electricity and so on. As man specialised more and more in these distinct subjects and established more and more scientific premises in them, there developed a compact, organised body of knowledge which concerned itself with the practical applications of such studies and this came to be called Engineering.

Knowledge of biology led to the sciences of anatomy, physiology, botany, zoology, evolution, genealogy, paleontology and so on. It led to the profession of modern medicine. Knowledge of geology led to the study of minerals and to metallurgy which again links up with chemistry, geography, seismology and so on.

Nobel Laureate Richard Feynman tells the story of a friend who objected to all this. You destroy the naturalness of things, the friend said. By bringing all these scientific considerations into subjects like, for example, the petals of a flower, you corrupt the purity of the scene and no longer allow the flower to be admired in all its pristine beauty. Feynman replies to his friend that scientific background does not and cannot take away from original beauty. He says that it adds and he cannot see how it should subtract. (4)

The friend with whom I used to go for a walk in the Hanging Gardens, Mumbai said that ever since man landed on the moon, he found it difficult to think of it as an object of romance. I have no such difficulty. I can romanticise about the moon as well as recognise that it is nothing but a satellite of the earth and that it shines with reflected glory from the sun. I think that this adds to my excitement about the moon; it does not and cannot detract from it.

My walking companion praised a mutual friend's knowledge of the passage of the moon across the night sky during the course of the whole month. He instinctively knows where the moon will appear on any particular night, my friend said. I am aware that this mutual friend is a devout Muslim, and I felt that if he were also a votary of science, he would not only be able to foretell the movements of the moon in the sky but would also be intensely aware—as I wanted him to be and as I knew for a fact that he was not—of the identity and motion of the different planets and stars, the movement of the tides, the presence of the Milky Way and the hugeness of the galaxy.

Greece and the Renaissance

You may still ask: what have the sciences got to do with painting and architecture? John Constable, a well-known English landscape painter, declared "Painting is a science and should be pursued as an inquiry into the laws of nature... Why not consider landscape painting a branch of natural philosophy, of which pictures are but the experiments?"

In the book *Art and Illusion*, from which this quotation is taken, E.H. Gombrich notes that Constable "knew what he was talking about. In the Western tradition, painting has indeed been pursued as a science. All the works of this tradition that we see displayed in our great collections apply discoveries that are the result of ceaseless experimentation. If this sounds a little paradoxical, it is only because much of the knowledge gained by these experiments in the past has become common property today." (5)

Gombrich discusses how effects in simple lace work like figure and ground, chiaroscura, modelling light and shade, foreshortening etc. were all devices which developed over the years and which had gradually been internalised by Western artists. Thus it will be seen that science and art are complementary and that a study of the former can only help in appreciation of the latter. (6) Some of the greatest artists of all time—men like Michelangelo, Leonardo da Vinci and Raphael—had a foot in each camp. They were self-trained experts in architecture and engineering as well as being great sculptors and painters. The anatomical studies carried out by these artists provided much of the inspiration for the painting and sculpture of that period. They were the original "Renaissance men," equally adept in the arts as well as in the sciences. Their predecessor, Paolo Ucello, mathematician as well as painter, was responsible for introducing perspective, a mathematical method of viewing, into painting. Prior to this innovation, painting was "flat-faced," or two-dimensional.

At the end of this chapter appears a list of such Renaissance men, showing their range of interests and skills which straddled both the arts and the sciences and showing that it was possible for them to pass easily from one discipline to the other.

As the years went by, the scope of both kingdoms of knowledge expanded considerably. Because of the increasing size and complexity of the sciences, a gap began to develop between these two cultures. Today, "Renaissance men" are few in number. This could be because we fail to remember the meaning and scope of science (we also earlier referred to it as the philosophy of science) as well as to the enormous increase in the sweep of the sciences themselves. If this argument is true, then knowledge of science or more precisely, the physical sciences, cannot but lead to a better understanding and appreciation of the arts.

What does the French word *Renaissance* mean? It means rebirth. Rebirth of what? During the period we call the Renaissance, it referenced the rebirth of "Greek" learning which, after the terrible interval of the Dark Ages, had again begun to command a kind of fascination for Europe. What we call modern science is supposed to have made its first stirrings about the time of the Renaissance. Therefore any study of the science of that time cannot but help in an understanding of the painting, sculpture, poetry, literature, architecture and history of that time. If you happen to be interested in history and 2would like to choose some period for closer or deeper scrutiny, whether for casual reading or planned study, I heartily recommend the Renaissance. It constitutes an excellent introduction to both arts as well as science and itself becomes a valuable investment in the journey of one's self-education.

What connection has science with geography, geology and anthropology? Well, geography and geology are both named after Gaia, the Greek goddess of the Earth. Geography was not always the more or less exact science that we know it to be today. For hundreds of years, man merely speculated about the shape and outline of the earth without hard evidence of any kind and proceeded to call it geography. The Portuguese for long hesitated to advance by sea beyond Cape Bojador, near Morocco, thinking that they would fall over the edge of the earth! They had crossed many barriers before and finally now there was to be "a crumbling of the medieval frontiers of their minds." (7) When maps were first drawn, even Paradise was boldly shown to exist somewhere or the other on Earth—at times somewhere in the Atlantic Ocean, at other times near Ireland or in the West Indies.(8)

Precision and accuracy of facts, and of the conclusions therefrom, the scientific attitude, had to come to geography before anthropology could be seriously undertaken as a course of study. Anthropology is the study of human societies and their development and its very existence requires a combination of science, history and geography.

the social sciences

We come to the social sciences. Economics and sociology became the study of man in economic and social groups in accordance with principles laid down earlier in the physical sciences. It was realised that in the social sciences there could not be anything like the same degree of precision because one was dealing with human beings. Nevertheless, when abstracting from the behaviour of different groups of humans, it was possible to arrive at certain broad conclusions. Also, if economic behavior and culture itself depended so heavily on the technology of each period, it followed that knowledge of technology and more particularly, the general science behind that technology, was critical for any true understanding of these social sciences.

Even from an historical point of view, science and economics had a great deal to do with each other. Economics first became necessary because developments in technology in the 1700s had begun to produce so much wealth for people in Britain that they needed to know what now to do in the matter. Should wealth be allowed to build up in the land? Should one promote exports and discourage imports? Or perhaps the other way around? What was to be done in respect of bullion? Was it better for the country to import more and more gold and silver or were the goods and commodities they represented a better alternative?

Samuel Johnson, English writer and lexicographer, called for a philosophy (science) to explain the phenomenon of trade (economics). Were there Newtonian " laws of motion" that regulated the economy? Scottish economist Adam Smith's An Inquiry into the Wealth of Nations (1776) was influenced by Newton's model of the physical universe, as he searched for the " natural order" of the economy. (9)

Now it is the turn of economics to influence the subject of biology and to help in the explanation of biological change. Charles Darwin borrowed the idea of self-interest and division of labour (i.e. individual differences) from Adam Smith and the idea of favourable variations from scholar Thomas Robert Malthus, "thus applying Malthus' iron law of human economics to the world of nature...and discovered the plausible mechanism of evolutionary change."(10)

Again, the wheel turns. Darwin's Origin of Species became the origin of "revolution" for Karl Marx. Marx freely admitted his debt to Darwin, even asking to dedicate the first volume of Das Kapital to him. Darwin demurred because he felt his family would be disturbed "to have dedicated to him a book that was so Godless!".(11) In this way, we see how physics influenced economics, which influenced the science of biology which, in turn, had a lasting effect on history and political science.

As should be clear by now, science itself advanced because of its successful attack on superstition, tradition, mystery and dogma, all of which had been encouraged by mythology and religion. Therefore, any study of mythology, theology and religion cannot subsist without also a proper understanding of the arguments of science.

The relationship between music and science is a more indirect one. The connection between Western music and science is clearer than perhaps that with music in our own country. This could be because modern science has existed in Europe for a much longer time than in India. The concept of the orchestra, notational music, harmony etc. are factors which follow from a scientific background. Then also, there is today the heavy dependence of music on electronic reproduction media. How terribly limited the world of music would be today without radio, TV, CDs, MP3s, streaming devices, and video recorders.

Aesthetic appreciation of the individual component parts of music again is only heightened by knowledge of the principles and background of music. Neuroscientist and musician Daniel Levitin asks : "I love music and I love science. Why would I want to mix the two?" Because, he explains, he is writing about music "from the perspective of cognitive neuroscience – the field that is at the intersection of psychology and neurology.(12) Levitin and his colleagues have conduc33ted research on music, musical meaning, and musical pleasure.

Literature and science are also connected. Take, for example, the novel. "The novel derived its form - and its name – from Northern Italy but first achieved prominence in the English language in the 1740s...The novel was, from the first, a commercial venture." And again: "the ability to read a book presupposes the availability of short but frequently recurring periods of free time." Both quotations are taken from Witold Rybczynski's Waiting for the Weekend . (13) Remember also that the weekend itself and the novel both became possible only because of the availability of leisure time consequent upon advances in industrial technology.

Cultural critic Edward Said observes that "Nearly everywhere in nin66eteenth and early twentieth century British and French culture we find allusions to the facts of empire... I am not trying to say that the novel or the culture in the broad sense 'caused' imperialism but that the novel, as a cultural artifact of bourgeois society, and imperialism are unthinkable without each other.(14) And as we have seen, European imperialism itself would not have been conceivable without the rapid development of science and technology in these European countries.

"It is impossible," writes novelist Orhan Pamuk, "not to see a connection between the great advances in the art of the novel in the mid-nineteenth century...and the sudden exponential increase in European affluence during the same period, which resulted in a veritable flood of material goods into cities and homes: an abundance and variety of objects unprecedented in the Western world. Especially in urban life, the massive wealth generated by the Industrial Revolution surrounded people with new devices, consumer goods, art objects, clothes, textiles, paintings, trinkets and bric-a-brac".(15)

We have seen that science and the humanities are intertwined at every stage, and therefore, it should now come as no surprise that even on the industrial side, for example, Denmark should be a world leader in insulin technology and in the manufacture of industrial enzymes while at the same time producing the largest number of professorships of furniture design; Germany's major exports should be passenger vehicles and products of the chemical industry—but also more than 50% of the world's exports of fresh milk and cream; and that Switzerland should have made such a success of banking, tourism and the premium watch industry while at the same time becoming a world leader in heavy chemicals, synthetic dyes, weaving machines and the pharmaceutical industry. Science advances over a wide front and if you succeed in one area, the chances are that you are also going to be equipped to succeed in other related and sometimes, not-so-clearly related areas. More on this later.

dynamics

So far in this chapter, we have tried to point to the complex pattern of linkages between science on the one hand and different branches of the humanities on the other. Complex, that is, until we find that with knowledge of the history of science as our guide, the relationships usually fall into place and therefore become that much easier to approach and to understand.

However, we are also obliged to study consequences. Therefore now, as before, we proceed to give practical examples concerning subjects as totally varied and diverse as (a) the "backwardness" or incompleteness of whole cultures (b) the current neglect of a feeling for creativity, aesthetics and visual beauty in many such cultures and finally (c) the lack of interest by their inhabitants in the flora and fauna of their countries. My submission is that just simply a knowledge of the history of science will help to explain all these anomalies.

Before I begin with this section, an explanatory note. My friend, who saw a draft of the book, objected strongly to my passing judgment on whole cultures. She found it objectionable that I should presume to speak about the "backwardness" of cultures. I totally understand this reaction but still I feel duty bound to go through with the exercise. Why? For several reasons.

1. because if you face a situation, you need to confront it and not turn away from it.
2. because the situation is urgent (lots of lives are at stake) and does not brook delay.
3. because I want to see if the science and technology solution fits and
4. because, for God's sake, I am not just commenting/ criticizing – I am proffering a possible solution.

Of course, when we speak about the backwardness of cultures, no permanent judgment is sought to be made. The whole point of this book is that if the role of modern science and technology is properly understood, entire economies and sub-sets of economies can be transformed and people and cultures changed within remarkably short periods of time. My claim is that no nation, no people, no one is exempt.

why Australia?

In Shiva Naipaul's book *An Unfinished Journey,* his father-in-law Douglas Stuart writes in the Introduction :

Shiva told me that he hoped to find an answer to the question : why didn't the Chinese, Japanese, Indians, Indonesians, Malayans and Filipinos find their way to the emptiness of Australia before the British? After all, they were much closer and yet so incurious about what might lie to the south.(16)

A similar thought had also earlier occurred to me. Remember that we began with the question: Why is India one of the poorest countries in the world? Our analysis now provides the answer to Shiva Naipaul's question. As mentioned earlier, "geography" in Europe before the advent of modern science was, in many ways, "a geography of the imagination," as Daniel Boorstin calls it. It was imprisoned by Christian dogma and further obscured by myths and pagan beliefs. Paradise itself, as stated earlier, was located in these maps. This was finally dispelled only after the coming of the printing machine, making available both more material and more exact material in the form of printed maps. In the sixteenth century, Mercator and Ortelius became the pioneers of modern cartography. The latter gladly incorporated in his atlases material sent in by sailors, mariners, agents and other admirers from their own, actual individual experiences. To these positive developments, was added the singular benefit of what Boorstin calls "negative discovery."

What was this negative discovery? Ever since Greek times, Europeans had believed that there existed a fabled Southern Continent to balance the large European land mass in the north of the globe. At one time or another, the northern tip of this large, imaginary land mass was even thought to be Ceylon in Asia or Tierra del Feugo in South America. In order to prove or disprove this, Capt. James Cook was secretly commissioned by the British government in 1772 to undertake his second, world-circumnavigating voyage. (In 1768, on his first voyage, Cook had "discovered" New Zealand and the east coast of Australia.) On this 1772 voyage, after satisfying himself that the Australian continent was separated from Tasmania, New Zealand and other islands in the Pacific, Cook was able to conclude in his Journal : "...I flater [sic] my Self that the intention of the Voyage has in every respect been fully Answered, the Southern Hemisphere sufficiently explored and a final end put to the searching after a Southern Continent which has at times engrossed the attention of the Maritime Powers for near two Centuries past and the Geographers of all ages."(17)

In addition to geography, Cook's expeditions in 1768 and 1772 were also greatly concerned with researches in natural history, botany, zoology and astronomy. All these sciences were attracting attention in Britain but were conspicuous by their absence in India. There was an intellectual ferment about all modern science in Europe which was absent in India.

Even the word "ocean" carried a different meaning at this time. Earlier Europeans made a sharp distinction between the ocean and a sea (mare). There was only one Ocean, the great circular stream that was supposed to encompass the disk of the earth. In those days, the

Ocean led nowhere; in the next centuries, people would see that it led everywhere. Only gradually, in the course of the fifteenth century, did "Ocean" come to have (this) revolutionary modern significance. (18)

Boorstin also tells us that "modern exploration had to be an adventure of the mind, a thrust of someone's imagination, before it became a world-wide adventure of seafaring. The great modern adventure—exploring—first had to be undertaken in the brain…The pioneer explorer was one lonely man thinking." (19) Exploration was driven and experienced by men who had both the curiosity and the discipline of modern science.

It follows, therefore, that far away Australia could not have been discovered by India or China or the other Asian countries. Indeed, by around the fourteenth or fifteenth centuries, the larger countries, India, China and Japan, each for its own reasons, had already begun to proscribe journeys across the seas ! (20)

There was no fear or aversion of water, of course. Hindu culture had spread in the seventh and eighth centuries to various places in Southeast Asia. Present day names like Singapore, Sumatra, Cambodia, Java, Sri Lanka, Laos are all derived from Sanskrit names. Then, the famous Chinese admiral, Cheng Ho, with his large collection of vessels, had visited many Indian Ocean and Persian Gulf ports from as early as 1405. Cheng Ho himself died in Calicut (now Kozhikhode) in 1433. For Japan, Japanese sailing vessels had been leaving from Japanese ports across the Pacific for hundreds of years, sometimes ending up as shipwrecks and their sailors as castaways on the west coast of the US. It was just that the three countries, India, China and Japan, each thought for their own reasons that their own cultures were the most important in the world and wanted to discourage intercourse with foreigners for fear of contamination.

What then was new? It was geography as a subject which was new , the "lonely man thinking" who was new and the "gunned ship" which was new and all three brought about the colonial invasions which we read about in the history books today.

prosperity bypasses India

What then about our other question? Why did prosperity bypass us in India and proceed instead to Australia and to New Zealand? We have already shown how science and technlogy influenced European man and it was this European man who was now transplanted to Australia and New Zealand and who paved the way to prosperity. It was this same European man who also was transported to North America and who then, when sought to be prevailed upon by Britain, stoutly resisted attempts at colonization by the mother country. It explains why the USA won freedom from Britain while at about the same time India slipped easily under the British yoke. Australia, New Zealand and Canada later became Dominions and did not suffer dimunition in status like colonized India or Burma or Ceylon or the Persian Gulf countries. The British sovereign was King of England and the dominions but Emperor of India!

Not far from Australia is New Guinea. Here there is a "cargo cult" of people who profess "cargo cult science". During World War II, they saw planes land with food, radios etc and so they arranged their land like runways, put fires at intervals along the runways, did other things that looked modern and waited for airplanes to land! Their leader was Yali and he kept wondering what the Westerners had done to deserve all these "goodies' which continued to be denied to his people. The short answer is modern science and technology. Reference is made to Yali and his people in "Guns, Germs and Steel" by Jared Diamond and in several other well known books – and as far as I can tell the simple answer still not provided. (21)

from backward to forward!

Let us now turn to a striking example from our own country. When in the 1950s, Dr. B.R.Ambedkar decided to convert to the Buddhist religion and to take half a million of his followers with him, it was probably in the entire history of mankind, one of the most spectacular attempts ever made to rescue a whole people, with one single, dramatic move, from the tentacles of centuries of poverty and backwardness. Dr Ambedkar's motives were wholly honourable and understandable. Hindu India had condemned parts of its own brethren to further backwardness! This too can be explained. If we had had an enlightened India, it would not have attempted and if it had been attempted, would not have succeeded, in keeping under bondage such a large part of its own people.

However today, nearly two generations later, we find that the Scheduled Castes, while they may automatically have discarded social stigma (not an insignificant achievement in itself) have certainly not obtained better economic status for themselves.. They still remain as poor as before. Beginning roughly from the start of the twentieth century, they have tried just about everything. First a demand for temple entry, then a demand for separate electorates, then the need for reservations in jobs and in education, then the glittering promise of a new religion (Buddhism) and, most recently, a demand for reservation in private sector companies. In economic terms, at any rate, all this has availed them little. As Arvind Das puts it: "they have gone through the stages of achhut (untouchable) to harijan (children of God) to dalit (oppressed) but unfortunately not much further(22).

Quotas and reservations has brought caste bounding back into the Indian social and political equation – where once the effort was to banish it from the scene! It has reached the absurd position that higher castes are asking to be classified as lower castes in order to be able to participate in the spoils e.g. the Gujjar agitation in 2008 and 2010 and the agitation of the Patel community more recently in Gujarat.

The explanation is that no religion contains a prescription for release from poverty. Indeed, the religions, wittingly or unwittingly, brought about the poverty in the first place. If we look around us, we find that there is not a single Buddhist country in the world which has succeeded in overcoming poverty as a result of its religion.

The thought naturally occurs to us : Might it not have been better for Dr. Ambedkar to take his followers in one single swoop from lowly status under Hinduism to the modern forces of science and technology? A friend of mine, with whom I happened to be discussing this, asked: "But what could he have called it?" What difference would it make what he could have called it. Ambedkarism, Modernism, Modway, whatever! Brilliant results could have been obtained in a single generation which would not only have yielded jobs, food, houses and so on for his people but would also have set, if they chose, and could still set the backward classes excellently poised for leadership of the entire nation in the future!

West Indians, East Indians!

These people are expatriates, compatriots, diaspora, so comment is permissible and should be considered in order. Richard Feynman relates how on a visit to Trinidad in the West Indies, he expressed a wish to be taken to see the poorer districts in the city. His black cab driver, at first surprised by this unusual request, promises to do his best but in return, would like the answer to one single question which, he says, he will put to the professor at the end of the tour. In the course of the tour, he points to the courtyard of the home of an East Indian family. An elderly woman is seen working on a sewing machine. The cabdriver explains that she is earning an income to help finance her son's education in the United States. At the end of the tour, the cabdriver's question is this : Why are these people who have come all the way from India working so hard to better their prospects while his own people, blacks, "aren't getting anywhere". Feynman thinks about it for a while and replies that he can only hazard an honest guess. He feels that with a two thousand or three thousand year old culture behind them, Indians realize the need for progress whereas, possibly, the blacks in Trinidad have so far failed to come to that realization.(23)

My own view, as an Indian, is that Feynman is being too kind. If Indian culture had served these people so well, why would they have needed to go as indentured labour to the West Indies in the first place? Indentured labour used to be known as "slavery under a different name." The cruel fact is that both we and the West Indians were left behind in history. We are both petitioners on the same side of the table while the Europeans and the Americans, helped by modern science and technology, confidently "glower" at us from the other side.

Yes, you can!

This brings us to the problems of African Americans in the USA. Why is it that this nine or ten percent of the population, in spite of being surrounded by modern science and technology for upwards of l00/150 years, has still not been able to bridge the gap between the whites and themselves? Even today they experience despair and anger. They feel 'boxed in and suffer from a siege mentality. They find it difficult to break into the power structure." (24)

Now an article in the Economist (April 21, 2018) says that half a century after Martin Luther King's assassination, "class divides" and "income segregation" is replacing overt racism in the US and that that itself should be a call for action. The article says that African Americans tend to be segregated in ghettos and poor neighbourhoods. They also have significantly higher rates of downward mobility and they are more likely to remain in poorer areas even when they have money to move.

I remain convinced that the sooner African Americans properly start down the path of modern science and technology, the sooner they are likely to overcome the "class divides" and "income segregation" which still separate them from the whites. Science and technology may appear to be two small words, just baby steps, but they have the wondrous capacity of blossoming into giant strides which alone can take them towards "the promised land."

Like us Indians, African Americans as a community need to discover that only by adopting the ways of modern science and technology, namely modernization, can they hope to separate themselves from their unfortunate history as victims of generations of prejudice and poverty.

I said properly starting down this path because living as they do in the USA, they have to a certain extent already been beneficially affected. The African American writer, Thomas Sowell, gives several examples of such human capital differences in his book "Conquests and Cultures".

1) "African Americans, being predominantly native-born even in colonial times, became the most culturally Europeanized of all African-origin populations in the world – and the most prosperous." Sowell says "Europeanized" but we know from the examples of Japan and now China that the explanation is not being European but

exposure to modern science and technology (which, of course, began with Europe).

2) African Americans who settled in Liberia in the early 19th century maintained ascendancy and despotic rule for over a century over indigenous Africans.

3) even the example of Africans moving in the opposite direction, namely, black emigrants from Jamaica, Trinidad, Barbados and Tobago moving into America itself , now boasting of median household incomes equalling or exceeding that of Americans in general. While agreeing that this might be partly because of selective immigration, Sowell shows that differences in racial income cannot be because of discrimination. This also shows that the fears about his people of our black Trinidad cabdriver, while understandable, were really unfounded. (25).

African American writers have themselves again and again hinted at this. Richard Wright in *Black Boy* says: whenever I thought of the essential bleakness of black life in America, I knew that Negroes had never been allowed to catch the full spirit of Western civilization, that they lived somehow in it but not of it." Maya Angelou, in *The Caged Bird Sings*, writes :"Momma could not take the smallest achievement for granted. People whose history and future were threatened each day by extinction considered that it was only by divine intervention that they were able to live at all.. I find it interesting that the meanest life, the poorest existence, is attributed to God's will but as human beings become more affluent, as their living standard and style begin to ascend the material scale, God descends the scale of responsibility at a commensurate speed." Another African American writer, Henry Louis Gates, Jr, argues that the causes of poverty within the black community are both structural and behavioural. He says: "A generation of well-meaning social scientists has made the notion of the 'culture of poverty' taboo, correctly observing that the concept, as originally introduced, ignored the economic and structural dimensions of the problem. But, having acknowledged those dimensions, it's time to concede that, yes, there is a culture of poverty. How could there not be? How could you think that culture matters and deny its relation to economic success? In general, a household made up of a 16-year old mother, a 32-year old grandmother and a 48-year old great-grandmother is not a site for hope and optimism. It's also true that not everyone in any society wants to work, that not all people are equally motivated. There! *Was that so hard to say*?" (italics in the original)(26).

What courage, what transparent honesty! I entirely agree but would like to enter one small caveat. If the charge is made today that (large) sections of the black population do not seem sufficiently motivated, this itself is a consequence of their confusion as to what is to be done, which direction to take. If the African Americans raise themselves from poverty as a result of modernization, then the section of their community which is insufficiently motivated will be neither greater or lesser than that of the white community in the USA or any developed community anywhere. Motivation itself is a consequence of modernization - and this includes "...a lessening of downward mobility and a strengthening of the motivation to move away from poorer neighborhoods (poorer schools, higher crime rates, less healthy places) into better ones."

American Indians, Indian Indians

The year is 1992. It is 500 years exactly since Columbus discovered America. But did he really discover America? Had not the American "Indians" already discovered it before him? There were over 50 million Native Americans when the white men began their colonisation of America. A verbal argument ensued in the USA between the two groups. In the process, it was/is generally overlooked that six years after Columbus' voyage, Vasco de Gama also sailed from Portugal via the Cape to arrive at Calicut (Kozhikode) in India.

Was this pure coincidence? Hardly! Diego Cao had sailed down the African coast in 1482, Bartholomew Dias had rounded the Cape of Good Hope in 1488, Pedro Cabral, on his way to India, had discovered Brazil in 1500, Vasco da Gama made a second voyage to Calicut in 1502 and Afonso de Albuquerque decided to make Goa the capital of all Portugese Asian possessions in 1510. How did all this happen ? As we noted earlier, it took multiple developments in astronomy, geography, shipbuilding, navigation and armaments manufacturing to make these pioneering voyages possible. Cipolla says:

" The gunned ship developed by Atlantic Europe in the course of the fourteenth and fifteenth centuries was the contrivance that made possible the European saga. It was essentially a compact device that allowed a relatively small crew to master unparalleled masses of inanimate energy for movement and destruction. The secret of the sudden and rapid European ascendancy was all there : in the skill acquired by Atlantic nations in the use of sailing ships and in their having understood that sea fight in these days come seldome(sic) to boarding or to great execution of bows, arrows, small shot and the sword but are chiefly performed by the great artillery." (27)

Today white America acknowledges that in the process of colonising America, it also considerably harmed the American Indian population. But how does it help the American Indians in redeeming themselves to merely know this? In his book, "A Voyage Long and Strange", Tony Horwitz, the American travel writer, at the end of his travels over the American continent, concludes sadly that the process in essence appeared to him as "grimly mechanistic: an inexorable grinding down of one world by another".(i.e. the Spanish world) and he quotes others as thinking that it finally amounted to "one society imposing its will on another." Today, the American Indians have accumulated problems of poverty, unemployment, alcoholism, drugs and even diabetes in a big way. An advertisement in the New York Times magazine shows a young, troubled American Indian student carrying a placard which says that one student, meaning he, can look after 12500 diabetics, that is, a whole tribe. I understand the sentiment but is it possible? Is it even enough?

Whether it be us Indian Indians or American Indians, history is, well, history and we must live with it. This kind of tape is neither rewound nor erased but it certainly does not prevent a fresh, new beginning from being made. The fact is that there's a whole new game in town and all of us trailing behind (inheritors of once great civilizations) need to get to know the rules, to play it properly and play it well. No people or nation is incapable of doing this.

In fact, unsurprisingly this may already be happening. Time magazine of Dec 21st, 2018 says : "Over 70% live in cities where an educated Indian middle class has emerged.

the woodcarvers of Nagina

We have been broadly studying the interplay of science and technology with geography, political happenings, religion and history. My claim is that if attention is paid to the forces behind science and technology, many economic and even cultural developments become meaningful and a general pattern observed where the picture may well have been unclear before.

Our next subject of study is what I would call the current comparative absence of a feeling for aesthetics, for creativity and for visual beauty in the cultures of developing countries. My object is to gradually approach the relationships between science and technology on the one hand and what we might consider as delicate, fragile, immanent, subjective, entirely individual, topics on the other. The idea is not only to try to demonstrate the effect of science and technology on the humanities but also to show how personal, individual matters can be influenced by impersonal technical forces in the long run.

I am not unaware of the strong existence of artistic qualities in our textiles, stonework, metalwork, woodcraft, architecture etc. but my argument is precisely that these qualities reflect the technology of an earlier period. Once artisans have fallen out of step with current technology, there is a paucity of new ideas and uncertainty as to how to deal with new materials, new techniques, new processes, new demands, new standards and so on. This may even constitute an explanation of what is called kitsch but our purpose is to go one step further and to try and trace out how such a gap occurs.

The woodcarvers of Nagina, a village in Uttar Pradesh, were a small community who had for at least two or three hundred years specialised in the production of carved wooden boxes and other wooden articles for sale in nearby districts and afar. Times have changed, demand has fallen and the traditional woods of the sheesham and other trees with which the craftsmen were most comfortable have been increasingly cut down and have now become scarce. Business has practically vanished and the woodcarvers are hopelessly unsuited and unprepared for any new trade.

Sanjeev Prakash (28) has studied how the inspiration and creativity of the woodcarvers of Nagina are mixed up with and dependent on the availability of supplies of wood of the kind to which they have been accustomed for generations. He complains that it is not enough for the authorities to only try and ameliorate their weakened financial and economic status or to try and secure other markets for their products; it is necessary to understand the technical factors involved such as loss of forest areas etc. which earlier provided their raw materials. All this is unobjectionable. However, it is not enough. My contention is that unless the author is fully informed by a sense of science and technology, he probably will not even guess at what steps are to be taken next.

Science can show how it is possible to take up where the author has stopped. The science of botany makes it possible to grow ten sheesham trees in place of each one that has been felled. Lack of a sense of the possibilities of science and technology engenders in this case, as in others, a negativism which not only destroyed an entire community dependent on a traditional livelihood but also prevented the author, although deeply concerned, from suggesting possible steps which might go beyond the mere bemoaning of their cruel fate.

The author explains how the craftsmen obtained their sense of design from the shapes of the leaves, their colouration, the grain of the wood and so on. It is interesting to recall that this is also the way in which European artisans and craftsmen used to receive their inspiration. And, after the coming of the printing machine, a veritable explosion of ideas occurred.

By encouraging a recurrent recycling of identical motifs, says Eisenstein in her history of the printing press, "the duplicative powers of print also placed an increasingly high premium on the development of new visual vocabularies. Images initially designed to be placed on walls or on parchment were duplicated in woodblocks and engravings, purveyed by print dealers, reworked by cabinet-makers, glaziers, potters and tapestry weavers, taken up by a new generation of artists as elements in large-scale compositions, only to be copied again by print-makers and redistributed for the benefit of craftsmen all over again."(29)

Einsenstein also quotes from George Kubler's *The Shape of Time:*

"About AD 1400 many technical discoveries in the pictorial representation of optical space allowed, or more probably, accompanied, the appearance of a different scheme of stating experience. This new scheme was more like a cornucopia than a funnel, and from it tumbled an immense new variety of types and theses, more directly related to daily sensation than the preceding modes of representation. The classical tradition and its reawakening formed only one current in the torrent of new forms embracing all experience. It has been at flood height and steadily rising ever since the fifteenth century." (30)

The woodcarvers of Nagina, on the other hand, were limited to their few master-themes and archetypical visual forms and once the source of their inspiration was lost, found that they lacked "the torrential outpouring of myriad diverse themes and forms" experienced in the West as an inevitable result of the coming of the printing machine.(31)

What then is the solution to this woodcarvers' problem? Not just further allocation of additional forest areas but also intensive, planned cultivation of those that are available and just generally an understanding of the rough direction in which future progress might lie. This kind of problem exists for many artisans in many fields and the measures for improvement that are to be undertaken would involve much less time, energy and expenditure if the general direction was already known.

colours from the paintbox

How does one define aesthetics? Surely this must depend on an individual's taste and sense of discrimination. Yet we all know and recognise that some things, whether in design or in arrangement or in colours can jar. Why does this happen? The explanation must be that we all build up within ourselves, some more than others, norms of judgment which, accumulated over a period of time, constitute current practice in good taste. We see metal railings and entire walls painted by the Bombay Municipal Corporation showing every colour in the paintbox—and we shudder. The lovely building of the State Bank of India on Bombay Samachar Marg, in between Ionian stone columns, sports horrible plastic letters announcing its name. These are only two out of hundreds of examples. Does this say something about us currently as a people?

If we break down aesthetics into separate elements like colour, proportion, arrangement, texture, symmetry, simplicity etc., it will be seen that only a close knowledge of the raw materials and techniques available at any particular time will enable us to build up an aesthetic sense. It follows, therefore, that if we have got left behind by several hundred years in modern science and technology, our sense of aesthetics must also suffer. If then a young British writer, deeply sympathetic to Nepal, writes about eccentric juxtaposition of pictures in a museum in Katmandu (32) or another speaks of a lack of a sense of visual man-made beauty in parts of modern North Africa(33) or a third writer points to the once great Chinese culture now producing kitsch in that country(34), these are also, all of them, only different cultural manifestations of a lagging science and technology in the respective countries.

how botany and zoology translate into flora and fauna

Jawaharlal Nehru often complained that, as a people, we lacked interest in our own flora and fauna. We are a tropical country with a large land-mass and nearly three thousand miles of coastline but very few among us know the birds or the trees which surround us. The immediate explanation is, of course, that we are poor and that the major part of the population is more concerned with getting two square meals each day. But even people who are better off and well above the poverty level, say, the middle and upper classes, remain totally uninterested.

To return to the theme, I suggest that a knowledge of the history of science could spark off interest in these matters. For example, if one reads about evolution, one becomes aware of, say, birds as warm-blooded creatures (as against fish, for instance, which are cold-blooded), the position of birds in the evolution of man himself, the development of the horse (for example) from the small eohippus to the animal it is today, the structure of the hooves of horses, the special four-chambered stomach of the cow and so on. Bird-watching as a hobby and ornithology as a subject do not generally develop in a vacuum. If one can acquire a sense of perspective with which to relate current events to the past, interest immediately creeps in. Different points in this perspective-view or history then act as hooks on which to hang current facts as they come to one's awareness. It will thus be seen that even a summary acquaintance with subjects like botany and zoology can lead to an abiding interest in the flora and fauna of our country. Actually, all of Asia could benefit from this. Poaching, smuggling, overhunting, trade in animal parts, encroachment by humans of forest reserves is taking a rapid depredatory toll.

A writer to the *Times of India* (35) says that although Bombay is surrounded by the ocean, its 90 lakh (then) people don't have more than a dozen privately owned sail-boats. Around that, three sailing clubs own another 14 or 16 boats. He contrasts this apathy with Australia or Europe or America where whole cities empty out as the population drives to the nearest beach. The fact is that Indians do lead a limited life. Few are interested in sailing or horse-riding or even riding on an elephant, like Mark Shands, from one part of India to another.(36) As we explained earlier, adventurousness or exploration starts in the mind and our minds have remained passive, uninterested and unused for too long. Science helps to spread sensibility about trees, forests, birds, ants, tigers, elephants, and interest in archaelogical sites, museums etc.

Writing in 1992, read what Paul Theroux, well known travel writer, has to say about the Polynesians:

"I tended to evaluate Pacific Islanders by the way they related to the ocean around them. Did they swim ? Did they fish with nets or spears? Did they build boats and paddle and sail ? Could they go from one island to another on their own in one of those boats ? Once these people had been among the greatest sailors in the world. But not now. I wondered whether they were afraid of the sea, whether they knew anything about it, whether they cared... No one went sailing. No one paddled. They jumped into the water and splashed—but they hardly swam.... It had been years since anyone had made an outrigger. It was as though the entire population (and this seemed pretty odd in the Pacific) was possessed by the most virulent form of hydrophobia."(37)

At the same time, as we have said so often before in this book, we must not suppose that these qualities always existed in the West. For example, Kirkpatrick Sale refers to Christopher Columbus' offhand treatment of nature on his voyage to the New World. He agrees with another writer, Elliot, that there was "a lack of interest among sixteenth century Europeans and especially those of the Mediterranean world, in landscape and in nature".(38)

Kenneth Clark says in *Civilisation*:

"For over two thousand years mountains had been considered simply a nuisance : unproductive, obstacles to communication, the refuge of bandits and heretics .... the thought of climbing a mountain for pleasure would have seemed ridiculous. The fact remains that when an ordinary traveller of the sixteenth and seventeenth centuries crossed the Alps, it never occurred to him to admire the scenery—until the year 1739, when the poet Thomas Gray, visiting the Grand Chartreuse, wrote in a letter : Not a precipice, not a torrent, not a cliff but is pregnant with religion and poetry."(39)

A friend of mine, who makes his own living by selling a minor consumer product, once complained about my obsession with science. I am cast unfairly in the role of a constant, tiresome crusader of science whereas my own purpose, when called upon, is to explain the comprehensive nature of science and to point out that it touches everything, absolutely everything, in our lives. It is all-pervasive. Science is in fact, as we have explained, a constant and comprehensive education and nothing shows this up better than when we argue, as we have tried to do in this chapter, how it can also create pathways to other disciplines in the humanities.

Multi-disciplinary interests

(1471-1528)	Albrecht Durer	Mathematics, geometry, optics, astronomy, architecture, wrote verse, painter
(1522?-1618)	Sir Walter Raleigh	Navigation, law, languages, chemistry, poet, historiographer
(1527-1608)	John Dee	mathematics, alchemy
(1560-1621)	Thomas Hariot	mathematics, astronomy, chemistry, naturalist,atheist
(1588-1679)	Thomas Hobbes	physiology, mathematics, geometry, Greek scholar, got to know Galileo and Descartes.
(1596-1650)	Rene Descartes	mathematics, astronomy, philosophy
(1605-1703)	Robert Hooke	Curator of Experiments to Royal Society,naturalist (Micrographia), architect
(1623-1662)	Blaise Pascal	geometry, physics, probability theory
(1632-1704)	John Locke	among first Fellows of Royal Society, Inspector General of Exports and Imports, Oxford, medicine, economics, education, contributed papers and carried out experiments ,made barometric observations for Boyle
(1627-1723)	Sir Christopher Wren	architecture, astronomy, geometry
(1642-1727)	Issac Newton	mathematician, physicist (optics, gravitation), author, inventor, Mintmaster of London Mint
(1646-1716)	Gottried Wilhelm von Leibnitz	law, religion, statecraft, history, literature,logic, metaphysics, philosophy, mathematics (calculus)
(1656-1742)	Edmond Halley	astronomer, publisher (Mathematica Principia, Samuel Pepys diary), founder of modern cosmology,

		geophysics, oceanography, meteorology and demography
(1724-1804)	Immanuel Kant	mathematics, physics and philosophy
(1731-1802)	Erasmus Darwin	poet and scientist
(1749-1832)	Johann Wolfgang Von Goethe	poet and scientist, Minister of Turingen

Chapter 7
"FITTING ONE CIVILIZATION TO ANOTHER"

The real voyage of discovery consists not in seeking new lands but in seeing with new eyes – Marcel Proust

The country that is more developed industrially only shows to the less developed the image of its own future. – Karl Marx, Das Kapital

The right to search for truth implies also a duty; one must not conceal any part of what one has recognized to be the truth. – Albert Einstein

• giant pygmy • reconstituting the future • the modern mindset • does technology affect culture (further visit) • certain qualities come to Western man • how nations change • tackling corruption • scientific knowledge vs scientific attitudes • MoSTly unaware • admitting the reality • old vs new light vs darkness • flight vs fancy • "the earth belongs to the living"

In this chapter, we list various "Western" ways which we take for granted and show how they happened to come about. We examine whether change can be wrought in India so that it is transformed from a poor, traditional, orthodox society to a forward thinking,

217

modern and more prosperous nation ready to take its place as one of the important powers of the twenty-first century world. The claim is made that if you simply follow a certain path, the initial fruits soon begin to rain on you. Then, like the Western world, you need to consolidate and build on this fundamental platform.

giant pygmy

As we know, a country is only as rich as its human resources. If its people are literate and educated, and then also possess creativity, skills and enterprise there is no reason why that country should not be able to generate wealth, adequately provide for its people and even go on to making them prosperous. If we agree that the developed countries in the West are well off because of different historical or geographical circumstances (or some similar alternative reason), then we should again ponder, as shown in the earlier chapter, why progress should have leapfrogged over us in Asia and reached far away Australia and New Zealand. With populations of 25 million and 5 million respectively, even these countries are, on a per capita basis, approximately twentysix and twenty times better off than us. (1)

It is customary in India to quickly reply: Our problem is that we are weighed down by numbers, The population is so large that it suffers from inertia and becomes unmanageable or at least, not easily organized. These are not futile but dangerous arguments. They come so readily to Indian lips that they have effectively suppressed all intelligent discussion of why we find ourselves left behind. China's recent rapid progress, despite its still larger population, is explained away by saying that it has a regimented, totalitarian society. The success of South Korea, Taiwan, Hong Kong, Singapore and Malaysia was dismissed as belonging to that of very small countries and therefore, not strictly comparable with India. (Now, we are eager to be admitted to the band of prosperous Southeast Asian nations!) The former USSR was supposed to be a special case because of its forced pace of industrialization, while the United States was considered an amalgam of various European peoples and a country which largely owed its preeminence to its large area, its insularity and its vast natural resources.

It seems next to impossible to get the average Indian to reflect over the fact that after two thousand years and more of our wondrous civilization – the solid past experience of which should count for something despite 200 years of colonialism - we are still among the poorest countries in the world! Our problems are mounting in size and complexity. It is true that we have made some progress in the last 70 years or so of independence but with the increasing population and the complications inherent in social change itself, we are obliged to see if there is not a fundamental problem with our very way of thinking.

reconstituting the future

They say that if tomorrow the United States were razed to the ground, it would take only about eight or nine years to put most of it back together again. This is because the people of that country already have the know-how, the expertise, the skills with which to re-build their agriculture, their industries, their institutions and their society.

Their people, their human resources, already have the tools with which to bring about replication. Naturally, these things can happen more quickly the second time around. Man struggled with methods for tracking time before he invented the mechanical clock around 1671 but from this simple beginning, we have today our modern digital and analog timepieces. If we deliberately took this kind of watch apart, it should take very little time for man to put back all the parts together again.

Surely this must also be the explanation for the so-called "economic miracle" of Germany, Japan and Italy after the Second World War. A writer to the *Times of India* in 1999 said bitterly:

"Even after almost 44 years of self-rule and management of the nation's affairs by its own elected leaders, India today stands among the 14 poorest countries in the world, seeking aid even from Germany, Japan and Italy – the very countries that were reduced to rubble in World War II. I happened to visit these countries as a young naval officer within three years of the war and have personally witnessed the havoc, deep distress and bleak prospects faced by their people". (2)

Actually, it was no miracle at all. It could and should have been fully anticipated. Germany, of course, was already a resurgent world power within only a few years of the debacle of the earlier World War, but even Japan began its long journey towards modernization and industrialization not after the Second World War, as is popularly imagined and as we discussed, but practically 150 years ago, starting approximately twenty to thirty years before the Meiji Restoration (1870-1890). All that these countries had to do was to change their objectives from war and military expansion to peacetime goals like rebuilding of their own countries and later, economic expansion by way of exports. The tools remained exactly the same. After the ignominy of 1945, both countries finally devoted themselves to butter instead of to guns and they have now emerged victorious in peace although defeated in war. As for Italy, the very preparation for war helped to industrialize the country and updated its infrastructure in a manner and in a period of time which otherwise might have taken much longer, possibly several decades. Today,

Italy's GDP per capita is US\$ 36,130 and it has rejoined the ranks of the developed nations.

It is a mistake, therefore, to compare these countries with India, where we have no more than about 65% literacy, where we lack previous experience of development and where we need to build things up newly and for the very first time. In those countries, there was reconstruction; in our case, it is development.

So much for the past. What about the future? For the exact reasons given above, we must look carefully at the competition we now face from the Eastern European countries and from Russia for the capital resources of the West. All these countries have a literate work-force, the necessary technical work skills and a substantive industrial infrastructure which is already in place.

What they lacked under Communism was a market economy and a free society. We happen to have these last attributes in India but lack or substantially lack all the earlier factors we have listed for a country of our size. Which group of nations will win the race to the future? By any reckoning, it will be admitted that getting a whole nation to become fully literate, educating it, endowing it with skills, modernising its outlook, etc. is likely to take a great amount of time.This is one further reason for us to get going and not to allow further loss of time in the development of the nation.

the modern mind-set

What is a modern mind? *The Random House Dictionary* of *the English Language* defines it as "pertaining to the present time, not ancient or remote." This is insufficient for our purposes. Richard D. Brown says about the concept of modernization:

"In the sixteenth and seventeenth century, 'modern' carried no technological or political connotations. The nineteenth century saw the rise of a concept of 'modernity' and endowed it with characteristic features of contemporary Western development. It was then that the idea of 'modern', of 'right now', became attached to the marvels of technology and nation-building. The Victorian Age became the 'modern age', while the burgeoning cities, the railroads, the mechanized production and the nation-state that so impressed the imagination of the time became 'the hallmarks of modernity'. (3)

So, what does the modern mind include? Is it the opposite of orthodox thinking? Does it include the skills and abilities which go into industry? Does it mean developing entrepreneurial ability? Financial acumen? Academic skills or scholarship? Simple political wisdom? Personal qualities? Exactly what? The answer is that it includes all of these to some degree but it now also includes something much more fundamental: a special point of view, a rational way of looking at things, a certain enquiring attitude, a special mind-set. If we wish to build a modern industrial nation, and there is no other way in which we can throw off our poverty, we must learn to think in a modern way.

How does such a mind-set come about?

does technology affect culture? (further visit)

In Chapter 2, we showed what technology meant and how it shaped culture. Let's develop that argument further and in doing so, attempt to answer the above questions. We've already noted that science is essentially *only* an unceasing search for truth. Sometimes, you need to give up your most cherished beliefs when they come up against the truth. Technology, for its part, yields a whole cornucopia of goods, products and services. It also comprises the methods by which these products are obtained and this we call *process technology*. But as we have seen and experienced, the most important consequence of technology is the transformative effect it has on its users. Every telephone, camera, TV set, bicycle, motorcar or computing device you use or learn to use changes you.

Technology not only does things *for* you but *to* you. Science and technology then, acting together, become a formidable combination for change. Imagine now 1400 million (or as few or as many as you like) motivated, purposeful human beings set to making up for lost ground and lost time in India.

Let's try and enumerate a few of the qualities associated with the West. Know that these did not come to Westerners (which, as a child, I used to think was the case) and will not come to us as a gift from the gods. Instead they resulted naturally, organically from the path of modern science and technology which the West chose to follow. We have already talked about how use of the telephone, the motor car and the camera affects us. What do contrivances like these and other things do?

Let's begin with a simple illustration. Most Indians would agree that one quality which Europeans are reputed to have and which Indians appear to lack is the simple habit of punctuality. We readily ascribe this quality to the West. We used to make jokes of the notorious absence of a sense of punctuality in India. "Indian Standard Time" acquired a popular, double meaning suggesting that an agreed time could be extended to suit one's convenience. Therefore, it is surprising when we learn that the very notion of punctuality did not always belong to Europe but came about only around 300 years ago. The word *punctuality* did exist but it was a variation on *punctiliousness*, meaning meticulousness. Only after the appearance in Europe of the clock or the timepiece did punctuality acquire its present meaning. As a result of the mechanical clock, European man now no longer thought of time as a flowing stream but instead as an accumulation of discrete, measured moments.(4) There developed a standard of time to which people could conform, hence the appearance and acceptance of punctuality.

Earlier clocks and watches were not manufactured in India. Instead, we imported them from overseas. It is still not unusual to have people stop you in the street and ask the time because they do not possess a watch themselves. Happily, clocks and watches of all descriptions are now made here. The average man in the street, in the cities at least, possesses a watch. It cannot but make a difference to his sense of time. Punctuality is no longer to be decried or sneered at – at least not to the same extent as earlier – and before long, it must follow that the Indian also will become conscious of the value of time and in this respect, will become no different from the European. In his book referenced earlier in this chapter, Richard D. Brown says that the eagerness with which Americans accepted concepts like punctuality was not coincidental but represented a "readiness for modernization... measuring time and self-consciously using it for whatever objective, secular, religious, public or private encompassed a new and modern attitude to life...a revolt against traditional ways." Machines like watches and timepieces affected thinking itself, in this case, say, punctuality also leading to a sense of precision and both together leading to a sense of efficiency, a concept that did not exist earlier .(5)

Here's another example, also having to do with Europe—since modern science and technology was born in Europe and any study of social habits in Europe and how they were created by the presence of particular machines becomes of interest to us. I was about to travel from Dusseldorf to Brussels and tried to telephone a business friend there to say that I wished to visit him. I was unable to get through. His line appeared to be busy. I flew anyway. He was happy to see me but sorry that I had not called from Dusseldorf because, as he explained, he would have liked to entertain me but he was due to have lunch that afternoon with some other visitor.

Naturally, I replied that I had tried to call several times from Dusseldorf but that his line had been busy. He looked puzzled. His expression clearly showed that he did not believe me. He said "That's impossible! We have ten lines and they could not all have been busy!" Fortunately, I had on me the slip of paper which carried his number and I produced it before him. It turned out that the telephone operator in Dusseldorf had told me to dial 32 for Belgium but had omitted an additional 2 for *Brussels* in Belgium. Or perhaps I had not understood her correctly. The point is that my friend had found it difficult to believe me. On the other hand, how many times in India do we not trot out the excuse that we tried to contact people but couldn't get through (less so these days because the system is improving). Because our telephone system was not as dependable as it ought have been, we were able to get away with this excuse but Europeans or Americans, because their telephone systems function more smoothly, cannot. It all goes to make up a social habit or expectation.

Perhaps the most obvious example of the influence of the machine on human thought and habit, an example readily accepted by all, is the annihilation of distance by jet travel. During the age of the steamship, it took between two to three weeks to reach India from Europe. Today, it takes less than eight to ten hours by air. The penetration of our way of life by Western clothes, hair styles, cosmetics, language and expressions, manners, music, education; the transmission of knowledge of science and technology; even our sense of smells, happens more quickly and more extensively than ever before. People fly for two- and three-day visits to Europe and America where earlier, less than even a generation ago, it was customary to consider a visit to Europe from India, at least for the average person, as a once-in-a-lifetime affair. The two worlds were so completely apart. Today, we see the global village being created before our very eyes!

Science and technology, which means also literacy and education, has brought untold benefits to Europe and America, not simply in terms of material comforts but also in the moulding and shaping of the minds, attitudes and personalities of the people. Every man, woman and child is influenced by this. Actually it is the most lasting benefit of all. If today we ascribe certain qualities to Western man, qualities such as individualism, self-reliance, enterprise, creativity, assertiveness, drive, willingness and ability to do manual work, self-discipline and so on, these are all attributes which have principally developed only during the last few hundred years: in other words, since the coming of modern science and technology.

certain qualities come to Western man

How? As with secularism, these other qualities also arrived in an indirect or roundabout way. The elevation of individuals to sainthood in the Christian religion had already put an end to centuries-old animism.(6) After the invention of the printing machine in 1448 and the consequent ready availability of books came the phenomenon of Martin Luther in 1520. Luther's single most important message to the people was that henceforth each man, (once the Bible was translated from the Latin into German and other languages), could study his own copy of the Bible. There was no longer need for clergy or other intermediaries who would help to interpret the word of God. Every man should use his own conscience as a guide.

This emphasis on personal faith and primacy of conscience turned out to be important. If conscience was to be the arbiter in matters of faith, why not intelligence in matters of knowledge? Seems a simple enough conclusion today but it did not exactly follow then. Knowledge did not always depend on intelligence or reasoning; sometimes, it did not even depend on observation.

Consider the following:

1. Albrecht Durer made mistakes in his famous woodcut of a rhinoceros because he had to rely on secondhand evidence which he filled in from his own imagination!

2. Leonardo da Vinci is shown to have made mistakes in his anatomical drawings. Apparently he drew features of the human heart which Galen's descriptions made him expect but which he could not have seen.

3. The so-called *Nuremberg Chronicle* (an illustrated world history including the history of a number of Western cities) with woodcuts by Durer's teacher, Wolgemut, shows the same image of a medieval city recurring with different captions as Damascus, Ferrara, Milan and Mantua! (7)

Over time, there was a general shift to modern forms of consciousness. Historian Elizabeth Eisenstein quotes Burckhardt in her book:

"In the Middle Ages both sides of human consciousness lay dreaming or half awake beneath a common veil. The veil was woven of faith, illusion and childish prepossession, through which the world and history were seen clad in strange hues. Man was conscious of himself only as a member of a race, people, party, family or corporation – only through some general category. In Italy this veil first melted into air; ...."

She does not agree that this phenomenon was to be credited to Italy alone. She believes that the shift—"an inability to discriminate between fantastic history and imaginary geography, between Paradise and Atlantis on the one hand and Cathay and Jerusalem on the other, between unicorns and rhinoceroses, the fabulous and the factual"—could be explained by the conditions of scribal culture and how they changed after print. (8)

With the development of printing, there was a growing sense of self-awareness, "an awakening of personality, with a new spirit of independence and a new claim to shape one's life – apart from one's parents and ancestors". Eisenstein tells us that sixteenth century literature had an avalanche of treatises which were issued to explain," by a variety of easy steps (often supplemented by sharp-edged diagrams) just how to draw a picture, compose a madrigal, mix paints, bake clay, keep accounts, survey a field, handle all manner of tools and instruments, work mines, assay metals, move armies or obelisks, design buildings, bridges and machines".(9)

This reliance of conscience in faith and of intelligence in knowledge brought about individualism, which brought about self-esteem which, in turn, led to self-reliance. Technology led to the new organization of knowledge within a person's mind. Traditional thinking, imp*ulsive thinking, old person's tales began to become unfashionable because un-useful. Precision in thinking began to count for more than before, numbers assumed much more importance than simple feeling.

When my daughter was studying at an US university, her American friend saw her address an envelope to me in India. The address said: Setalvad Lane, off Nepean Sea Rd., Mumbai. The friend commented ...so you also have to give directions to the postman!

Aha!, but this also used to be the case in Europe! In those days, "diction, grammar and orthography were fluid; they had barely begun to crystallize. Even proper names lacked approved spelling. Weights and measures were a hodgepodge. Travellers and mail made their way without addresses, unique names and numbers as coordinates for places. When Newton sent a letter to the Secretary of the Royal Society, he directed it To Mr Henry Oldenburge at his house about the middle of the old Palmail in St Jamses Fields in Westminster." (10)

Creativity? Alan Bloom writes: "We have become so accustomed to this word (creativity) that it has no more effect on us than the most banal Fourth of July oratory....But when it was first used by man, it had the odor of blasphemy and paradox. God alone had been called a Creator.....The very expression dignity of man, even when Pico della Mirandola coined it in the fifteenth century, had a blasphemous ring to it. Man as man had not been understood to be particularly dignified." (11)

The very notion of creativity was, therefore, new. With the mind having been organized and at the same time, set free, creativity followed. Creativity, invention, innovation occur when the mind leaps to an idea. Such leaps are often the result of chance or serendipity. That can happen to anyone. However, as Pasteur said, ideas come more easily to a prepared mind. And from this and as the history of Europe itself over the last 300 years has demonstrated, it is possible to prepare oneself for a modern mind and it is also possible to foster such an attitude in individual persons.

All this was in respect of thinking. On the material side, the position was not very different. Rights of purchase and alienation of land had been severely limited. Business activity had been confined to fixed channels. These values reflected the view that saw wealth as more or less fixed. It was assumed that the only way to get rich was at the expense of one's neighbours. There was no idea that generation of new wealth was possible and that there could also be increasing productivity. In the sphere of law, there was change in the relations of men with each other. In matters of property, disputes came to be decided on the basis of argument rather than force. Contracts were now drawn up between nominal equals rather than in the nature of personal bonds between superior and inferior. There was a general shift in legal exactness from diffuse obligation to explicit content.(12)

Assertiveness? This also has to be a direct consequence of individualism. We can point out in our own times to examples of even little Indian children who have been transformed after the experience of a prolonged stay overseas. Is it the exposure to more advanced and more varied technology that causes the change? (We saw earlier that just the experience of a telephone in the house brought about psychological changes in the child.) Such children are much more confident and much less submissive after they return. No longer for them the instinctive timidity of earlier times. I met one such Indian child, about four or five years old, in the lift of my building a few years ago. I had not met him before. I patted him on the head in a friendly way and said: How are you? He looked straight up at me and replied: I am good, thanks, how are you? No Indian child had said that to me before!

Nothing succeeds like success. With creativity on the one hand and assertiveness on the other, a sense of drive surely must follow. There is increasing reluctance to allow matters to be decided by Fate or Chance or Providence. There is an eagerness to take matters into one's own hands, to impel oneself, to persevere, to press ahead. The men of the Renaissance knew that the key to their problems "(was) rooted in the lives and actions of men, not in universal mysteries or the attributes of God. ...the range of their enquiries, the freshness of the scepticism and the sharpness of their observation gave impetus to and helped to acquire intellectual acceptance for the search for truth on earth instead of in heaven." (13)

The willingness to do manual work has a slightly longer history. By the thirteenth century, it had already been made respectable by Christian monks in the Benedictine and Cistercian monasteries. People were poor and hence the monks suggested work. The Cistercian slogan was Ora et labora - playing and working. The words were those of St. Benedict of Nursia but were adopted by St. Bernard of Clairvaux for his nearly 340 Cistercian abbeys all over Europe. (14)

Barriers between scholar and artisan having fallen, there was a preparedness, a readiness to do manual work. Elizabeth Eisenstein explains in her book how, after the coming of the printing machine in 1448, the difference between head and hand, between town and gown and between scholar and artisan quickly started disappearing.

In our own times, early in the twentieth century, with more leisure time available and no servants around to do manual work in the developed countries in Europe, it first became necessary and then became "fashionable" to do one's own work.

Contrast this with one of my own experiences a few years ago in a Mumbai hotel. A British business visitor and I were visiting an Indian customer in the latter's hotel room. Our host consulted us and ordered tea. After a while, the waiter knocked at the door, entered and placed the tea things on the table. He turned around to leave but our host said to him rather sharply: Aren't you forgetting something? He wanted the waiter to pour out and make the tea! It could be that our host was asserting status but there was an element in it of the feeling that manual work was manual work and not something to be done by "respectable" people. My British visitor later said that he was absolutely amazed. Generally speaking, the way we bark out our commands even to our domestic servants seems to confirm this.

In our country, I feel that equally with a physical reluctance to do manual work (the truth of which cannot be denied), there is also a general confusion in people's minds as to what constitutes good form. This is probably another aspect of Acute Bewilderment. Mahatma Gandhi's personal examples as well as exhortations about the need for manual work sound fine to Western ears but always seemed a little quaint to the elite Indian. If manual work was made to appear fashionable as part of the tradition of modern science, perhaps the efforts would be more lasting. If abundant opportunities for alternative employment for household servants were also to become available, the efforts would be permanent and total.

This was also, of course, the way it happened in European countries. In Britain, for example, the most common job for women in the 1880s and 1890s was domestic service : about one in three unmarried women were servants. For men, it was the second most important occupation, after agriculture. (15)

Indians often say about themselves that they lack self-discipline as a people. Self-discipline, by definition, must come from within. It cannot be imposed from outside. However, only a sense of self-esteem can bring about self-discipline. Thus self-esteem, self-reliance, self-discipline. Mark Tully gives an example of such self-discipline in his book No Fullstops in India. This is as related to him by an Indian. Apparently, this Indian, in his youth, and a few friends were walking down the street late one evening in Delhi. A Tommy on his bicycle coming from the opposite direction crashed into them. The Indians remonstrated strongly. The British soldier said that they had no business walking on the street and that they should have been using the footpath. The Indians equally indignantly replied that his bicycle was obliged to carry a headlight. Upon being told this, the Britisher said : You are quite right, Sir and cycled away. This apparently had made a deep impression on the Indians.(16)

Nirad Chaudhari writes about how Rabindranath Tagore reflected on the disaster on the *Titanic* when men and women brought up and steeped in luxury, used to thinking of themselves alone and to all appearance, oblivious to the rest of mankind, stepped back to make way for women and children to the lifeboats and deliberately chose death. What better example of self-discipline? Some may characterize this as a reaction to an extreme occurrence but one has to admit that there definitely is an element of discipline involved.(17)

Tagore could not help comparing it with several horrifying examples from his own experience, of which Nirad Chaudhari cites only two: Tagore was living in a houseboat in central Bengal. One morning it was moored to the bank. The previous night had been stormy and the river was in spate. He noticed the body of a woman being carried away by the swift current and called out to the men on the bank to take out his jollyboat and rescue her. Not one man stirred. Then he offered five rupees to anyone who would volunteer. A whole crowd jumped into the jollyboat. The woman was brought up and resuscitated.

The other example was of a fire in the bazaar of Bolpur near Santiniketan. Tagore's students went to put out the fire but could not get help from the local men. Only four Afghan usurers came. And then the Hindus refused to lend pitchers to fetch water lest they should be polluted by the Muslims. Nirad Chaudhuri writes:

Tagore travelled to Europe, the land of gross materialism, in search of spirituality. Tagore asked : Is there no connection between self-sacrifice and spirituality, is it not a sign of the strength which comes from religion? Does spirituality consist solely in avoiding contact with other men, in keeping the body uncontaminated or in telling beads?(18)

Kenneth Clark states that the tradition of chivalry - women to come before men – probably began in Persia, in the East. (19) If true, it is another example of how far we in the developing world have moved away from those high standards. Today, whether India or Iran, whether as a passenger in a bus queue, as a motorist on the road or even as customer at a crowded shop counter, it is a veritable free-for-all. Self-discipline is conspicuous by its absence. It can only be restored by an improvement in economic circumstance occasioned by the coming of modern science and technology which together then proceed to shape the behaviour and consciousness of a people.

The purpose of self-discipline must remain essentially, therefore, a concern for others. This concern for others is thus also brought about and fostered by technology. In time, this concern for others can lead to a sense of kindness. Clark writes :

" We are so much accustomed to the humanitarian outlook that we forget how little it counted in earlier ages of civilisation. Ask any decent person in England or America what he thinks matters most in human conduct: five to one his answer will be 'kindness'. It's not a word that would have crossed the lips of any of the earlier heroes of this series. If you had asked St. Francis what mattered in life, he would, we know, have answered 'chastity, obedience and poverty'; if you had asked Dante or Michelangelo they might have answered 'disdain of baseness and injustice'; if you had asked Goethe, he would have said 'to live in the whole and the beautiful'. But kindness, never. Our ancestors didn't use the word, and they did not greatly value the quality—except perhaps in so far as they valued compassion. Nowadays, I think we under-estimate the humanitarian achievement of the nineteenth century. We forget the horrors that were taken for granted in early Victorian England: the hundreds of lashes inflicted daily on perfectly harmless men in the army and navy; the women chained together in threes, rumbling through the streets in open carts on their way to transportation. These and other even more unspeakable cruelties were carried out by agents of the Establishment, usually in defence of property." (20)

how nations change

How did entire nations get to acquire this kind of modern mind-cast? The instrument here is nothing other than an impersonal, disembodied, non-subjective science and technology. Its influence can be intensive as well as extensive. It works on every individual and on all people, it applies at all points, it applies at every level of society and its pressure is continuing and relentless. Each nation subjected to this kind of treatment found itself radically changed in the process. It bred a more confident, a more skilled, a different kind of man. It was men and women of this kind who then took the nation forward, away from the poverty of centuries and on to the prosperity which we see today.

We have already seen a multitude of benefits conferred by technology on individuals and groups. Armed with these qualities, is it any surprise that some nations surged forward and others, now caught on the wrong foot, stayed backward and eventually fell victim? Of course, it did not all happen in a flash. It took years and years, even centuries. It may even have been unclear in the beginning but before long, nations in Europe had discovered that there were on to something special, something not known before in history and they not merely clung to it but pushed it forward with all their might.

What were these qualities which affected the nation as a whole? Elizabeth Eisenstein shows how one technology alone, the printing machine, circa 1480, led to a better setting out and organization of knowledge in human minds. We have referred often to this revolutionary moment. The printed book led to the notion of antiquity as a distant historical milieu. Earlier, all experience was supposed to reside in the past. This experience needed to be borrowed from the past to be applied to present times. Now people were able to think clearly, the past as past but also about the present and the future.

But how did it actually happen? Father Ong in *The Presence of the Word* demonstrates how technology led to change within the mind. The skills associated with dialectics and the art of discourse (as in Cicero's times) gave way to the habit of personal enquiry, silent cerebration and the art of thinking so much more characteristic of our times. "Without literacy man tends to solve problems in terms of what people do or say – in the tradition of the tribe, without much personal analysis...(however) reading of any sort forces the individual into himself, by confronting him with thought in isolation, alone." (21)

Now it was possible to tell much more easily which rights fell in the public domain and those which did not . There was a drive towards uniformity and rationalization including things like weights and measures and systems of coinage. Mass literacy and nationalism also developed together. Printing weakened fear of disapproval, people increasingly questioned the earlier habit of respectful submission to traditional authority.

Printing also had a great deal to do with the creation and encouragement of a collective consciousness. At first sight, this seems like a paradoxical thing to happen but not if, as Eisenstein explains "...the relationship between communication systems and community structures (is) more carefully explored...To hear an address delivered, people have to come together, to read a printed report encourages individuals to draw apart... and yet: the wide distribution of identical bits of information provided an impersonal link between people who were unknown to each other... even while communal solidarity was diminished, vicarious participation in more distant events was also enhanced; even while local ties were loosened, links to larger collective units were being forged. Printed materials encouraged silent adherence to causes whose advocates could not be found in any one parish and who addressed an invisible public from afar. New forms of group identity began to compete with an older, more localized nexus of loyalties." (22)

Acquisition of self-esteem by individual persons led to an esteem for others and for their rights. If I am as good as everyone else, it follows that everyone else is as good as I am. In a word, republicanism.

Curiosity, a sense of adventure, a need for discovery (new lands as well as increased knowledge), soaring imagination, all received impetus. This was driven by the need to do hard work and by a sense of ambition. There was a willingness, even a desire to follow rules. People were prepared to give way, to yield to others.

There are important implications. As we have noted, science is essentially a constant search for truth. At a personal level, this means being honest, utterly honest with oneself at all times. It means not deceiving others, not cheating the law and not even being untruthful with oneself in respect of one's motives. This is much more than just an "inner voice." It is the institutionalization of it. It is the secret policeman or policewoman within each one of us. When you have produced a people like this, it acts as an incentive for honesty and it becomes a bulwark or even a preventative against corruption. Because use of technology also created confidence, one gradually became choosy, one wanted to do things the "right" way, not a corrupt kind of way. More people now instinctively preferred to insist on and to fight for what they considered to be their rights instead of taking the easy way out. Of course, all these are truly only ideals but science is probably the best way of constantly hammering away at the message while all the while aspiring to get there.

tackling corruption

For us in India, in discussing the subject of corruption, there's an additional, interesting historical angle. It is also an excellent example of how whole nations change. We have already explained that economic growth in a nation ultimately takes place because of science and technology. It does not happen because of the government's benediction. A developing nation, therefore, is to be viewed as a work-in-progress. If growth is more than corruption, one is heading towards developed country. If corruption exceeds growth, one is going in the direction of developing. There is no reason why corruption and growth cannot co-exist. However, whatever the protective defences you put in place – whether clean government, good enforcement, rapid economic growth or well-functioning institutions (and these must continue) – your ultimate objective will always be to try and arrive at a people endowed with moral and ethical principles, a polity with integrity.

How does this come about? What cultural or societal changes are required to make this happen? There are two paths, one short-term and the other a rather longer path. The first requires you to build individual self-esteem, as mentioned above. The longer route is illustrated in a book called *Warfare and Weaponry in South Asia, 1000-1800.* Earlier, sedition, intrigue, looting and plunder were common to the Indians, the Afghans and the British. (Loot is an Indian word.) However, during the 17th and 18th centuries, European warfare had gradually become the exclusive domain of the modern nation state. Warfare was taken out of the hands of the military contractors. Individual apportionment of loot and plunder was disallowed. Soldiers were now paid wages. They were required to take an oath to serve the state. The Europeans had now a completely different attitude towards warfare as such. On the Indian and Afghan side, however, 'collaboration', 'treason' 'intrigue' and 'corruption' continued apace. (23) This then is the historical background. The lesson for us today should be that a nation embarked on a road paved by science and technology is positioned to secure gain for itself in each of both these ways, gradually shaping itself into a more and more modern nation.

With all these qualities in tow distinguishing him from the peoples of other countries, European man developed a habit of mind which gave him a coherent way of thinking, a way of looking at the world (his own and that of others), a world-view which was necessarily and markedly different from the Hindu, Muslim, Buddhist and Chinese way of looking at things.

European nations learned that "planning, information and the general notion of secular improvement enabled humans to better their condition on earth and that this could be secured by state action...The notion developed of the state as an initiator of legislative and administrative rules designed to improve society and increase its resources... Administration began to be conceived in terms of legal precedent. The power of the state began to be understood in terms of consent as well as coercion...(and) the concept was increasingly grasped that government could be used as a means of mobilizing resources of society in order to maximize public welfare."(24)

If we agree that science accompanied by technology helped to propel nations forward, it follows that there is little hope for our country until it also becomes science-minded and more modern-minded. We asked whether we could prepare ourselves to acquire a modern mind. We wondered whether such a mind could be grafted onto other persons. In each case, the answer must be an emphatic yes. Follow the prescribed course and you automatically begin to acquire the qualities of a modern mind. Indeed, it is possible to say : ... "follow the path and the fruit trees will rain their fruit on you!".

We have studied how this process came about in the West. It need not take quite as long in India. Change will eventually come to India, whether we like it or not, such is the power of technology. It already surrounds us on all sides – we are not an antiquated nation any more; we could not remain that way if we chose. The problem is that we are seriously short of time. For this reason, it is essential that we recognize both the cause and agent of change, accept it wholeheartedly and help it along in transforming the life and character of our nation.

scientific knowledge vs. scientific attitudes

One difference requires to be constantly kept in mind: this is the difference between scientific knowledge and scientific attitudes. In the beginning, scientific knowledge was restricted to only a few. Later, as the body of science itself began to grow and science increasingly began to be taught in schools, colleges and universities, it attracted more adherents for itself. Scientific knowledge in such people and the technological achievements that science now produced, began to breed scientific attitudes on the part of the people as a whole. It is these scientific attitudes that represent the collective mind of a modern nation. In The Conquest of Paradise, Kirkpatrick Sale quotes Peter Mathias as saying: "It is the spread not of scientific *knowledge*, which is truly possessed by only a few, but of scientific *attitudes*, which are absorbed by many, that characterizes Europe from the fifteenth century on. (emphasis in the original)" (25)

Today, with the proliferation of science in all directions, attitudes toward the subject have even become blasé. The discipline of science is infinitely larger today than it was in the fifteenth century and it is also more complex. This is why, even in developed countries, there are large masses of people who claim either to be uninterested in science or intimidated by it. Scientific *attitudes*, on the other hand, once implanted, cannot be shaken off or forgotten. Once you have begun to think along logical, rational lines, it is difficult, if not impossible, to stop doing so.

Can we in India turn this around and use it to our advantage? We know that specialized scientific knowledge is difficult to comprehend and to make popular. It is also expensive to extend to the people of the country as a whole. Therefore, is it possible to work backwards and begin by trying to inculcate scientific attitudes in the people? One example: while science education for children and students is important, should a *simulous* effort be made to gradually convert parents? Such a programme would be much easier to explain and much easier to administer. In other words, we try to promote science literacy side by side with ordinary literacy. It could quicken the overall process of development with far smaller outlay of resources.

MoSTly unaware

As we have discussed, science is largely a cerebral, intellectual endeavour. The artifacts of technology, derived from science, are however all too real—they can be felt, experienced. The expansion of mind and motor skills that comes from use of these artifacts is, again, in the nature of an unseen thing. You cannot put your finger on it, you cannot hold it in your hands. It is impalpable. Consequently, the danger of overlooking it or missing it altogether is great. Here are several striking examples, in my opinion, where it was never considered:

(1) World War II was drawing to an end. Before occupying Japan, the U.S. government needed to know what kind of people the Japanese really were. Ruth Benedict, one of the most eminent anthropologists of the twentieth century, was deputed to travel to Japan and make a study of the Japanese people. In her bestselling book *The Chrysanthemum and the Sword,* she explains how good Japan was at importing foreign cultures and adapting to them. She has in mind – as she makes clear in the book – Japan's adoption of Buddhism from China in the first or second century AD. She says: " It is difficult to find anywhere in the history of the world any other such successfully planned importation of civilization by a sovereign nation."(26) The other, more recent importation was right there but totally unseen by her. There is no mention of Japan's borrowing of Western science and technology and consequently, Western ways of thinking starting from as early as the 1850s. This import has shown itself, for good or for bad, to be of even greater significance. Because of it Japan could equip itself for war, took over practically all of Asia and even today, in peacetime, has one of the largest economies, one of the highest per capita incomes and the highest life expectancy for men and women in the world.

(2) As noted in Part 1, in *Sea of Poppies* Amitav Ghosh provides a searing account of how hapless indentured labour from Bihar and Uttar Pradesh was first recruited and then transported to Mauritius. The British rulers, a mere joint stock company, are the bossmen and

we are the directed. Cannot some thought be given as to why the British took over our country and why we fell victim? MoST made possible Britain's travel to India and its occupation of India and the lack of it made us the supreme vanquished in our own country. The author has a different explanation but I suspect that he offers it because it is easy to miss the very existence of MoST.

(3) The World Bank exhortation to allow (Indian) migrants to flock to urban and other centres –even encouraging migration, in search of economic health, from states that do not provide sufficient growth opportunities (27)—in my view, betrays ignorance of what MoST can do to transform people – any people, anywhere!

(4) In Ezra Vogel's book "Deng Xiaoping and the Transformation of China" which we have referenced earlier, towards the end there is the following paragraph:

"As the boat passed by the remains of a Qing dynasty customs house, Deng again passed on the essence of his departing message: China had been humiliated by the foreign imperialists, but that era had passed: "Those who are backward get beaten...We've been poor for thousands of years, but we won't be poor again. If we don't emphasize science, technology and education, we will be beaten again." This is indicated as the key to China's transformation in numerous places in the book. Nevertheless, the late Fang Lizhi, famous Chinese astrophysicist, a proponent of human rights, in a two page review of the book, makes no mention of it and instead laments the fact that there is no mention of human rights. Pray how does one ensure human rights in the real sense unless there also is economic growth and development!?

admitting the reality

We have argued that because of the manner in which we in India have grown, we have been left crushingly behind in history. Actually, this statement applies to all developing countries without exception. Whether we look at it as the developing countries having been left behind or as developed countries having shot forward – the net result remains the same.

Was this an unfeeling and unpatriotic statement to make? I continued to harbour serious doubts within myself until I read the following passage in E.H. Carr's *What is History?*:

" More than thirty years ago a high military officer visiting the Soviet Union listened to some illuminating remarks from a Soviet officer concerned with the building up of the Red air force : 'We Russians have to do with still primitive human material. We are compelled to adapt the flying machine to the type of flyer who is at our disposal. To the extent to which we are successful in developing a new type of men, the technical development of the material will also be perfected. The two factors condition each other. Primitive men cannot be put into complicated machines". (28)

Here the Soviets are saying that their people were "primitive material," that their aircraft had to be tailored to the kind of pilots they happened to have, that as the quality of their people improved, so also would the capacity and speed of their airplanes. What refreshing candour when a country boldly admits that many of its people still constitute primitive material! Had they not summoned the courage to admit to their condition and to diagnose their illness, they could never have embarked on the subsequent treatment. Carr wrote this when the Soviets were still reeling from the effects of the German onslaught during the War. They went on to win the war. Seven decades later, in our own times, the Soviets have again bravely admitted that the entire experiment of communism as a political and economic system, spread over seventy years in their country, had not worked. Perestroika and glasnost will remain as monuments to man's ability to look inwards, to criticize and if necessary, to correct his course.

Earlier, we examined Japan's growth as a modern nation. Masao Miyoshi was a professor of Japanese and English in 1979 at the University of California. His comments about his countrymen are interesting. In a study of the first Japanese embassy (delegation) on its voyage to the USA in 1860, he finds there were "insufficient powers of observation, insufficient use of 'I', lack of a sense of comparison, and lack of perceptual abilities [demonstrated] compared to Americans travelling in the opposite direction (Commodore Perry's men on their visit to Japan in 1853). They were making the voyage for the first time. They were seeing new things. Yet Miyoshi finds that there was this inclination towards mechanical bookkeeping: "...little evidence of any will to interpret or impose any imaginative structure on raw experience. They tended to describe geographic movement only and that often in unadorned, mechanical terms. Even as regards landscape description, there is much evidence of the writer's wonder at the beauty of the places they visit but they seem unconcerned with verbalizing their observations in detail." Altogether, he finds their reports "disconcertingly mechanical and uncoordinated" and attributes it to " lack of a sense of individualism and absence of self-consciousness". This was, of course, 1860 Japan.(29)

Scotland was no different. Prior to the eighteenth century, they were "conscious to a painful degree of their backwardness, their poverty, their lack of polish, their provinciality." In a later era, "the Scots did not simply imitate the English but eventually forged to the forefront of British culture and world civilization." (Adam Smith in economics, David Hume in philosophy, Joseph Black in chemistry,

James Watt in engineering.). They forged past the British in industrial engineering and created some of the leading medical schools of the world in colonial America, the first medical school in Philadelphia, Kings College (renamed Columbia University) and at Dartmouth." (30)

Modern science and technology has changed Western countries and the thinking, habits and values of Western people – and we have seen how grave the consequences for countries such as India has been.

For all of us, therefore, left behind, whether Hernando de Soto's Peru or China or India or Egypt or Turkey, we have all, every one of us, by forsaking modern science and technology and the change in human beings that that brings about, reduced ourselves, let's face it, to becoming weaker peoples. It is only if we do this, only if we recognize our incompleteness and how this happened to us that we can begin to take the proper steps on the road to our recovery.

old vs. new

Let's us now look at some illustrations showing the difference between a modern mindset (rational, scientific, logical) and our traditional way of thinking. Remember that the former dovetails neatly into all the equipment, the appliances, the conveniences surrounding you, that is, it accords with reality, whereas the latter is a stand-alone and at best can only offer faith and/or spiritual solace.

An advertisement by a commercial firm in the *Times of India* catalogues various optical products that a firm sells on behalf of an overseas company. The point here is the products they sell, not the fact that these are manufactured overseas. *Right next to it* on the same page is an item stating that a group of Indians in Houston, Texas, have gathered a sum of Rs 1.25 crores for the purpose of putting up a Meenaxshi temple in that city.(31)

It seems to me that these esteemed Indians who have gone overseas and who have so easily fitted into life in prosperous America are unclear about the reason why they needed to go there in the first place. If goddess worship was able to accomplish goals, there should be no paucity of jobs and no lack of opportunities right here in our own country for these talented sons and daughters of India. There would be no need to go abroad in search of a better future.

What I mean when I describe this advertisement is that the one represents a feverish search for truth (although at first sight it may not appear to be so) while the attempt at temple-building in the U.S is an unthinking, misdirected effort, at least in my opinion, in the general direction of God and Providence.

light vs. darkness

Let's examine the slow process over the centuries (32) which culminated in the optical instruments listed in this plain advertisement. It is a gradual process but it is worth examination because of the intense, underlying search for truth that it was:

(1) The first lenses are devised. The word lens comes from lentis, the Latin word for lentil seed. Roger Bacon (1220-1292) suggests the wearing of lenses to aid vision, and about 1300 AD spectacles come into use in Italy. We take spectacles for granted today but at the time that their use was first suggested, there were religious obstacles to their being used—they were considered unnecessary and were even said to go against the laws of nature. (33)

(2)Hans Lippershey invents the telescope. The name comes from tēleskópos – a Greek word meaning "to see at a distance"

(3)Galileo Galilei constructs his own telescope by placing two lenses in a tube. His first thought is to use it as a weapon at sea. Then,great event,he turns the telescope on the sky and the moon. Until now it was thought possible to count all the stars which could be seen. Now the telescope is able to see stars which have never been seen before, and the diameter of the moon appears much greater than when seen with the naked eye. The telescope also reveals several moons of Jupiter. Galileo allows his guests to see inscriptions on a cathedral nearly 3 miles away! His instrument is christened telescope, beginning the practice of naming instruments of modern science after names borrowed from ancient Greece. Now, man is *seeing* other worlds instead of merely thinking about them. The telescope arouses enormous interest in the science of optics.

(4)Isaac Newton (1642-1727) views light through a prism and finds a progression of colours. He passes these colours through a second prism, held upside down and obtains white light! He concludes that the array of colours is not an inherent property of light but is an effect of that kind of light on the retina of the eye. Thus, some people are colour-blind but light doesn't disappear for them—only colour does.

(5) Herschel,(1738-1822) with his large telescopes, becomes the father of astronomy beyond the solar system and discoverer of the galaxy. He finds that the sun is not the centre of the universe at all.

(6) Photography enters upon the stage and makes light do more.(1840) Light is persuaded to make a *permanent* image. In initial telescopic astronomy, the impression on the retina is temporary. The impression on the photographic plate, on the other hand, is now permanent and even cumulative.

(7) Enter spectroscopy (1814), Each element is found to have its own characteristic spectrum. Light from a star can now be analysed and made to yield its chemical composition. It is found that the composition of stars and planets is not different from that of Earth.

(8) The element helium is predicted in advance in the sun (in India, in 1895, by a visiting English scientist) as a new element 28 years before it is discovered on Earth!

(9) Edwin Hubble's (1888-1953)work on the Mount Wilson, California telescope initiates new studies on cosmology (properties of the universe as a whole) and cosmogony(the origin and evolution of the universe).

(10) So far, we have had light from visible bodies. Now comes light that cannot be seen. Infra-red ("below the red") radiation in 1800 all the way to ultra-violet ("beyond the violet") in 1801.

(11)James Clerk Maxwell's electromagnetic spectrum (1870) This was only a theory when first proposed but Hertz in 1886 finds radio waves exactly as predicted. Marconi (and Bose [1858-1937] in India) develop the modern radio.

(12) Radioactivity (property of certain chemical elements causing them to emit radiation due to changes in the nuclei of atoms of the element) is discovered in 1896.

(13) Radio Telescope (1932) - shows, even in infancy, how it can outdo three centuries of refinement of optical astronomy at a single stroke.

(14) Radar (radio detection and ranging) invented in 1935 and used in the Battle of Britain in World War II

(15) Today, even the space telescope (launched 1990)

This then was the slow, tortuous process by which the truth was won from nature in the science of optics. This forms the background for the development of various instruments in spectrometry, meteorology, documentation, opthalmology, photogrammetry and astronomy set out in the advertisement.

Contrast with this the *kumbhabhishekam* of the newly built Hindu temple in America. At best, it represents, at least in my view, a mindless, thoughtless, endless repetition of the name of God. We have been invoking the name of God in this tireless fashion for more than 2000 years and we need to conclude that either the gods are not listening to our entreaties or that our prayers are misdirected and that we are appealing to the wrong gods. The stark consequences of this mindlessness are to be seen, by way of photograph and description, on the very next day, 30th June 1982 in the same newspaper! It shows a dead body, apparently unattended, lying on the platform at Gaya railway station and crowds looking for their seats in the train milling all around it! (newspaper cutting with author).

Swami Agnivesh, who was debating the practice of sati in the pages of a Bombay magazine, with the illustrious Shankaracharya of Puri (who agreed with the practice!) argues that it is ironical that India is the only country where there is a goddess of wealth and yet we are one of the poorest countries in the world and that there is a goddess of learning and yet we are one of the least literate in the world. I submit that it is not ironical, it is inevitable. Both cause and effect are to be seen throughout the length and breadth of this country.

flight vs. fancy

Let's take another example and trace out a modern phenomenon while distinguishing it from the age-old way of thinking in India. We are told about Hanuman carrying the mountain of Meru and we are informed about Pushpak transporting the gods by air. Mind you, I am not saying that these are not delightful tales. I say it in all seriousness. They are fascinating stories, showing a fertile imagination and they make for excellent mythology. But it is not how flight came about. Even in Europe (as elsewhere), man thought that he could put on wings, jump off from the edge of a cliff and soar in the air like a bird. He usually landed very quickly with disastrous consequences to himself.

Flight came to man in an entirely different manner. There is an excellent exhibit at St. Louis Airport in the United States showing the beginnings and progress of flight. It all began with the simple discovery (in chemistry, if you please!) that all matter has weight. Even air, it was realized, has weight. In that case, they reasoned, if something has to float in air, it needs to have less weight than air, something, for example, that rises even in air. Was there such a thing! Indeed there was and the woman of the house (and the man as well) had been seeing it for long, only not in this particular way. This thing was smoke, which all of us have seen to rise even in air. Chemists began to think: Was there a chemical element which was lighter than air and would rise in air? Yes, there was. Thus was born the balloon filled with hydrogen. Then, since helium was safer and less inflammable than hydrogen, helium began to be used. However, although balloons could float about in the air, they were painfully slow in covering distance and in finding direction. Meanwhile, the steam locomotive was already in use but it was, of course, too heavy to be used for powered flight. Therefore, when the internal combustion engine became popular with the coming of the motorcar, it was only a matter of time before the engine was used to power flight. After the biplane, came the monoplane, then in our own lifetimes, the turboprop, the pure jet and now, the jumbo jet.

So it will be seen that flight became possible for man due to the combination of a number of seemingly unrelated sciences. Chemistry, physics and metallurgy were equally as necessary as aerodynamics. It might never have happened if man had just sat back and made up fanciful stories (that they are lovely stories is a different thing altogether) or merely dreamed of flying in the same way as birds!

the earth belongs to the living

Let's now conclude our comparison of modern vs. traditional with a look at the area of social custom and practice. In all cultures, the tradition has always been that one should respect one's elders. What could possibly be wrong with such a wonderful sentiment? Age represented knowledge, experience and wisdom and these qualities commanded respect. But a certain change came about in this happy state of affairs with the invention of the printing machine. Gifted students no longer needed to sit at the feet of a given master in order to learn a language or academic skill. Now it was possible to have books which included both knowledge and experience and transmitted these to their readers in a much better manner than fathers could do to children or elders could do to others. Wisdom too was now available by filtering knowledge not only from one's own experience but also, if one read books, from the experience of other people.

Venice, in Italy, was the place where publishers began to gather. By 1500, about 25 German printing houses had opened there. More books were published in fifteenth century Venice than in any other city in Europe (perhaps as many as 4500 titles, accounting for some 2.5 million copies). Interestingly, the technology apparently came to Venice early because of the pepper routes that long connected her to Central Europe.(34)

From the fifteenth century onwards in Europe, therefore, young people with access to books, developed a potential for knowledge and experience far in excess of older generations who earlier did not have the same recourse to books and were thus restricted in the scope for expanding their minds. The printing machine turned out more books and better books on all manner of subjects. Each generation became better informed than the one before and as a consequence, whole countries, as we have said earlier, started on the path to progress.

Books also exist in India, of course. It follows from this that each generation is better schooled, more educated and generally speaking, much better informed than the earlier one. But, regardless of who today is educated or not, many still believe in total submission to fathers and elders, of all siblings to the eldest, of sisters to brother, of shishya (pupil) to guru and wife to husband. Times have changed for some, but most continue to blindly follow tradition.

Should this mean disrespect for one's elders? Absolutely not. But respect for the older generation should be accompanied by the knowledge that times have indeed changed, tradition must give way to modernity and old must make way for new. Such a development must not only not be obstructed by the older generation but, as in Europe, must be actively encouraged by the elders themselves because only then can each family benefit, each generation progress and the entire country move forward.

This is the real meaning of the Jeffersonian belief that the earth belongs to the living. One of the things that he said, specifically followed from this principle, was that no generation had the right to bind another. For example, speaking of our own society, should the father be dependent on his children for support in his old age? Wouldn't it be better if the father earned enough for himself and his family during his working life and was also able to provide for old age, thereby preserving his own self-esteem and also avoiding the need for burdening his children with the responsibility for himself and wife. It all depends on the economic system. If the economic system does not provide the means for the production of enough wealth, the father is unable to look after himself in his old age. Society then twists logic around so that his eldest son becomes obligated to look after him. The child is told that he is lucky to be brought into this world and even more lucky to be brought up because of the sacrifices that his parents have had to make. It is an unending refrain in millions of Indian homes. It produces the further distortion that children are brought into the world to provide more pairs of working hands and to act as economic assets for the parents.

Of course, every economic system is dependent on the science and technology of the age. If the technology has fallen behind or is otherwise deficient, job opportunities are lacking and the social system gradually gets distorted in the process. This is one more example of how technology affects culture and is perhaps a good point at which to end our discussion of how desperately we need a modern, forward, progressive way of looking at our country and the world.

I have tried to show the fateful consequences for our country of the presence of non-science in different areas of our life. I have tried to outline, with examples from everyday life, why we are held back and why developed nations, having liberated themselves from this type of bondage, have shot forward and succeeded in obtaining a good standard of living for themselves.

Can we follow their example? Is it at all possible for India to take the same path and rapidly become a developed, more prosperous country? While preserving all that is good and sweet and useful in our own culture, we are now called upon to also adopt the culture of modern science and technology and in doing that, perhaps showing the best way, as Naipaul has so properly called it, of the "fitting of one civilization to another." (35) And this is also what I consider to be true multiculturalism, intelligent multiculturalism. Embrace the best, discard the rest! What can be so wrong with that?

PART 3

(agenda for a nation)

Chapter 8
RALLYING THE COUNTRY:

wooing the teachers,

working with parents,

involving the people.

For it is a certain maxim, no man sees what things are that knows not what they ought to be. – Jonathan Richardson, quoted by E.H. Gombrich, Art and Illusion

The change implied by economic growth is not then simply a change from one set of values to another—from love of cattle to love of money, from respect for seniority to respect for education, from faith in custom to faith in science—but a more profound change in the nature of social skills. – Development in a Divided World, Dudley Seers and Leonard Joy, Eds.

Failing to prepare is like preparing to fail. - Benjamin Franklin

• can India change? • what kind of change? • the 4 Es • new jobs and old • MASK • is knowledge manageable ? • organizing for change • creating a climate • beyond consumerism • wooing the teachers • what students can do • working with parents • the special role of women • a feminist agenda • involving the people • helping change to happen

In this chapter, we will further demonstrate how the adoption of the path of modern science and technology brings about transformation of society. India is a large country and there is a great deal of ground to cover. Hence I will avoid going into details and instead will try to paint with broad-brush strokes; these will, however, contain suggestions about goals we should set before ourselves as well as methods we might adopt to achieve them.

can India change?

Can India really change? Is it possible? Can our observations, our arguments and our conclusions apply to this highly religious country which has stoutly resisted change over the years? Such fears are unfounded. There isn't a country in the world not amenable to change. Besides, the change which we now seek to usher in is no larger than, although significantly different from, the changes which have already transformed the face of the country over the last hundred years.

First, who would have believed that independence would come to India so abruptly and that too in such an essentially non-violent way? Who would have credited a short, frail, half-clothed man with the ability to start a mass movement for freedom in a vastly illiterate country in the teeth of the opposition of the mighty British Empire? Yet it did happen.

The economic changes that we have already undergone over the last seventy or so years have transformed us in many ways. A simple way to confirm this is to look at everything around you in your room. The chances are that before independence many goods (and the producer goods by which they were made) were imported from overseas. Every single item is made in India today. Imagine the industries that have been set up in order to provide these products, the employment they offer, the families that grew up together with the wage-earners and the invisible bonds that tie it all together. The sinews of our economy are these strings that bind us together as a nation. The state of India, I mean by this the condition of India which it represents, is a far cry from the shattered, diffident, uncertain, economically stagnant nation that existed on Independence Day.

There are other examples of our capacity for change. First, family planning. If anything, we left this until very late. There was the fear that India, with its religious, traditional background, would not accept public discussion of such an intimate issue. Today, the slogan Hum do, hamare do is known in every part of the country, so familiar that it has now almost become a cliché.

Then, central planning. When first mooted for our country, it was said to be indicative of a strong, leftist tilt in the country. Planned economies were only for communist nations. They had no place in a free society! There was national and international clamour against our adoption of the concept. Today, it is conceded that planning is perhaps even more necessary in a democratic, liberal, free society and in a mixed economy than in a totalitarian society. If planning is necessary for individual families, for commerce and for industry, then it is a sine qua non for the nation as a whole.

Another example of a concept which seemed foreign to a country like India and which has succeeded beyond expectation is secularism. I don't mean, of course, that the concept has been realized. Far from it. The idea is very much under siege while the country even today furiously debates the pros and cons of religion and secularism. But the very fact that the debate is raging shows how, even in a highly religious country like India, the ideal of secularism can be placed before the people as an objective worthy of being striven for.

When the country was partitioned in 1947, portions were hived out to form the basis of a theocratic state. Yet the remainder of India, despite horrendous communal killings and the serious dislocations that go with any partition, remained steadfast to an anti-religious or non-religious idea and in due course of time, proudly consecrated it in the form of a secular state. If this could happen, then persuading the people about the benefits to be gained from the kind of change we have been discussing, should not be incapable of achievement. The people of India realize that they are at a crossroads. They want to know what modernization means, what it really represents, which way the nation ought to be going and they are anxious for economic, political and other leadership to point the direction.

Therefore, when we have already engineered such enormous change for ourselves, what needs to be done today should not deter us, however large the change may be in itself. We now require to think afresh and then once again bind together, adapt, adjust, consolidate and build upon the progress already achieved.

Change in our thinking must precede all other kinds of change. Why? Because one can sometimes be enveloped in a sea of modernity and still find it difficult to change. The arrangements and conveniences of modern life are so easily at hand and taken for granted that it often makes it that much more difficult to change. For example, most Indians will readily agree that certain tribal groups in say, Central India or Eastern India might need to modernize their thinking. But will these same people agree that those who put up Ganesh idols or Durga idols every year at great financial and environmental expense, which seem so little to advance their material well-being, should similarly re-visit their thinking?

Change will come to this country, like it or not. The compulsive force of science and technology is like a powerful undercurrent in all countries, unseen onthe surface and whose existence may sometimes be doubted, but carries all before it effortlessly. This same compulsion operates in India, and will continue to do so, gathering strength as it does. It will stop at no obstacle although it may be slowed down a little now and again. Eventually, it will grind down every barrier in its way and achieve its end.

The question then before us is whether we should prepare and organize for change or whether we should simply allow change to overtake us. The enormousness, the depth and the seriousness of this kind of social change should not be underestimated. To allow such forces to come upon us suddenly (different sections of society are being affected at different times in different ways) and in an unplanned way is to tempt Fate in a dangerous fashion. If we fail to anticipate, if we do not prepare our society for it, if we do not mould and guide these forces as they exert their unseen pressure on us, the consequences could be calamitous. There is more need for such cerebral planning in our country than there is even for the central economic planning that we have been practising. As noted earlier (see Chapter 2), a perceptual or cerebral revolution of this kind should preferably precede or if not that, at least accompany an economic or political revolution.

what kind of change?

What kind of change do we seek? We need to modernize. Like corporations and whole nations, we need a mission statement, a national vision. Our mission statement is very simply put: Our mission is that India from now on pursue the path of modern science and technology. A sense of direction is vital to a democracy. Especially a large democracy like ours with major variations in language, script, religion, regional culture, history, clothes, food habits etc. J.K. Galbraith once described India as perhaps the world's only example of a functioning anarchy. It is still quoted with gleeful approval by many Indians. This kind of back-handed compliment will no longer suffice. From now on, we need to work purposefully and with determination and what better purpose than MoST? Remember science is a search for truth. This has to be an ever-present guide to our actions. Japan forgot this most important concomitant when it created its Greater East Asia Co-Prosperity Sphere with dire results for itself and the rest of the world. It put technology to use but forgot science! (1) We cannot allow this to happen. We have to be clear in our minds how we are going to attain our goal and a careful understanding of the direction of MoST will undoubtedly help.

Do we use political parties as our vehicle for change or do we allow large masses of people to merely band together with vague, inchoate ideas about our common mission and thus, in effect, permit a nation-wide free for all? Actually, it is remarkable how every political party, each trumpeting a certain, exclusive ism for itself has, at the bottom of it all, the standard platform of science and technology. I advocate: Forget ideology, consider idea-logy! (see Chapter 8, Appendix 1) Each party, in addition to whatever else it wishes to state, should be compelled to define its role in terms of the common goal of modern science and technology. The expectation would be that in the course of time a common platform based on MoST and bounded by MoST would emerge, thus reducing considerably the partisan proclivities of each party.

In our own lifetimes, we have seen the spectacular collapse of fascism and communism. Fabian socialism practised, after World War II, practically all over the world including in India, was finally given the go by in the 1960s with the increasing success of countries like the fabled South East Asian tigers. More recently, in 2008, we witnessed the near collapse of the entire world's capitalist economies.

What ought we to do? Should we opt for capitalism because, in the same way that Churchill spoke about democracy, it is probably the most beneficial and the least harmful ism of all? What essentially are the freedoms that capitalism truly confers on its practitioners? The Economist suggested: To travel, to shop, to exchange currency, to change jobs, to move house, to think, to speak.(2) But also to hold property, to accept the pursuit of profit and especially, to criticize.

Is there need for the market? If you do away with the market, what do you use in its place? Without a doubt, it is the best kind of system for resource allocation. Sylvia Nasar writes about the market:

" ... The trouble with substituting planners for market, (Ludwig von) Mises argued, is that without markets there are no longer market prices to use for making your calculation. Can't you just make some up? Sure, but if no one was producing for, or buying in markets, they wouldn't be market prices. They wouldn't reflect the subjective preferences of the consumers who are demanding a good or the calculations of the businesses deciding whether to supply the good – in real time too. They wouldn't give you the information you needed to make a rational decision. You'd have no way of knowing whether you were making the most of your resources or squandering them heedlessly." (3)

The communist countries dispensed with the market and brought near ruin to their economies. In recent years China, transformed in a mere thirty years, went to great lengths to gently re-introduce the market into its economy. Imagine what a powerful formula it would make for the market to be combined with a clear understanding of the forces of science and technology. Supply and demand forces constantly controlled by, monitored by and working clearly and in tandem with the forces behind modern science and technology. What would we call this? Call it what you like. Social democracy (as in Europe), creative capitalism (a la Bill Gates), modern day capitalism, stakeholder capitalism, whatever!

So much for a general sense of purpose. What now of the specific problems that we need to examine?

the 4 Es

In our country, there is the question of demographic dividend. We are well placed to benefit by this. As Raj Jain has written in the Economic Times: We currently have 500 million in the workforce and this is expected to grow by about 20 million each year for the next 10 years. By 2020, India will account for a fourth of the world's total workforce. And it will be a young workforce. By then, the average working age is projected to be 60 in both the US and Europe, 45 in China and merely 29 in India" (4)

But Jain goes on to say " this workforce has a serious problem. A little more than half (around 270 million) is employed in rural areas, primarily in agriculture, 40% of the total workforce is illiterate and another 40% constitutes school dropouts...Of the 455 million jobs available, 90% require some level of skills, 9% are knowledge-based and 1% require a combination of both skills and knowledge"(5) Therefore, apart from the problem of employment, we also have the problem of unemployability. Further, 80% of all new entrants to the workforce have had no opportunity for skill training." (6) Even with respect to the existing workforce, it turns out that only about 2% has had skill training as against 96% in Korea, 75% in Germany and 68% in the U.K. (7) Like other writers, Jain emphasizes that there is in effect, therefore, a " big disconnect between what the industry needs and what the students learn through the education system".

According to him, the 4 Es which need to be in place are Education, Employment, Employability and Excellence. (8) A foundational course in MoST (along the general lines suggested in this book) combined with skill training could put things in the right perspective, transform outlook and prepare students/workers for different slots in the employment system. It would contribute the very flexibility which Mr Anil Kakodkar, former Chairman of the Atomic Energy Commission, meant when he once said, "I would worry if a graduate in a particular discipline can't adapt to another discipline. A good education is where a student learns to adapt to changing scenarios." (9) This reasoning applies whether the applicant is a graduate, a student, a worker or even an apprentice. Even in the USA only approximately 1% of jobs requires or demands an MBA degree. Degrees offering technical or entrepreneurship background are better. "Education is still incredibly important, but specialized skills matter more than ever".(10)

new jobs and old

Of all our multifarious needs, jobs should be the topmost priority. If we make certain that jobs are available for people and that, increasingly, candidates are trained, shaped and made suitable for these jobs, a large part of our work will have been done. Food, clothing and shelter can follow. Men and women with jobs will acquire the confidence to organize housing, education and health care for themselves or ensure that they are organized for them.

Mr. Sudhakar Ram, writing in the Economic Times, suggests four ways to encourage entrepreneurship in order to create jobs:

1. since 60% of the population lives in rural areas, we need to create employment opportunities closer to home for our youth;

2. education and research institutions need to create appropriate technologies based on renewable materials and energy sources;

3. private enterprises and public private partnerships need to provide training for specific areas of work and finally

4. banks and financial institutions require to provide financial, logistical and other support.(11)

Every one of these areas can be strengthened and deepened if individual and group are inducted into the processes of science – youth can then create its own opportunities, research and development will not merely exist but will flourish and public private partnerships and banks can reflect the large strides which come easily with an understanding of the enormous economic potential of science. On the same day on which Ram's article appeared, its sister newspaper, The Times of India, reported that the Mumbai police had advertised for 3,600 jobs. 75,000 candidates had applied, there was a stampede and one person died. Familiar stuff, but is this kind of thing any longer acceptable? So unless we get cracking, there is nothing magical about demographic dividend. If we do not prepare for it, the consequences could be fearful. Instead of demographic dividend, we might well have demographic devastation on our hands.

I'd like to end on a happy note, though. Let me, therefore, summarize here, author J.A.Chowdhary's quick account of how Hyderabad in Andhra Pradesh grew before his very eyes:

"As the (information) technology industry grew, the support segments, such as hospitality, travel, medicare, retail, to name a few, grew as well...The technology industry forms the backbone of the modern economy as we know it. For every one job that it creates, there is associated growth in other segments and hence more jobs and thereby more wealth creation opportunities. The once risk wary citizen, who saw savings only in the form of a savings account, now began to venture out into more wealth creation avenues, with enhanced risk.(12)

We spoke about how 20 million people were expected to be added to India's workforce every year for the next ten years. This means that during this period alone a total of 200 million new jobs will be called for. It is enough to strike terror in any heart – except if you consider that MoST, if properly harnessed and put to use, can make jobs available and provide candidates to fill those jobs. But for this nothing less than a huge national initiative is called for.

We also earlier pointed out how unemployability due to lack of skills existed side by side with existing employment availability. But there is further complication. Latha Jishnu showed up this paradox even as early as in 2005: Newer and newer sectors were looking for specially skilled staff while at the same time, hundreds of old-time professionals were unable to find employment! Jishnu said that there were plentiful vacancies in the health care industry, in telecom, in the automobile and auto-ancillary industry, the pharmaceutical industry, hotels, oil and petrochemicals, the power generation industry, in education, training and consulting (ETC), in textiles, in IT services and in the gaming, design and animation industry. But companies could not find design engineers, engineers with project management experience, financial managers and candidates with experience in embedded software and chip design.

Multi-disciplinary skills were usually called for but these were not often to be found. (13) This situation still obtains.

The bio-technology industry needed specialists in many fields: biology, chemistry, physics, molecular biology, microbiology, pharmacology, toxicology, computer science, biochemistry and biophysics.

The financial services sector had /has vacancies in investment banking, commercial banking, in stock-broking jobs, in the mutual fund industry and hedge funds. Jobs were available for relationship managers, wealth managers, research analysts, operations managers, financial planners and portfolio managers.

The newspaper industry required editors, bureau chiefs and industry analysts at attractive salaries but there was a shortage of candidates.

Jishnu said the health care industry was growing at 13% annually. It required doctors, nurses, medical technicians, hospital managers and administrators. It also needed super-specialised junior doctors, supervisory nursing staff, bio-medical engineers, service line administrators, quality assurance experts and chemists conversant with good clinical practices.

The legal sector offered a great number of new possibilities: Young lawyers, buoyed by globalization, were making careers in private equity, competition law, corporate crime and regulatory practices, intellectual property rights, M & A (mergers and acquisitions) deals, arbitration, corporate and commercial law, capital markets, litigation law, SEBI laws, foreign exchange, management laws, maritime law and international trade and finance. This is still true.

I would just point out that in every one of the above industries and even in the legal sector, not one of these jobs would exist unless it was meant to service operations created in the first place by modern science and technology—but candidates with only an arts background were to be found! Familiarity with MoST and the flexibility we referred to a little earlier on in such jobs would be invaluable.

We also referred to the need for encouraging entrepreneurial enterprises so that candidates could start businesses of their own, thereby employing both themselves and further staff. Campaigns have to be begun for the creation of jobs in agriculture, in commerce, in the retail industry, in the tourism industry, in the distribution trade and towards industries with careers in project management, supply chain management, logistics and transportation etc. The concept of education itself has to be expanded with online education being emphasized because of its greater reach, more limited expenditure and higher potential.

So, of course, all this means that we have a huge task ahead of us. Something that can be boldly faced by a thorough understanding of the enormous power that only science and technology can provide. The foregoing, therefore, is by way of broad declaratory statements about the kind of fierce intellectual excitement we must generate in order for this kind of change to be made. Our objective should be job opportunities, job availabilities, job possibilities galore! An understanding of MoST will not only help to stimulate existing possibilities in our minds but will lead to the conjuring up of more and more possibilities.

MASK

Although our acronym is MASK—designating manufacturing, agriculture, services and the knowledge sector—historically, of course, if you exclude the hunter-gatherer stage, it was agriculture with which man began.

MASK—Agriculture: As mentioned earlier, the Physiocrats of nineteenth century France, who popularized the phrase "laissez faire" (minimal government interference in the economic affairs of individuals), also fervently believed that agriculture was at the back of it all. Even manufacturing was to be traced back to the land. They never would have imagined that today the very opposite has happened and that agriculture itself has become a large industry.

For too long after independence, our concentration was on industry. So we are big time laggards in agriculture. How did this happen? Because, for all the reasons outlined here and elsewhere in this book, we remained stagnant in our thinking and failed to go through the several stages required for agriculture to become an industry.

Actually, the early history of agriculture in England and America was no different from that of India. In the early part of the 17th century, older patterns of life prevailed: "Self sufficiency, the medieval economic standard was still the goal of English agriculture." This complacency said:

"We are too wise, holding it ridiculous to innovate anything not approved by cultural practice." Innovation was risky. People believed that "tis not the husbandman but the good weather that makes the corn grow."

Farmers were willing to emigrate to new lands but resisted "book farming". They favoured traditional practices such as word of mouth and neighbor practices to print. Rational management of resources, ideas of time-thrift and efficiency were new to Europe and therefore also played a minor role in America. Like in India, there was opposition to the creation of central markets. Thus, Britain and the USA also began with subsistence farming but unlike India which never went any further, both Western countries in stages went on to

1) market farming (catering to the needs of the market)

2) to book farming (guided by botany)

3) to the "factory farm" (with purchased raw material like feed, fertilizer and livestock)

4) to mechanized farming and

5) to precision farming or smart farming. (14)

But even this is insufficient now. It is said that the fundamental character of agriculture has changed. The Dutch, a small but pioneering country in agriculture, are claiming that traditional farming as practiced in most of the world is both unsustainable and environmentally damaging and that sustainable and intensive production is the only way forward. Thus, Dutch cows produce twice as much milk as they did in 1960. Their scientists work with government to boost productivity and develop high value products. Hovering cameras tell the Dutch which tomato plants need pesticide, reducing pesticide use by at least 85%. Greenhouses have solar panels and are energy producers rather than consumers, excess heat is recycled and stored for winter or turned into power for neighbouring houses. The value of the agricultural exports of this small country makes it second only to America. Denmark, another small country, which is similar, has actually been called an "agricultural superpower" by the Economist. (15)

In the U.S. itself, even at the start of the 19th century, a full 50% was engaged in agriculture. Today, the corresponding figure is only about 1.5%. With it, not only does America feed itself but it also exports large quantities of food to other countries. On the other hand, what do we have in India? A full half of a large population, both by way of income as well as employment is engaged in agriculture but the contribution to GDP is only of the order of 13 to 14%. There are many cultural obstacles which have accumulated over the years. Fatalism has to be removed. Farmers have to be constantly reminded that their fate lies in their own hands and is not determined by an unseen Providence. They have to be repeatedly told that tomorrow can be better than today and that their children and grandchildren's future requires them to adopt such an outlook. A real effort has to be made to gradually induct the traditional farmer class into modern ways of thinking.

All this could be backed up with a massive attempt at agro-industry. If agriculture isn't profitable as a vocation and large industry not a feasible proposition for small farmers or even collectives, there are plentiful opportunities in agro industry. These would range from cereals and pulses to spices to fruit and vegetable, to edible oils, to cut flowers and dairy products, to meat and poultry, to processed food and snacks, fish farms, marine products etc. Each of these items constitutes a mini-industry in itself and has to be undertaken with confidence, with aplomb and with a striving for excellence. This will only be possible if farmers are equipped themselves or employ intermediaries with knowledge of the basic principles of botany and zoology and other related sciences as suggested in this book.

Raj Jain points out in the Economic Times that India's biggest challenge is productivity per acre. China produces 400 million tons of grain with only 100 million hectares of agricultural land whereas India produces only about 108 million tonnes with 146 million hectares of agricultural land. But, Jain says,[even] if the next Green Revolution is based on the use of newer technologies, better yielding seeds and sustainable agricultural practices, the results will take longer than we have time to spare! So, he concludes, the next big revolution in India may (could) well take place outside the farm. Jain suggests three main ways of doing this:

1) Liberalized farm markets through direct marketing and contract farming, collective linkages between farm production, food processing industries, retail chains and end consumers.

2) He says the next Green Revolution will not be triggered pre-harvest but post-harvest. (For example), India produces over 600 million tonnes of food products, is the largest producer of rice and wheat, pulses and milk (but) only 2% of India's fruit and vegetable output is processed as against 70% in Brazil and 60-70% in developed countries. Processed foods as a whole account for only 2% of total production.

3) Farm to fork post-farm management – understanding of consumer demand and production demand and matching of demand with supply. This means supply-chain efficiencies. Farmers need to get access to technical know-how including new varieties of seeds, soil testing, crop calendar planning, correct and timely use of fertilizer and post-harvest guidance (16)

The undertaking of all these steps can only benefit from an increasing acquaintance with the methods of modern science and technology. We may have run short of time to work on the land but it is never too late to work on farmer-thinking. Together with efforts made to introduce modern methods on farms, we must work on the farmers themselves –to get them to see how they got left behind, to appreciate that only modern methods can bring quick results.

If you think that this represents drastic change, impossible to achieve in the India of the present, consider that what we will finally really need is nimbleness of response to the fact that agriculture itself is changing dramatically. Else, tiny Denmark would not be called an "agricultural superpower" by the Economist nor, as we have said, the Netherlands, its neighbour, qualify in agricultural exports as second only to the U.S., a country which is 200 times its size.

MASK—Manufacturing: As noted, countries traditionally advance through a cycle of agriculture, manufacturing, services and now they promise to go on to a knowledge economy. After graduating from agriculture, America had its own heyday in manufacturing. As long ago as 1865, about the time of the end of the Civil War, the US already had gathered for itself the makings of a world industrial power. From the early twentieth century, the automobile industry, the electricity industry, the airline industry, the oil and natural gas industry, the refrigeration and airconditioning industry, even the entertainment industry, all commenced with America. These and many other industries provided gainful employment to America's people and contributed to a common pool of manufacturing knowledge which has been called the country's industrial commons, namely, the collective R&D, engineering and manufacturing capabilities that sustain innovation.

However, in several more recent industries like semi-conductors, lighting, energy storage, green energy production, computing and communications, advanced materials etc., critical knowledge—together, sometimes, with entire supporting industries—has been or was on the verge of being lost by the USA to Southeast Asian countries, to Japan, and more recently to China. As a result, not only was employment in American manufacturing seriously affected—worsening the effects of the 2008 recession when that occurred—but, more importantly, the country's capacity for innovation was eroded. Not just present products but even future products were affected because it was found that manufacturing and innovation in one business (could) spawn whole new industries. (17)

Some economists like Jagdish Bhagwati do not agree. His argument is that, starting with Adam Smith, services (e.g. the " labours of churchmen, lawyers, physicians, and men of letters, players, buffoons, musicians, opera singers, etc".) have always been condemned as unproductive. It was thought that manufacturers were technologically progressive while services were technologically stagnant. Bhagwati argues that massive technical changes in the retail sector soon produced FedEx, faxes, mobile phones and the Internet. He offers as further example the cases of Argentina, Australia, New Zealand and Chile all of whom have vigorous transportation industries (using) trucks, rail and cargo to move agricultural produce with and across nations.(18)

This appears to me to be a strange argument. Whatever the service industry, whether tourism, communications, transportation or even the production of potato chips (another example offered by Bhagwati in his article), who can dispute that all are themselves based on the products of manufacture? The more sophisticated or developed the service, the more the dependency on newer and newer components or products of manufacture. Naturally, each country would like to have both manufacture and services but this may not always be possible. For example, not every country can have its own aircraft manufacturing or shipbuilding industry, so in such cases products have to be got from overseas. Gene Sperling, Economic Advisor to the Obama administration, says that U.S. experience in manufacturing policy has been that 90% of patents, 70% of private R&D and things like the acquisition of skills, availability of jobs and development of not just present but even future products were all direct consequences of manufacturing. (19)

Michael Dell, Chairman and CEO of the computer company, appears to be in broad agreement. Visiting India, he was asked how India compared with China and Taiwan in manufacturing, and he replied: "We don't have many of the suppliers in India that we would like to have as we have around our factories in China.... Let me be clear, we have a success story in manufacturing in India but it could be more. The opportunity lies in attracting component suppliers."

(20) So, just as happened in the Indian automobile industry, there also have to be parts suppliers and components suppliers for a particular industry to take hold. No country which has them can risk gifting away any one of the constituent parts overseas.

Is it too late then for India to now get into manufacturing? To organize for manufacturing? It is never too late although, from the sluggish way we seem to react to even important developments in other countries, one would almost think so. China's belated but spectacular rise to power was, of course, based on an export-led economy and it is perhaps too late for India to attempt that. But the example of China does prove two points: first, that if one chooses to follow the right path, which we have shown is that of modern science and technology (MoST), the results for even large countries can be quite impressive; and second, that such a transformation, or at least a substantial transformation does not take three hundred years any more. It can be achieved in about thirty years or so, in more or less one generation!

It is remarkable how China, whatever its protestations ("socialism with Chinese characteristics"), changed from being a totalitarian, regimented, autarchic economy to one based on manufactured exports mainly directed to the US and Europe. China began with an experimental scheme in the form of a Special Economic Zone (SEZ) in Shenzen and after that, there was no looking back. But it should have been us! It was we in India who boasted of democracy and a mixed economy—not to mention the fact that we had the British right here in India for nearly 200 years during a large part of which Britain was "the workshop of the world".

Also where once, in the realm of political events, news used to travel rapidly from China to India, as in the case of China's early years, then during the Korean War and in the case of the Viet Nam war and subsequent peace negotiations, a fundamental change in the very platform for the whole of China's economy took long to register with us. We were so confounded that even the opportunity of emulating China's example was missed! If they began with pilot SEZs, surely the same could have been organized in India as well. So India both missed the bus and also missed the realization that we had effectively missed the bus. All this needed to be said, although a serious digression from our discussion, simply because we cannot, we absolutely cannot, be caught flat-footed in this way in the future.

Luckily, India still remains a large country, with a large population and can easily direct any large manufacturing effort towards its own people. There is a huge national market available and it is crying out for plentiful goods and for quality goods. Scrupulously following the path of science and technology will mean that not only will India be properly set on the road to manufacturing but the consequent creation of jobs and the rise of consumer demand will stimulate more intensive and more expansive manufacturing.

Then there is what is called reverse innovation. Pointing to the enormous demand waiting to be assuaged in emerging countries, it has been suggested that overseas multinational companies should begin tailoring products for emerging countries like India and then, having tasted success, tweak these products for sale to sections of populations in their own countries. But this could equally well be undertaken by Indian companies. In fact, they would be better placed to do this. Import whatever components you wish but add value so that you export!

There is defence production. Nearly 70% of our defence production is said to be imported from overseas. This presents yet another opportunity for manufacturing in India. How? The book Freedom's Forge, by popular historian Arthur Herman actually carries a whole blueprint for defence production in peacetime and this can easily be developed further. We have all heard about wartime economies changing rapidly to peacetime requirements. But the opposite? The USA itself represents an excellent example of a peacetime economy being converted to wartime purposes—in the nick of time, just before the Japanese attack on Pearl Harbour in 1941! (21)

There is 3-D manufacturing. According to the Harvard Business Review of May 2015, quoting a PwC survey of more than 100 manufacuring companies, 11% had already switched to volume production of 3-D printed parts or products. The U.S. hearing aid industry converted to 100% additive manufacturing in less than 500 days.

There are jobs to be created in space research, in climate change industries, in refurbishing existing infrastructure and building new infrastructure, in the transport industry, in the vast fields of education (proper education) and health care. The Japanese are already creating new jobs in providing for the problems of ageing populations (in Japan as well as other countries), in customization and individualization (eg. in hospitality) etc. There is no reason why India should not eagerly seek out every new possibility in manufacturing.

Looking to the digital age, there will be possibilities in artificial intelligence, data analytics, network engineering, cybersecurity, virtual and augmented reality, robotics and automation, logistics and supply chain management and the enormous potential of the Internet of Things. John Chambers of Cisco says that in the US, they are already putting in place the right infrastructure to capitalize on the 15 billion things that are connected today, which will rapidly move to 50 billion by 2020 and 500 billion by 2030. He says that in the USA, the estimate is that 65% of children entering primary school today will work in job types that don't even exist yet and that, therefore, to set up children for success, education needs to refocus on technology. (22) In India, we cannot even begin to contemplate this until the foundations are got right, namely, those based on a proper understanding of science and technology ie MoST.

(A thought: When India becomes a developed nation, whenever that is to be, one expects that because of its economic growth and its sheer size, it would automatically take its place with its immediate neighbour, China, and the United States, as one of the three leading powers in the world. At that time, would there be a better chance than there is at present for the two democratic nations to also persuade China of the unmitigated benefits of a peacetime world?)

Probably the best way to spread manufacuring is through MSMEs (micro, small and medium enterprises). There are already 51 million in India. Even in the USA, they are called small businesses but their impact is huge...over 50% of the working population is employed by small businesses, so you can judge the possibilities for India. (23)

The guidance may have to come from Government but the impetus has to come from the small and medium scale industry itself. Armed with the tools provided by MoST, there is no reason why the spread should not happen more rapidly, more systematically, more extensively and even more enthusiastically than at present.

As is often said in India, the country's development so far has happened despite one heavy foot being solidly on the brake! Consider now, therefore, financial journalist Harish Damodaran's excellent account of India's new capitalists – and they are not the Birlas, the Tatas, the Goenkas, the Ambanis or the Godrejs. Here is a "review" of towns like Coimbatore, Tirupur and Sivakasi, all in Tamilnadu: (24)

Unlike Mumbai, Surat or Kolkata, Coimbatore in Tamilnadu did not have locational advantages, wasn't a political or administrative headquarters, financial capital or even a temple town. And yet it soon came to be known as the Manchester of India and transformed itself into a land of foundries, machine shops and engineering units producing castings, motors and compressors to pumpsets and wet grinders for food – all this by budding industrialists from two communities, the Naidus and the Gounders, whose primary vocation was farming!

Coimbatore also prospered in textiles. Unlike the composite spinning-weaving units in Mumbai, the Coimbatore units were primarily spinning units, now selling mill yarn to the many handloom weavers in the region. This, in turn, boosted the cottage weaving industry extending later to the powerloom and knitwear clusters in the area adjoining towns like Tirupur. Damodaran shows how in Coimbatore, the textiles as well as engineering industry had its origins in the commercialization of its agriculture. These two communities then went on to founding educational institutions and medical establishments including the now world famous Aravind Eye Care system with hospitals in Madurai, Coimbatore, Tirunelveli, Theni and Pondicherry.

Tirupur itself is just 42 km from Coimbatore. Tirupur began with manufacture of banians (undershirts)! One small manufacturer actually received his biggest order for T-shirts from Uganda where new elections had been called after Idi Amin had been deposed and Milton Obote had taken his place. Tirupur is still known as the banian capital of India although it quickly progressed to supplying undergarments and knitwear and now stylish sportswear, jackets, sweatshirts, Bermudas, children's wear, skirts and lingerie to global buyers in America, Europe and elsewhere.

Damodaran explains that, apart from textiles, the Gounders also are in the engineering business (Shanti Gears), in agribusiness and now also in the basic seeds business.

Sivakasi, on its part, began with production of safety matches but quickly went on to the fireworks and pyrotechnic industries. Because of increasing requirements for trademark labels and posters, it became a centre for offset printing and now has begun to cater to the world market for premium diaries, notebooks, technical and religious books (Bible, Koran, Bhagavad Gita) and other paper products.

All this happened before this book was written. Earlier, even in my own case, this kind of backward integration and sideways expansion used to be just a furious blur in my mind and never stood for what it really was – boldness, innovation, dynamism, advancement, connectivity in every sense of the term and of course, for the region itself where there had been desperation before: now, jobs, jobs and more jobs. This is another illustration of what science and technology can do for the country as a whole.

So what does MoST do and how does it really help the small businessman? As the Ameritrade ad says: When you understand the details, it's easier to see the big picture. MoST can teach you to

1. approach knowledge in such situations and to at least understand the fundamental ideas of science.
2. compartmentalize knowledge into groupings, classifications etc.
3. understand the connection between the different sciences themselves
4. judge the potential size and shape of markets
5. understand the manufacturing process of component or constituent suppliers

6. provide a secure technical platform, however elementary, for commercial success

7. make for a bolder, more confident, more understanding businessman and

8. thus, spur innovation.

Once again, if the goal is to create jobs, then every branch has to be looked into, whether manufacturing, services or knowledge.

MASK—Services: Lee Kuan Yew made Singapore a garden city before it became a financial centre. International bankers, driving into the city from the airport, did not need much to convince them that this city meant to deliver. Cannot we tackle the question of Swach India with the same earnestness?

We have had the problem of lack of indoor toilets for many years. A full 50% of the country's population (no less) was affected. What this would have done to the dignity and self-esteem of especially girls and women can only be imagined. But our government finally woke up to this problem only a few years ago. However, just generally, I think it will be agreed that the entire country needs a massive clean-up. Is it all that difficult to start off with, say, sustained, nation-wide anti-littering, anti-spitting and anti-noise campaigns? Is it difficult to see why these must begin in all seriousness before we take on the gigantic problem of cleaning up the Ganga? The results could be dramatic and the surest sign of an India on the move!

Take the tourist industry. It's an apology for what tourism could become in India. China receives 57 million tourists every year. Even Malaysia gets 24 million tourists annually. India gets all of 6 million arrivals. Comparisons are odious but we in India possibly have an even greater share than China of monuments and historical and archaeological sites. (Similar sites in China were apparently destroyed during the Cultural Revolution although the ruins of some have been preserved in museums like the one in Beijng.)

Some four or five years ago, I bought two books from my favourite bookstore in Mumbai (alas, now closed),one a Thames and Hudson book on Hindu architecture (not even including extensive Buddhist and Jain architecture) and the other a Marg publication on Muslim sultanate architecture – not Delhi, Agra or Fatehpur Sikri, if you please, but the history and architecture of places like Ahmednagar, Daulatabad, Bijapur, Gulbarga, Bidar and so on. There are other places in Bengal that come to mind: Bankura, Bishnupur, Chandernagore, Burdwan, Malda, Murshidabad etc. There are hundreds or perhaps thousands of tourist places of interest and it is high time that we put them to use to create much-needed jobs for our economy.

Fashion, as an agent of change! How does that strike you as a service? Gandhiji might have demurred – at first. But think of it. If it was pointed out to him that India in 2019 was still a young nation with an average age of 29 years, youth unemployment at about 13% (156 million people), would he not readily have agreed? Fashion and design are, after all, attempts by the young, male and female, to look their best, to get ahead, to modernize. What can be wrong with an attempt to marshal this energy, to direct it, guide it into productive channels for the advancement of the nation – especially if it also meant more job opportunities were being created. Even some developed countries continue to discover new possibilities in design – New Zealand, geographically secluded from the rest of the world, in the case of the apparel industry and tiny Denmark, in respect of eyewear (spectacle frames). India, with its centuries' long experience in attractive textiles for example, absolutely cannot afford to be left behind.

So whether it be tourism, BPOs, finance, legal or educational work, the health care industry, translation services, accountancy or actors and supporting staff participating in an already well-established film industry, the possibilities for jobs in a well-thought out and organized services sector are enormous.

MASK—Knowledge: We are told that we are heading for a knowledge economy. There was a time when there were only thr2222ee factors of production in economics: land, labour and capital. No longer. Now it is a question of how to "unlock" human potential or build up human capital or intellectual capital. We are told that eventually it's knowledge that will make the economy go around but as far as I know, we are not told how such human capital is to be created or cultivated. We have plentiful supply of potential human capital - and MoST happens to be the way to develop it.

Mr Jeff Stemke is a knowledge strategist who has spent 35 years with the oil company, Chevron. His view is that knowledge is not something you can manage. You can accelerate the flow of knowledge from one person to another, he says, but you can't manage knowledge. (25) My belief is that you can manage even knowledge. In this book, we have looked at how you can plant the seeds of knowledge, point to the direction to be taken, allow those seeds to sprout and then spread among different disciplines. You simply need to follow the trail. You may not always know the absolute, exact path to be taken but you know the general direction in which you want to go. You can choose to be in box or silo mode (where you are carefully organizing your own knowledge) and the next moment you can decide to put yourself in spillover or straddle mode. At will!

In this sense, knowledge is manageable and therefore portable. Consequently, if we have 600,000 villages in India and they are doing poorly – small landholdings, poor harvests, external dependency for seeds, fertilizer, market, power and water – we can take knowledge to them instead of having them come to miserable shantytown conditions in the cities as they are now doing in very large numbers. You cannot at present take it to them direct, of course, because many are not even literate and the few that are are not even properly educated. But you can certainly take it to the government bodies who do this type of work, to the NGOs giving this kind of social service, corporate bodies like e-Choupal, dedicated teachers who can be trained for the purpose and so on. If wealth is generated in the rural economy in this manner, it has a higher chance, as C.S.Ramalakshmi says, of its being distributed right there. (26)

When you do this, what you are then really doing is preparing the path for the journey from the bullock-cart to a knowledge economy! Seems formidable? incapable of achievement? Mr. Steven Geiger, COO of the Skolkova Foundation, Russia, faced with a similar nation-wide situation, says "Is changing culture and mind-set easy?... Large countries are like battleships. Get them turning even a few degrees in the right direction and you've changed their course. (27)

If direction is important, if new kinds of knowledge are involved, if knowledge is shown to be portable, we then require more than ever to hew closely to the basic, fundamental platform of MoST. Here, therefore, are some more examples of a knowledge economy - some already in existence but several more yet to be created.

We ourselves already have a software industry. This used to fall in the services compartment but now probably more appropriately belongs to the knowledge side. Kiran Karnik writes that direct employment provided by India's software and service sector is over 2 million but the indirect jobs created are estimated to be three or four time this number. (28). There are further enormous possibilities in pharmaceuticals, in health bio-tech, in the medical equipment industry, in precision medicine, in new materials science, in the food industry, in information technology, in the transportation industry, etc. (29) (30)

We have been highlighting the important role played by science and technology. If one were not to appreciate this, not to keep the big picture constantly in mind, it would be difficult to understand, for example, the various nuances and shadings of the present debate in respect of a manufacturing vs a knowledge economy. And as we have seen, the technology of manufacturing and services changes people and people don't change if it is absent. For each country, therefore, a wide-spectrum effort becomes necessary ranging from agriculture to manufacturing through services going on to knowledge. Certainly for India this should be our aim. MoST and MASK runs as a streak through all forms and actually assist us in constantly keeping in mind the history of - you know what? - the very concept of progress.

Earlier in the book (see pg 57), we spoke about how the meaning of words can change with the passage of time and so it is also with the word progress. Even in Europe, the very scientists whose discoveries would create the modern world were not conscious of it. (31) Progress was used " in the simple physical sense of an onward movement in space or onward movement of a story or narrative ...(however) by the seventeenth or early eighteenth century, the word had commonly come to mean advancement to a higher stage, advancement to better and better conditions, continuous improvement." - progress as we know it today. (32)

Marx in his day focused on social progress. He considered that the conflict of economic classes (class struggle) was the road to human economic advancement and progress. In our own times, we know now in the case of China, the largest Communist country, that

Chairman Mao insisted that class struggle really was the key but Deng Xiaoping, initially at very great cost to himself, believed that modern science and technology should not be ignored as an equally important, if not more important, force of production. (33)

organizing for change

Having stated our mission, outlined what we wish to change to, gone into employability and unemployment, explained why a careful journey through MASK is so necessary, how even something as impalpable as knowledge is capable of being identified, exploited and made portable, if then it is agreed that we must organize for change, how do we go about it?

When we speak of design, we usually do so in respect of its application to physical objects or artifacts. We spoke about it in this sense when we included it earlier under Services. We even extended this skill to fashion and especially if fashion was considered as an agent of change.

But design in recent days has begun to be applied to shaping thinking itself. They call it design thinking. It happened in this way: Good design has always been known to contribute to the success of commercial products. From hardware, companies then asked the firms doing design to look at user-interface(s). Soon firms were treating corporate strategy as an exercise in design. Today design is even applied to helping multiple stakeholders and organizations work better as a system. Tim Brown and Roger Martin, authors of the Harvard Business Review article (34) from which this information has been taken, show how each design process became more complicated and sophisticated than the one before it because each was enabled by learning from the earlier stage.

However, in a given situation, as the design process got more complicated, a new difficulty arose. This was the acceptance by the different stakeholders of the designed artifact, whether it was product, user experience, strategy or complex system. The planners concluded that the design of their intervention was even more critical than the design of the artifacts themselves.

The authors proceed to demonstrate how design thinking in this way was used by Intercorp Group, one of Peru's biggest corporations, to first put their own bank and its personnel on a proper footing and then extended the experience to successfully introducing an entire schools system and even a modern retail business in frontier towns in Peru where the owners of Intercorp, itself a private company, wanted social transformation to take place and for a middle class, as in Peru's cities, to emerge.

The authors call it Designing a New Peru. No reason why we should not attempt to design a new India and endeavor to introduce similar systems whether they be in education, in health care, in banking itself, in transportation, in the retail business and so on.

This way all stakeholders are taken into account and got involved. For example, in the case of schools, the stakeholders would be students, parents, teachers, civil servants and finally, whoever was sponsoring and shepherding the project, whether private company or government body. In the case of health care, it could be patients, doctors, hospitals, insurance companies and again, whoever was responsible for the project, private company or government. Each of these stakeholders would be consulted about successive designs until all were persuaded or had agreed. Everyone felt that this way of organizing had a much better chance of success.

creating a climate

Of course, in introducing change certain basic truths have to be kept in mind. There should be a lively sense of dissatisfaction with the current situation. Despite this, there is always likely to be resistance to change. Wherever possible, change should be in bite-sized chunks and not in indigestible lumps. The dictum should be "People change, we don't change people. (35)

Our task is to wean people away from traditionalism, orthodoxy, superstition and to point the way to a modern future. Old habits and old thinking are deeply ingrained in our people. It is necessary to step carefully and to avoid treading on too many toes. And yet the need is urgent and cannot brook any delay. A plan must be drawn up about how small doses of change are initially to be administered, leading to larger changes later with the willing help of the people themselves.

The question soon becomes: How does one in actual practice begin to change such a large expanse of society? How does one persuade people to exchange their beliefs in myths, superstition, miracles, swamis and babas for reasoned, scientific, logical thinking? Actually, it isn't even total exchange of one for the other. At present, we find ourselves in something of a half-way house where both types of belief exist at one and the same time. With an urbanising and industrialising India, logical and scientific beliefs exist cheerfully alongside blind faith, obscurantism and total non-reason.

In studying the effects of science on society, we must expect that the results cannot be immediate. Society comprises a collection of individuals, each with different mind, different background, different experience, different values, different aims, different circumstances and so on. Yet all of these individuals and all of these groups can be influenced by science. The results of the treatment are certain but because it deals with a mass of individuals, it cannot be immediate or instantaneous - although initial results should be seen remarkably quickly.

How we do it is by way of a one-two punch. This requires that we put the proposition to the people and allow them to reach their own conclusions. We set out the arguments for and the arguments against and allow them, each one of them, to make their own inferences, to arrive at their own decisions. In adopting such a course, we can be confident about the therapeutic effects of science and of scientific thinking. We needn't worry whether people will go off at a tangent or even in the opposite direction or whether they will, for long, remain just plainly indifferent.

If we are successful, they will quickly see reason. Mind you, there are bound to be people who will object. There will be resistance. After all, to try and change a person's thinking is to subject him or her to the most severe wrench that that person is likely to experience. It is nothing less than an attack on the person's identity—but it is a task which must be undertaken, and which is best undertaken by the person himself. If anyone wishes to be perverse and fly in the face of facts, he will quickly be brought to reason. By whom? By himself! As we have said, it is rather like driving a motor-car down a one-way street—in the wrong direction! You quickly discover that all the other cars are ranged against you. You see the error of your ways and are obliged to reverse course! Scientific thinking, the plentiful artifacts of science which surround us and above all, an understanding of the reasoning which helped to build these goods, will together compel you to achieve the right direction.

Example: If you want to solve the problem of India's unemployed millions, no amount of religion is going to help. Jobs are conceived and provided by science and technology operating in the fields of agriculture, industry, commerce, the distributive and service trades and the knowledge industry of the future. Exactly as has happened in the developed countries. There's no other way. Ask the person who resists : Do you wish to carry on the way you have been doing or do you wish to equip yourself with a job, a living and thereby forever benefit yourself, your children and family, your community and your country?

I call this the Pied Piper approach. The Pied Piper played his pipe and the children in their hundreds simply followed. The lure of jobs will entice people to follow. With jobs they will be able to carve out careers for themselves and secure a better future for kith and kin. If we have success in this field, they will more readily listen to arguments for change in other ways.

Another way of persuading people is to point to the effortless gains made by Western medicine, allopathy (now well established in most developing countries, including India) over different kinds of indigenous medicine. This happened because the methods and general reasoning behind the medicine and therefore the facilities offered by it (hospitals, clinics, maternity homes, vaccines, surgery, public health measures, countless lives saved) were more advantageous to the people (patients).

This is more than just another effort at persuasion. It carries the weight of history behind it. We have already alluded to the fact that, of the three large nations in Asia, it was Japan, not China, which first got off the mark. Japan was the first to acknowledge that the West possessed something which nations in the East lacked, namely, modern science and technology. And it then systematically set about getting that something. But what was the particular thing that set Japan thinking? "It began with medicine." (36) Doctors of medicine in Japan, then greatly influenced by Confucian thinking and generally Chinese culture, were impressed with the fact that visiting Western doctors studied and learnt and attempted diagnoses from actual study of their patients and not from mere books. Europe itself, ever so slowly, had learned that "the sick should be the doctor's books...close observation of human bodies, not verbal formulation about them." (37)

To return to our argument, the advantage of allowing people to reach their own decision is, of course, that their resolve is that much more strengthened. This is the basic principle of motivation. Any change in a person's thinking must come from within. It cannot be forced on him or her. Science itself requires the change to come from within; the idea of force or compulsion is repugnant to science. Additionally, in a democratic society, it is never possible to push change; it is only possible to suggest it. The people must be carried with you. They must be helped to bring about change on their own.

beyond consumerism

Nor is this kind of change limited only to material progress. We are not speaking about a blind, mindless pursuit of consumer goods and individual riches. With large masses of the population severely deprived of the basic necessities of life, without homes, transportation, sanitation facilities and so on, who dare say that we are on the road to consumerism! While jobs are to be our topmost priority if we follow the path of science, this type of change goes hand in hand with more clean surroundings, more parks, more public libraries, more hospitals, more museums and art galleries, more theatres and concert halls, more organized sports etc. These social services are concomitants of industrial growth and wealth creation and of course, this is also the way it happened in the West. (38) All fall squarely within the domain of science and allow themselves to be subjects of change through the means of science. Inclusive growth should involve not only the mobilization of all sections of society (and especially the lower strata of society) but also rapid growth along broad economic, social and cultural lines.

It goes without saying that the Government must institute such change. Once agreed that it is only science and technology which will take us towards a modern state, then Government must proclaim that change is necessary, explain why it is necessary and take steps to cause change to happen. Propaganda by newspapers, magazines, radio, TV, cinema, the internet and social media must support such steps for change and ensure that the momentum is kept up, that an atmosphere for continuous change is created. State Governments, municipal bodies, schools, colleges, universities, institutions, social organizations, trade unions, trade bodies, the armed forces, citizen groups, offices, factories - all must be encouraged to adopt this movement for change and to accelerate it. If a proper climate is created, it is bound to result in the total involvement of the people. This is one way of consolidating and building upon the not inconsiderable achievements of the last seventy years instead of the argumentation, the bickering, the endless accusations of majority and minority communalists, not to speak of communal riots themselves!

In the USA, they call it "speaking from the bully pulpit." The office of the President of the United States carries enormous prestige and speeches from that office have considerable effect on all sections of society. Some may agree, others may disagree but the speech is heard out carefully and a lot of discussions follow each speech. President Obama addressed even the schoolchildren of that country, exhorting them, in a global competitive world, to work hard at their studies and to set educational goals for themselves. In China, slogans have been used to motivate the population viz "the half of China movement", " the 4 Modernisations"," to get rich is glorious", "it doesn't matter if a cat is black or white so long as it catches mice "and so on. The current blandishment offered for Tibet is "leapfrog development"! An interesting comparison was made in the Chinese TV documentary "River Elegy" where criticism was made of the Yellow River, a symbol of traditional China – and there was praise for the Blue Ocean which had brought "innovative foreign ideas and modern practices to China's shores" (39)

A great number of these kinds of motivational slogans will need to be employed to help the country achieve its goals. The people of India are totally ready for it, but insufficient use is being made of our bully pulpit.

Of course, in addition to all this there is also planned, structured change. This is not an alternative to what has already been suggested but is an important complement to it. This change can be of two kinds. One is change of a historical kind, change which is involved at every level in any country which sets out to change. I have kept this in an appendix as a separate narrative (see Appendix 2 at the end of this chapter) in order not to confuse it with the special steps outlined earlier and discussed hereafter for India. The other kind of change, which we now consider, involves teachers and students, involves parents and finally, would involve the people themselves.

Teachers and parents respectively would prepare for change in students and for change in children and wards finally culminating in change in the people as a whole. People as a category, would organise for change and consciously bring it about themselves while at the same time they would be exposed to the propaganda and publicity from Government of which we have spoken earlier. If and when change reaches the people, in other words, when people start changing, then only can we say that the experiment has properly begun.

wooing the teachers

We begin by discussing teachers as a group because obviously, so much depends on them. They can make or break any visionary ideas of change we may have. There is great need for converting teachers to our cause. Our ultimate goal is nothing less than trying to change the thinking habits of an entire people. If teachers are convinced about the need for change and about the direction in which change is to be got going, then impressive results can be expected.

In the experiment in Peru to which we referred earlier and where laptops were used, the role of teacher was changed, as they put it, from "a sage on stage to a guide by your side." Our circumstances in India are different and would probably require a judicious combination of both these roles.

It oughtn't to be difficult to convince teachers of the benefits of science and technology. After all, the subjects which need to be pushed, subjects like botany, zoology, physiology, biology, astronomy (night sky watching) and other natural sciences as well as the humanities are already familiar to them. They are well experienced in the ways in which to handle them. All that is now needed, if the arguments set out in this book are agreed upon, is the realization that the logic and the philosophy which constitutes the foundation of each one of these subjects needs to be traced out and placed before the students.

Why? In order to demonstrate to students that science is nothing but a constant search for truth. If a single new discovery or invention were not to correspond to the principles that already exist - tested over and over again by a whole community of researchers and scientists - then the entire edifice is threatened, would crumble and would require to be discarded. Science constitutes a direct and indirect commitment to intellectual truth. It is of the greatest importance that students from an early age be exposed to this fact and that it be drilled into their minds.

Again you may ask why? Because it then becomes, sometimes without their even being aware of it, a constant inner voice. It can fire them up with a burning zeal to excel in their studies, and it can provide them with a lifelong interest in their chosen subjects. At the other end of the spectrum, just to give a few examples, as principled young citizens, it may make them reluctant to jump bus queues or may even may make them look with disfavour on their parents' attempts at dissembling (say, tax evasion). We did explain that our definition of science—to go where the argument leads –was capable of enforcing a rigorous sense of discipline.

Just an understanding of the process and demands of science are worth more than a whole semester's worth of lectures. The subjects remain the same but the reasoning behind all that science needs to be brought out and elucidated much more than is being done at present.

You know what? There's an easy way of doing this. To teach the real lessons of science, it is sometimes not even necessary that you teach science! Instead, it is possible to learn about the history of science. The innumerable episodes from real life that are to be found in the history of any science make for exciting, thrilling reading. The lessons that are contained in these various episodes make an indelible impression on the minds of readers, young and old. The effect is all the more powerful because it is not specially sought to be made; it is indirect, roundabout and oblique. It is for the reader to make the deductions or not to make them – and it is precisely this that makes it effective. Such is human nature. Recall the dictum: People change, we don't change people! This blends in with what we suggested in Chapter 7 where, in order to make maximum use of the nation's resources, both parent and child together learn about science. Names of some recommended books for the history of science appear in the Notes (40)

what students can do

There is need at all times to show students how these subjects which are studied in school and college are the very supports of modern life. True that these are academic subjects requiring to be studied in some detail. Therefore, in the course of doing this, students are apt to forget that the content and the reasoning behind these subjects are the foundation on which all modern life is based. Without them there can be no banishment of poverty and no material progress. I would remind the reader of PSSP which needs to be constantly brought out before students throughout their course of study.

Students must be shown that the drive towards modernization not only brings about economic growth, thus lessening economic competition between groups, but that by striving for a common, neutral, secular goal, also to that extent takes people away from narrow considerations of religion, ethnicity, region and language. This doesn't mean that we refuse to recognize the existence of these categories. On the contrary, each of these areas can be later taken up for careful, detached, scholarly study. Some of the best writers on these subjects are the ones who are least prone to be swayed by emotions: one might say that it is precisely the lack of subjectivity and emotion which qualifies them to write sensitively and with depth and authority on these subjects. The idea is to remove these and other differences from the marketplace and to make them serve the cause of consolidation of the nation and its people.

At this very time, a whole new area of development and change lies right in front of us in the form of climate change. New York Times journalist Thomas Friedman makes a plea for science education in his book Hot, Flat and Crowded, in which he asserts that healthy ecosystems and healthy economies have to go together. He says we need companies that view climate change not as a threat but as an opportunity, and pushes not just for projects but for a revival of the USA.(41) How about revival of this country which desperately calls out for it since it missed out on the earlier development in the first place?

Students in college and university find themselves at an important crossroads in their lives. Their years in education are about to end. There is need for careful study of the various choices open to them. A mistaken step could prove catastrophic, perhaps destroying for life their chances of the right career. At a minimum, there could be loss of precious years in pursuit of the wrong choice. Serious damage could be caused to the student's morale and to his preparation for his life's vocation.

It becomes critically important, therefore, that the attention of students be aroused early on in life and not left to the last years of school or college. The challenge should be that there is so much of potential interest to the student, so much out there, that he/she should be hard put to choose between different courses of study, different careers and different vocations. Instead what we find in our country is that, to speak the truth, the very opposite is the case and many students sadly end up equally uninterested in all courses of study !

Let's face it. The fact is that teachers as a whole are themselves sometimes unclear about the connection between different subjects in science or the even more important relationship between science and the humanities. As we have seen, it is necessary to acknowledge the paramount importance of science in our lives; its history, the process by which the products of science have come about; the logic which made them possible and the manner in which all other non-science subjects have organized themselves around this startling new body of knowledge. Both arts and science teachers must be fully schooled in the scope, the philosophy and the reach of their subjects. Unless this is done, the teachers cannot teach with conviction. Unless they are enthusiastic themselves, they cannot convey enthusiasm to their pupils. Enthusiasm only comes with understanding and this is true of both teachers and pupils.

One of the big differences to be found between education in India and that in developed countries is the approach of students to education itself. It is ironical that where we in India seriously need more and varied education, the approach in classrooms is casual and almost frivolous whereas in other countries where so much has already been achieved, the approach is serious and determined. This is one of the surprising differences which strikes any Indian who has ever attended a classroom overseas.

This difference in approach shows up in different ways. Let me illustrate one such manifestation. Mr. Venkatraman Ramakrishnan was awarded the 2009 Nobel Prize for Chemistry together with two other U.K. colleagues. While visiting India from the U.K., here's what he told the interviewer from the Times of India: "Students wanted to take pictures with me and get autographs. I told them I was not a film star. Being attracted to a scientist is the wrong way to be attracted to science...What I am trying to explain is that there was a good chance I would not have got the Nobel. There are many scientists doing good work. Not all of them win the Nobel. I have to say I was fabulously lucky to be where I am today. It's a mistake to judge science by Nobel prizes. Students should take up science for the love of the subject." (42)

Students in our country have become disengaged from school, to quote Laurence Steinberg's Beyond the Classroom, (43) which discusses the problems with education in his own country, the USA. These problems are, of course, of a much smaller magnitude than those we face in our country and yet Steinberg concludes at the end of his book:

"No curricular overhaul, no instructional motivation, no change in school organization, no tightening of standards, no rethinking of teacher training or compensation will succeed if students do not come to school interested in, and committed to, learning".

But how? What needs to be done? You cannot command students to become interested! In our country, we have debated for years whether it is the fault of the students or the teachers. My submission is that it really is neither. Often it isn't even a question of funds. The Economist in October 2009 reported Arab countries now spend as much or more on education, as a share of GDP, than the world average. " They have made great strides in eradicating illiteracy, boosting university enrolment and reducing gaps between the sexes.... but the gap in the quality of education between Arabs and other people at a similar level of development is still frightening." (44)

In my view, the fault clearly lies in the pedagogy, in the premises or reasoning behind our teaching. Unless we acknowledge the predominant role of modern science in our lives and until we recognize that all other subjects either branch off from it or are tied to it in one way or another, we cannot give education in India the special meaning which all education must have and the supreme boost to the individual that its possession will give. Education has to be made more relevant to life itself and I believe that this is the quickest and most effective way of doing it.

When this has been accomplished, students will not find it necessary to bunk classes, and mass copying in examination rooms and leakage of examination papers (a more scandalous commentary on Indian life and education cannot be found) will hopefully be a thing of the past. Instead, there will be more self-dictated learning, student-to-student learning and student-group learning. Education must be seen as a continuum, a lifelong, pleasurable learning process with first, the parent and teacher dispensing knowledge to the student, then the student as adult and parent passing on that excitement to his/her children while the parent effortlessly continues his /her own "education" till the very end of life. Science is fully suited to providing such long-lasting, continuing inspiration.

If the Government agrees that there is a close connection between the content of what is taught, the quality of the teaching, the direction in which that teaching is taking us and on the other hand, the very future of the nation, it is essential that teaching as a profession be made respectable and remunerative. There are many ways of doing this besides increases in salaries and benefits. This book is however not the place to elaborate on how this objective can be reached.

For a long time, there has been a debate on whether students should follow vocational and professional or scientific courses, thus preparing themselves for a career in life or whether they should acquire a liberal arts education which would equip them in very general terms for whatever choice they would wish to make later or even perhaps for a situation, not uncommon in India, where a career or a job opportunity was forced upon them by circumstances and which they had not really chosen for themselves. We have suggested that if interest in general science is aroused in the child from early on in life, it ought not to be difficult to get its various subjects to interface with liberal arts subjects or with the humanities in general. We have seen how interest in, for example, the stars or the human body or in Earth or in Nature can be turned into a consuming interest in subjects like history or geography or economics or philosophy or even art and painting. A study of the Renaissance period in history can be invaluable for pursuit of study in biology and painting as well as, say, archaeology and architecture. No use repeating ad nauseam that all disciplines are inter-dependent. This must be demonstrated over and over again. From the many subjects in which they are now deeply involved, students should find it pleasantly difficult to choose the one (or few) subjects for specialization and indeed for a lifetime's career.

Finally, a quick word on the perceived gulf between science and the humanities. This, in my opinion, could only have come about because of a sustained lack of appreciation, possibly starting some 100 to 150 years ago, of the true nature of that problem-child, science. A real understanding of science does not and cannot mean an estrangement from the arts or the humanities; it can only mean a truer, deeper appreciation of the humanities. Once the separation began, more and more teachers were bound to get affected and in course of time, there grew up two separate streams in colleges and universities, lacking in understanding of each other and even academically antagonistic to each other. If this enormous misunderstanding is removed from teachers' minds, in course of time it must spread to students and then at last the excitement and fascination of all learning, arts and science, will be restored to our children.

These are not wishful, theoretical aspirations. They will prove critically important later for innovation. Meaningful innovation can only happen when one straddles the humanities, art and science says the Economic Times once again, this time quoting P.R. Venketrama Raja of Ramco Systems who speaks of the need to appreciate" the inter-linkage between knowledge verticals." (45)

Dr. APJ Abdul Kalam, former President of India, constantly spoke about the need to promote a culture of innovation in the country. He said: "A creative mind has the ability to imagine or invent something new by combining, changing or reapplying existing ideas. A creative person has an attitude to accept change and newness, a willingness to play with ideas and possibilities, a flexibility of outlook, the habit of enjoying the good while looking for ways to improve it." (46) It seems to me that you can really, truly do this only if you give students and others the essential background they need with an overview of science (and the humanities). Innovation may oftentimes be the result of chance but as Louis Pasteur said and as we quoted earlier, chance favours the prepared mind.

Our goal should be that education should be made as exciting as a hobby. In India, on the other hand, centuries of movement away from reality has left us totally drained of all interest in life itself. As we discussed in Part 2, there are not even enough people with hobbies. It is not enough to reply that when one is occupied in barely existing and making a living, there is neither time nor money to indulge in hobbies. What investment can be required, for example, in merely watching the night-sky, in marvelling at it, in learning to appreciate the drama and grandeur of the stars? Similarly, if you happen to know about evolution in general, how reptiles came before birds and bird feathers and how forearm bones in bird feathers and in humans evolved from the same ancestor, it is easier to get started on the hobby of bird-watching or even the science of ornithology.

Parents and teachers can make studies as interesting as hobbies. We have a great amount of work to do and if we go about it properly, a glorious future awaits us. Time spent in school and college for the fortunate few who go there is altogether too valuable an asset to be frittered away. Both for themselves as well as in the larger interests of the country, it is essential that this time be put to good use. In this section on students and teachers, all we have sought to do is to point to some very general directions in which we could move. The practical, more detailed proposals for these to be put into effect must come from the educators and the authorities - with perhaps the ready assistance of the students themselves.

working with parents

We all agree that if a child is to be brought up with an enquiring mind, his parents must create a suitable environment for this purpose. They must provide an atmosphere at home in which he/she is encouraged to question and they as parents are equipped to provide answers. Generally, very little needs to be done to encourage children to ask questions. This comes naturally. If it gradually fades away before the child becomes much older, it is usually because parents grow tired of answering a myriad questions and often later, because parents run short of answers. This is no cause for embarrassment. If the parent doesn't know the answer to a child's question, it could become the start of a joint search for the answer. In organizing such a search, an unspoken bond is created between parent and child. This very bond stands for the co-operative attitude so necessary in the search for knowledge and which is what the parent is trying to foster. If the child is small and does not understand that books, pictures, dictionaries, encyclopaedias, radio, TV and the computer and internet can be used as resource(s), he can be promised an answer and the answer provided later. It then becomes a joint adventure between parent and child.

Some basic learning on the part of parents is, of course, necessary. The learning is undertaken because the parent himself/herself is curious. Often, it is a rehash of what may have been learned in school or college, knowledge of which did not remain with one because it was not properly presented or because the relevance to one's everyday life was not pointed out or perhaps even because learning the simplest, most interesting things was made such a chore.

The idea is to encourage learning from one's everyday environment. If the child is alone with a parent under a night-sky, there is no reason why he cannot be introduced, in very small doses, to the excitement of star-gazing or astronomy. To be able to do this, the parent must himself understand the excitement, let us say, of the speed of light. In my own mind, I can never stop comparing the speed of my motorcar (say, 35 miles per hour) with the speed of light (186,000 miles per second)! Gripped by this kind of excitement, it is possible to explain to the child why some stars appear bigger than others although they are much smaller, how our sun is only an average-sized star, why the light which reaches from the stars actually began its journey a long time ago and so on. This kind of exercise builds up many different dimensions in a child's mind at the same time as it gets him involved in his own everyday scene.

When the toddler first understands the difference between today, yesterday and tomorrow, every parent joyfully recognizes that an important milestone has been crossed. Similarly, just the exposure of the child to the principle of the passage of light from the stars to us on Earth can be an excellent introduction to a sense of history. It is not necessary to rush things. This would be to spoil everything. Allow the child, in his own time, to cast his mind back on the beam that brings sunlight or moonlight or starlight to him and an excellent, strong foundation for a sense of history and geography has been laid down.

When the child goes into the garden and see bushes, trees, plants and flowers he should be explained the beauty of botany. When he sees birds or fish or animals, he should be told about the fascination of zoology. When he plays with sand on the beach or asks questions about the earth, he should be insinuated into the wonders of geology. If the child is sick or unwell, it could be treated as an opportunity to explain the meaning of health (ease) and its opposite, dis-ease. From here , it is only a small step to simple anatomy, physiology, the role of medicines and so on.

Before long the child is on his own and he now begins the great journey of the exploration of knowledge, both intensively, that is, delving deeper and deeper into subjects to which he has already been exposed as well as extensively, venturing into subjects that he has not known before, discovering new facts for himself, stumbling into still more subjects and so on. Whatever the nature of the joys that the child will know later in his long life, few will rival the exquisite joy that he will experience in this pure, unending search for knowledge.

Here we should put in a pitch for reading. Just reading, planned reading, as distinguished from observing, experimenting, visiting explorataria etc. We made brief mention of this in the Introduction. Nowadays, we take it for granted that reading is one way of obtaining knowledge. But, once again, this was not always the case. In the late 15th century, when printed books had already been around for some 50 years, European man suddenly realized that one could develop a keen sense of discovery through reading. An analogy was made out between the book of God's words (the Bible) and the book of God's works (Nature). The set of tools employed was also thought to be familiar – literacy and linguistic knowledge in the one case and mathematics applied to careful observation in the other. Anyone could now read not only the Bible but also Nature. Daniel Danielson writes that even at that time, equipped with the tools "...whole new possibilities of understanding (would) emerge in the natural sciences as well as in theology". (47)

The question is hardly limited to India. It even is present in developed countries where despite the economic and other prosperity already achieved, they too need from generation to generation to re-ignite children's interest in science and science subjects. Can we in India profit from their experience? Here is a list of practical suggestions made on a USA National Public Radio discussion:

Get them engaged in ideas, then the reading follows:

1. Reading should be made part of children's lifestyle, not just part of their education.
2. There should be a planned outreach to schools from libraries.
3. Children/students should be taught how to find resources quickly.
4. Teachers themselves should be helped to find out all that's out there.

Before making this slight digression into the merits of reading, we indicated how parent could work with child. But is there a way of tying this up with work for the nation as a whole? Mr Sam Pitroda of the National Knowledge Commission puts it expressively: "We aim to convert India into a knowledge economy. This is the journey of a nation and it is going to take about 20-25 years for the recommendations to show results. But we require groundswell." He also says that "India is one place where parents will not eat (in order) to provide good education for their children.... There is a demand but the supply has not been created."

Pitroda's solution is smaller universities, better faculty, deregulation in education and some good liberal arts universities to ring in a 'generational change in education'. But he feels change has to be brought about at ground level. (48) It is my view that " groundswell" and " change at ground level" will readily be available if all reforms are based on a proper understanding of the foundational platform of modern science and technology.

Also, if you wish for groundswell, what better way than pressing parents themselves into service, a ready but hitherto unused resource? And, instead of smaller universities, what can be more compact and more comprehensive than science, the one-word definition for pursuit of all knowledge? As for liberal arts, which take time to blossom, germinate and bear fruit, once again what better than science for more direct connection to our most urgent need – jobs, jobs and more jobs?

the special role of women

Mahatma Gandhi said: "Educate a man and you educate an individual; educate a woman and you educate a family." The children of a household usually spend more time during their formative years in the company of their mother. It is vital that women of our country are empowered in their thinking, their mental and intellectual horizons widened, as they play a critical role in preparing themselves and our children for the development of our country.

Unfortunately, in our country, the horrifying statistic is that one out of every three women is unable to even read or write. How then are they going to help their children? This terrible ignorance, a result of their illiteracy, is to be visited upon their children. Some of these children may break out of the mould, acquire an education and do well on their own but banerally the children of illiterate or semi-literate mothers are burdened with a severe handicap.

Since women make up approximately 50% of the population of every country, no country can expect to make progress which neglects to educate its women. This applies equally to Islamic and Hindu countries. Wearing of purdahs or veils is not in itself anti-education, of course, but it is usually symptomatic of orthodoxy and anti-modernism. It often goes hand in hand with denial of education, with forced marriages, polygamy, restrictions on movement and even severe punishments. The Economist (September 26, 2015) states that the potential GDP increase in India with gender equality could be of the order of 60%!

Denied access to various branches of education and knowledge, unwilling or unable to obtain jobs, more and more such women then become experts in religious procedure, ritual and orthodoxy. In millions of families in India, women will set the religious tone and the menfolk will unquestioningly follow. What rituals are to be practised for birth, for naming ceremonies, thread ceremonies, marriage, death and even shraddha, not to mention satyanarayans and other such ceremonies are often the special province of women. Himani Dalmia argues that women's undertaking of ritual fasts like Karva Chauth, Ahoi Ashtami, Mangalvar Vrat etc represents their essential powerlessness and their hunger for an agency which could affect the destinies of all (themselves and their families). She asks if there are not, in today's world, other means to feed that hunger? (49) What better way than if they were gradually made votaries of science?

The men in these households, busy as they are with the business of earning a living, increasingly leave it to the women to pronounce judgment or offer guidance in matters of religious ritual. No one takes the trouble to think, nobody sees the blatant contradictions, everyone fears the consequences of breaking with tradition and all are removed from reality! In such a situation, the initial role must inevitably pass to the male parent, if literate and educated. He has the twin job of educating both his wife and their child. As far as the government is concerned, the education of women and particularly their education about the true meaning of science and the benefits to be obtained from it for their children and for the country, must constitute one of the subjects of the highest priority.

The Chinese, whose problems are not far different from ours, realized the critical role to be played by women. They have long had a movement for the education and modernization of women. In their own special, dramatic fashion and recognizing, of course, that nearly half of the population of their country consisted of women, they call(ed) it the Half of China movement! We desperately need a Half of India movement in our country.

a feminist agenda

Women in poor, developing countries like India are a woefully oppressed group. It seems to me that if women's empowerment and upliftment is the goal, there is no better way of achieving this than by their getting on to the modern science and technology bandwagon. Instead of having to fight injustice at every turn and for every slight, women could become part of a giant tidal wave of modernization which follows when you adopt the very simple, rational rules involved. In doing this, women could not only transform themselves but help to transform their husbands and their families and in time could shake off all the inequities accumulated over centuries (abortion rights, child marriage, female foeticide, female infanticide, domestic violence, dowry deaths, lack of indoor toilets etc.). This kind of flanking movement could sidestep all the obstacles presented, directly and indirectly, by a patriarchal society's vested interests. There is no point in merely condemning gang-rape incidents. This is the way to set up structures and institutions to fight it.

We talk about democratic dividend but not so much about child malnutrition. Neeraj Kaushal writes in a Economic Times article that one third of the world's underweight and stunted children under the age of five are in India—twice the number in even sub-Saharan Africa! And it isn't just poverty—child nutrition affects 20% of even the wealthiest families! She asks: Are we less caring about our children? Is there something in our cultural values? She says yes, even compared to sub-Saharan Africa! Malnutrition of children in our country starts early; during a woman's pregnancy and through the effects of her overall health and nourishment in childhood. According to the author, the problem can only be solved by improving the health, opportunities and rights of the mother, the primary caregiver of children. Not just legislative rights, but rights to participate in decision-making both at home and outside it, opportunities for social interactions, rights to improve their lives through education and employment.(50)

The situation seems irretrievable – until you think of science as a medium, a vehicle, a ready tool. You use science as an innocuous way of insinuating modern thinking and attitudes into people enabling them to tackle immediate problems while at the same time it constantly works on their minds assisting them to batter down centuries-old, archaic attitudes. Foreground, background!

Writing about the Arab spring, an article in Time magazine (51) commented on the Arab woman's struggle for equal rights: "Women are good for revolutions but historically, revolutions haven't been so good for women." After the revolution in Iran, Ayatollah Khomeini insisted that they wear the veil. In Afghanistan, Mullah Omar's men beat women with sticks if even their ankles sometimes showed under their burkhas. In Tunisia, women are guaranteed birth control, abortion rights nend equal pay but they are worried that it could all be set back by Islamist groups who may call for Sharia.

In her recent memoir, Elizabeth Warren, the presidential candidate says that nearly 25% of the US GDP was due to the women (working full time) in the work force! How then can a poor country like Afghanistan, now free of US occupation, not see the clear advantage of having women receive education and then participate in full measure as equal partners in the economy? Inspite of all the confusion which resulted when the Americans recently gave over, one (Afghan) woman on the radio tearfully described the American stewardship as the 'golden years' of Afghanistan. What a nice tribute. Remember there is no alternative, whatever maybe prescribed by *any* religion.

Fighting for women's rights under the constant, unwavering banner of MoST is probably the most effective, least adversarial and most durable way of going about it. Men can't want jobs—which men, especially young men, desperately do in the above countries—and still set themselves up against women's rights. There is an underlying contradiction. The two don't go together. Once women begin looking for jobs themselves, men's ideas will have changed and there will be simply be more jobs available. We have used Muslim countries as an example but the same arguments apply with equal force to India.

involving the people

From working with parents and teachers and helping women as a group, we are now required to take the message to the people as a whole. How do we go about this?

With a population of over one billion, of which nearly 20% is still illiterate, this is an enormous task. There is no need to lose heart. We can set about the job with courage and confidence because:

(1) every single artifact of science which surrounds us - and this is true in even in the remotest villages - is all the evidence we require. These products of science constitute a veritable army and nothing can stop its march. The electric bulb, the bus or the motorcar, the motor pump, the newspaper, the TV, the watch or clock or timepiece are but a few of the soldiers in this arsenal to be seen in even the smallest village in the country;

(2) our conviction that the way of science is the only way. There is no other way in which we can pull this country up from the deep morass into which it has fallen over the last three to four hundred years. The unshakeable belief that science presents the only way to modernization is itself enough argument before the people of India, sufficient to persuade them to ponder the consequences of their choice. The cry should now be : Modernize with science or perish!

In his book The Idea of India, Ajit Khilnani writes: "To Visweswaraya's technocratic battle-cry Industrialize or Perish!, Gandhi replied Industrialize and Perish." (52) Nearly seventy years after independence, it is no longer merely a matter of rival slogans. The people of India are called upon to decide.

The exact manner in which the Government and other interested organisations go about this need not detain us for long. I repeat: It is necessary to start an intellectual ferment among the people. Radio, TV, magazines, newspapers, the cinema, the internet, every possible medium in both urban and rural areas must be pressed into service. Even in a country like India, nearly 75% of the population is serviced by TV. The reach of radio is even greater. Assuming that we have demonstrated in this book that lack of science is the chief reason for our ills, it oughn't to be difficult to drive home this message to the people. We have shown how this matter which makes up what we call the culture of us all can be broken down into smaller pieces and then analysed and therefore, tackled.

helping change to happen

In getting his country to try out the capitalist road, Deng Xiaoping first secured the support of various groups in his country such as farmers, managers and workers, intellectuals and students, the military leadership, the financial and the top leadership of the Government and the Communist Party. To change course from that already firmly set by a regimented, totalitarian, ideologically-bound, wholly Communist country was an incomparably more difficult task than the one that we in India are now called upon to undertake. The great advantage of a mixed economy and a free society is that we are free to choose and free to speak our minds. In our own country, therefore, we could even add to the above groups others like government employees, professionals, trade-unionists, office workers, shopkeepers, artisans, farmers and so on.

We have a large and thriving middle class. The Economist estimates it to have been 264 million in 2005. (Mr. Shashi Tharoor thinks the category is more sociological than logical.) Sufficient, however, to propagate and carry forward the message of science. The middle class is concerned about matters like children's health and is prepared to invest its time and resources on education. We have to secure the willing support of the middle class and use it to give a powerful thrust in our efforts to take science to the people.

No stone is to be left unturned. Even expectant mothers could constitute one such group! In his book, The Passionate Mind - Building up an Intelligent and Creative Child, Michael Schulman shows in great detail how infants, yes infants, and Nobel Laureates alike seem to want to discover the same four things:

WHAT IS OUT THERE?

WHAT LEADS TO WHAT?

WHAT MAKES THINGS HAPPEN?

WHAT'S CONTROLLABLE?

He argues that the same four concerns underlie the scientists'search for knowledge and the artists' search for truth and indeed in all of our attempts at work and daily activities to learn more and perform better.(53)

With our population showing no sign of immediate abatement, there is an army of expectant mothers available at any given time. Granted that while not all of these would be literate, educated mothers, there is no reason why a beginning cannot be made with such as are available. Later, armed with the fruits of our experience, the project could be expanded to include all expectant and recent mothers. I make this small suggestion in all seriousness and in an effort to show that in this all important work, no group should be neglected, no possibility overlooked, no stone unturned.

Government should equip its publicity machinery suitably and get them to gear up for the enormous task. The initial effect will be available before long and in course of time, a multiplier effect will set in thereby accelerating progress. Before long, the entire population of the country could become engaged in the enterprise of suggesting improvements along broad lines to be indicated by Government. In place of mere messages about integration set to music on radio and television, this would make for an excellent way in which to actually weld the nation together. It is no use just decrying gang rapes, communal riots or caste or regional differences. It is necessary to replace them with a positive, constructive programme. What better way than to show how only modern science and technology can do the job for the nation?

Let's end this chapter on change with a brief portrait of a small country, Denmark, which already, it can be said, appears to have constituted itself in this way. I first refer to an article in the Economic Times supplement, CD, of June 11, 2010. The sub-title reads: "United Spirits is set to become the world's biggest booze company." The writer is referring to the fact of the company's having achieved a sales target of 100 million cases, making it No 2 in the world (after Diageo) and on the verge of soon becoming No 1 in the world.

Is this all we should aim for? Let's look at the potential. It's possible to relate it to far, far bigger things. These become apparent only if you understand the scope of modern science and technology. Mr. Vijay Mallya exults: "We've come a long way since I joined the company 20 years ago. Liquor was a commodity then and politicians wanted to ban it. We have turned it into a branded product linked to aspiration."

The Danish-made Carlsberg beer was introduced in India in 2006. In Denmark itself, they of course treated liquor not as sin but to be taken in moderation, like all other food and drink. One of the consequences of manufacturing beer turned out to be that the country also became an expert in yeast and fermentation technology and in industrial enzyme technology. It's not an accident, therefore, that a tiny country like Denmark, therefore, becomes the second largest producer of insulin in the world. Apparently, insulin is difficult to make and we have been importing it for years from overseas. (More recently, India has come to an arrangement with Denmark's Novo Nordisk for it to be produced locally under licence.)

The total number of diabetics in India is slated to go up to double its number, 75 million, in another few years.(54) The article which provided the figure described it as the price of progress and that added to it is the genetic vulnerability of Indians to the disease. Isn't that all the more reason for us to be vigilant, to be on top of the science and to take all possible science steps to shield ourselves? Is it acceptable that we have a situation where a small country like Denmark makes the medicine (thank God for it!) and all we do is to offer ourselves up in the millions as patients?

Two of the world's most innovative manufacturers of enzymes for converting biomass to fuel – Danisco and Novozymes – come from Denmark.(55) The country is also a world leader in the cooperative farm movement. Earlier in this book, we quoted from Dr. Kurien's speech on the excellent work Amul was doing in Gujarat. Denmark was a pioneering country in the cooperative farm movement as long ago as in the 1880s. Building on this, it did the same for the pork industry (1887), in which today it is a world leader. And judging from the way, science can and does spill over into the arts and the humanities, should it then surprise you that while Denmark is now classified as an agricultural superpower (as mentioned earlier), it also manufactures furniture for export and at any given time can boast of several professorships of furniture design? (56)

In our own times, Denmark has become a world leader in the wind power industry. It gets more than 19% of its electricity from the breeze, and Danish companies control a whopping one-third of the global wind market, earning billions in exports and creating a national champion from scratch.(57) It is also one of the world's most energy efficient economies. It has grown 70% since 1981 but its energy consumption has kept almost flat all these years. In 1973, 99% of Denmark's energy came from the Middle East. Today, that percentage is zero.(58)

So we've painted a picture of Denmark, one small example out of many developed countries and shown how it is able to exploit its capabilities. This realization that progress, when it comes, comes in the form of a broad, wide-ranging, many-splendoured force came to me a few years ago as a result of my readings in this subject of what modern science and technology does to you. I kept on thinking to myself: Is that possible? can it really be true? Imagine my total surprise, therefore, when only in 2011, while going through a biography of Adam Smith, I come across the following quite remarkable prediction, made as long ago as 1738, by Lord David Hume, the famous Scottish philosopher and mentor of Adam Smith :

In times when industry and the arts flourish, men are kept in perpetual occupation and enjoy, as their reward, the occupation itself, as well as those pleasures which are the fruit of their labour. The mind acquires new vigour; enlarges its powers and faculties; and by an assuidity in honest industry, both satisfies its natural appetites and prevents the growth of unnatural ones, which commonly spring up, when nourished by ease and idleness. Banish those arts from society, you deprive men both of action and of pleasure; and leaving nothing but indolence in their place, you even destroy the relish of indolence, which never is agreeable, but when it succeeds to labour, and recruits the spirits, exhausted by too much application and fatigue.

Another advantage of industry and of refinements in the mechanical arts, is, that they commonly produce some refinements in the liberal; nor can one be carried to perfection, without being accompanied, in some degree, with the other. The same age, which produces great philosophers and politicians, renowned generals and poets, usually abounds with skilfull weavers and ship-carpenters. We cannot reasonably expect, that a piece of woollen cloth will be wrought to perfection in a nation, which is ignorant of astronomy, or where ethics are neglected...

The more these refined arts advance, the more sociable men become: nor is it possible, that, when enriched with science, and possessed of a fund of conversation, they should be contented to remain in solitude, or live with their fellow-citizens in that distant manner, which is peculiar to ignorant and barbarous nations. They flock into cities; love to receive and communicate knowledge; to show their wit or their breeding; their taste in conversation or living, in clothes or furniture. Curiosity allures the wise; vanity the foolish; and pleasure both. Particular clubs and societies are everywhere formed: Both sexes meet in an easy and sociable manner; and the tempers of men, as well as their behaviour, refine apace. So that, beside the improvements which they receive from knowledge and the liberal arts, it is impossible but they must feel an increase of humanity, from the very habit of conversing together, and contributing to each other's pleasure and entertainment. Thus industry, knowledge and humanity, are linked together by an indissoluble chain, and are found, from experience as well as reason, to be peculiar to the more polished, and, what are commonly denominated, the more luxurious ages.(59)

Denmark is a small country, with a population of five and a half million. I leave you, dear reader, to imagine the possibilities for India.

APPENDIX 1 to Chapter 8

FORGET IDEOLOGY, CONSIDER IDEA-LOGY!

(The approach to politics, economics and society differs when looked at from Kuala Lumpur or Shanghai or from London but all are in agreement when it comes to scientific and technical advance.)

LOOKING BACK, IT IS easy to see that practically the whole of the twentieth century was racked by a keen tussle between the forces of capitalism and socialism on the one hand and mostly fascism on the other and then, after the two World Wars had ended and the Cold War had begun, between the forces of capitalism on the one hand and communism on the other. But what did all these political ideologies have in common and in the end, with what tools or implements did they venture to wage their fights? What gave them their economic strength and their military means, the twin props without which no nation can dare to challenge another in our modern-day world? The forces of science and technology, of course.

It is customary to chart the economic progress of a developed nation by detailing its mastery of agriculture, its journey through manufacturing and industrialization, its graduation into a variety of services and now, even by the tracing of the emergence of its creative class. All these are recognized as stages of economic growth. What do all these stages have in common and what was that special element which enabled transition (slow or rapid, depending upon how the attempt at development was going) from one stage to another? The forces of modern science and technology, of course.

We speak about the political, economic, social and cultural dimensions of a given situation or a stated problem. While all aspects are important and often inter-dependent and while it is good to be multi-dimensional in one's outlook, can any one of them claim to be the seed-bed of the others? Is not the approach to political, economic and social aspects likely to be altogether different in, say, an Islamic culture from that in a Confucian culture or from that in a Calvinist Protestant culture? Despite these differences, with the economic and technological progress of nations in today's world, what is it that drives them towards a certain, inevitable convergence? The skyline of modern Kuala Lumpur does not look all that different from that of modern Shanghai or modern London. The forces of modern science and technology have given them all a common mien.

There's no escaping the fact. Whatever you do, wherever you turn, you are thrown back on, or rather speeded forward by, the forces of modern science and technology. Not education, not history, not economics, not religion or philosophy can avoid being deeply influenced by it. Was it worth fighting all those bitter wars and developing all that enmity when the mighty force behind all that exhibition of strength was one and the same? Are we overly swayed by ideologies (capitalism vs communism, conservatism vs liberalism, Hindu vs Muslim, Singhalese vs Tamil, Western vs Asian) when we should really be focusing our sights on idea-logy? Because that is what modern science and technology is all about. It is not merely the artifacts or products of science we see all around us. Modern science and technology is essentially a corpus of ideas, a framework of thinking, an unceasing quest for truth.

(First appeared as an article by the author in the Bombay magazine, One India One People, February 2004)

APPENDIX 2 to Chapter 8

There is an additional, historical perspective: the kind of structured change involved at every level in any country which sets out to change. It can supplement our efforts in instituting change in India. This way, we also learn from the experience of Western countries. I have kept this here in an appendix as a separate narrative in order not to confuse it with the special steps earlier outlined for India.

change in education curricula

Immediately following the Industrial Revolution, education and skills were not seen as important to the success of capitalism. Capital equipment was the thing. Lester Thurow says that Adam Smith barely mentioned education in his Wealth of Nations – only as "an antidote to the mind-numbing boredom of factory work". (1) J.K.Galbraith agrees with this. According to him, Adam Smith, writing at the very start of the Industrial Revolution, spoke more admiringly of the division of labour (and the productivity flowing from it) than even capital or the question of application of power/ energy to production. (2) However, times change, agriculture has been overtaken by industry and now, in many countries, industry has given way to services. Some are working towards a knowledge economy. Consequently, educational curricula also have to change and must reflect this change.

change in industry categories

Entire nations changed from being producers of crafts to being nations of great entrepreneurial tinkerers (Watt, Bessemer, Arkwright etc) (3), from this to learning how to service their own and foreign markets and finally as shown below to economies based on R&D. We do not ourselves have to go through these phases but it helps to keep them in mind.

change in social organization

Thurow states that whole cultures (have) to be rebuilt to accept rapid technical change. How true this is for countries like India! He shows how, during the nineteenth century, in creating its chemical industry, Germany developed the concept of systematic industrial R&D. Large numbers of scientists, engineers, trained managers and skilled workers had to be generated (as) an old religious or political elite would not do. (4) This called for changes in educational curricula and in the educational system itself. Great Britain, unable to do this, fell behind. Early in the twentieth century, the USA went even further by going from elite classics-based education (Latin, Greek) to mass technological education... although it was not the world's technological leader. (5) The U.S. even discovered that in a free market economy, universal, compulsory, publicly funded education (was essential) to finally break the link between family income and education. (6)

change within industry

We saw earlier how agriculture gives way to industry and industry, in turn, yields to services. As part of his work on health and poverty issues, Bill Gates has said "today no country of any size has been able to sustain a transition out of poverty without substanially raising productivity in the agricultural sector. It can have a transformative impact". (7) True and certainly applicable to countries like India which have so many still engaged in agriculture. But, remember, agriculture itself is changing. So we need to keep that in mind as well. Even in agriculture, we spoke about how the next green revolution in India might need to take place outside of farming (better roads, better communications, better cold storage facilities, better marketing structures etc.)

change in economy

In step with the above changes, economies of whole countries have changed from local to national to global. But here's the paradox. From global because of the computer and the Internet, to also being personal and individual. In an article titled "Israel discovers oil", Friedman writes about how an Israeli professor took him to meet several young Israeli high-tech students of Ben Gurion University. Introducing the students to Friedman, the professor exclaims: " These are our oil-wells!" Friedman writes about how these days the next important competition is between you and your imagination...now, countries and companies have to empower their individuals to imagine and act quickly on their imagination. Friedman concludes: These are oil-wells that don't run dry! (8)

This is the kind of human capital we should strive for – capital which will pay dividends over and over and over again. Whether or not this will happen we cannot know for sure. But when this kind of change is imminent, can India afford not to organize itself as an entire country for the first planned, strident efforts in science?

knowledge creation and knowledge deployment

The USA did not need to create all its knowledge in order to get started. It learned to gather knowledge quickly and to deploy it effectively. Thurow says:" Knowledge creation requires highly educated creative skills at the very top of the skill distribution. Knowledge deployment requires widespread high quality skills and education in the middle and bottom of the skill distribution. The same country need not lead in both." (9) All along it was the case that scientific knowledge might be restricted to a few but scientific attitudes could be and needed to be widespread among the people.

Is all this too complicated to keep in mind? Not really. The trick is to understand that it all gets covered under one banner, namely, modern science and technology. Now you can see clearly the powerful forces which are unleashed and so you are in a position to better control and guide the enormous thrust that they generate.

In India, we have to take it one or two steps further. From literacy to conventional education to science literacy. In other words, taking the nation from agriculture or its present bullock-cart economy status (let's be hard on ourselves) to helping it to achieving an industrial revolution (in places the process has already begun) to ensuring that it becomes a knowledge economy, the economy of tomorrow. This may seem difficult, some would say impossible, to do in a country like India left so largely behind. But if you do it in stages as we have indicated above, it realizes itself, it increasingly happens on its own, it happens rapidly and it cannot but happen. The important thing is to identify, to boldly acknowledge the path to be taken, to promote, to coordinate and then to combine it with the huge will-power of 1400 million people so that that enormous effort is bent towards the common goal of rapid advancement of the nation.

Chapter 9
CONCLUSION

Society is not made up just of thinking individuals. There are structures and institutions and mechanisms within which – or between which – individuals think. – Edward de Bono, I am Right, you are Wrong

Men are themselves the source of their own fortune or misfortune. – Leon Battista Alberti

I do not want India to be an economic superpower. I want India to be a happy country. –J.R.D.Tata, after receiving the Bharat Ratna, 1992

*• modern science and technology • not race *not colour • or economic system • or religion • or geographical location • not national resources • not East or West • not agriculture or industry • nor form of government • not even ideology • the magic key • North vs South • backlash against Science • using MoST as a tool • astrology vs astronomy • what can the individual do? • the completion of change*

Let's go back to where we began. We said that modern science was the solution to India's accumulated problems, a multiple cure for a long-standing illness. We listed certain characteristics for the cure, saying that it:

• was simple; nothing extraordinary

- wasn't unusual or novel; was right there, staring us in the face

- was comprehensive; brought about a general sense of well-being

- wasn't instantaneous but could begin to show results quickly even when offered to large bodies of individuals

- wasn't bitter; was sweet-tasting and enjoyable to take

- inexpensive and needed little by way of resources

- was personal, self-administered and individual; and finally:

- had an irreversible effect— once successful, there was no real possibility of relapse

I hope that the reader will now find it possible to agree with all that has been claimed for the cure. We went on to say that it was the only cure and that there was no other. I hope that this too has been established.

modern science and technology

Mantra is an Indian word which has been accepted and is now commonly used in the English language. Our mantra in India should be modern science and technology. The mantras from the scripture books which we have been reciting tirelessly for hundreds of years are unfortunately unable to rescue us from our sorrowful condition.

The fruits of modern science and technology, which means better material conditions and a better people, are available to all who seek them. No one is barred. Ethnicity or colour or gender is no obstacle.

The economic system at hand, the form of government adopted, the geographical area, although they do matter, are not a serious barrier and do not have preponderant importance.

The way of modern science and technology is also the most direct way of obtaining results. It gets straight to the heart of the matter which concerns us in this book, namely, the eradication of poverty in India, the commencement of the journey towards prosperity and the consequent and simultaneous liberation and upliftment of the people of our country.

In Chapter 1, we began by answering some of the standard explanations raised when it comes to discussing the backwardness of India. In this last chapter, let us tackle some of the other more technical objections that are brought up, both in India and overseas:

not race

When, in the course of writing this book, I have sometimes been asked to provide a brief synopsis, I have become accustomed to receiving, by now, two predictable reactions: When I have spoken to Indians , the response has been that the solution surely cannot be quite so simple or so easy. My reply is that surely the solution does not have to be complicated and untried just because they think it cannot be otherwise. The response from European and American friends, although here one would expect more understanding, has often been one of sheer disbelief. There is still the lingering feeling that coloured people would somehow find it difficult to make the grade. This kind of reluctance is quickly despatched by my insistence that if Japan and now China could do it (and nobody questions that any longer!), there was no reason why India could not do so or even countries in Africa or Latin America could not do so. Therefore, if the path of modern science and technology is adopted, race or nationality does not matter. You can be Asian Indian or American

Indian, African African or African American, Hispanic, Chinese, Japanese, Korean, Iranian, whoever.

not colour

Colour does not matter. You can be any colour. In the exact ways which we have suggested, modern science and technology will transform you as surely as the dawn will come tomorrow.

or economic system

It is of some consequence what kind of economic system you follow, whether mercantilism, capitalism, socialism, communism or fascism but in itself the type of system is less important than, once again, the forces of science and technology which give any system its thrust and act as the true engine of its growth.

For example, it has long been debated whether Britain would have had its Industrial Revolution if capital had not been extracted from colonies like India. Or whether capitalism itself would have been possible in Europe without the silver obtained from South America. The answer to this surely should be that without the coming of modern science and technology, neither source of riches would have been accessible and even if accessible, could not and would not have been able to be put to use for purposes of growth and development.

Furthermore, capital is not all that is required or all that is involved. What about the advances in astronomy, physics, physiology, anatomy, medicine, chemistry, cartography etc. which also came about at around the same time? How do we explain these developments? The answer is that modern science and technology advances on a wide-ranging front, intellectual as well as practical, and capitalism itself as a system benefited from the possibilities which were now offered by the new forces which drove both man and machine.

or religion

Once it is decided that the march is to be begun, religion too cannot stop progress. Whether a people are Protestant or Catholic, whether Buddhist or Confucian, Tao, Shinto, Jew, Muslim or Hindu, Zorastrian, Sikh or Jain, science applies to the followers of them all.

Let's consider some further illustrations to show how this affects us in India. For example, it is often thought by Indian parents that Westernisation for their children was best obtained by sending them to Christian missionary (convent) schools. What is not understood is that the Christian missionaries in these schools, earlier German or Spanish or Italian or Irish (to mention only a few nationalities) or now Indian, were not themselves the cause of this Westernisation, only its effect. To see a white cassocked priest driving a Matador van (earlier, a frequent sight in Mumbai) was only to witness this foreigner himself benefiting from modern science and technology. He was no more responsible for the van (the internal combustion engine) than a pig-tailed Hindu priest might be for his scooter (another common sight in South India). Christianity happened to be the religion of (Western) Europe and therefore, adapted to the demands of modern science and technology much more and much earlier than other religions had the opportunity to do.

The Catholic Church is still adapting, as when the Vatican announced in 1992 that Galileo had been wrongly condemned and that the Pope would now formally close the 13-year old investigation into its condemnation of the scientist in 1633! To look at it in another way, if modern science and technology had been born in India instead of in Europe, Hinduism would have been the first to require to adapt to it, not Christianity, and then perhaps there might have been Hindu missionary schools in Europe and European children might have gone to them for modernization or Easternization.

or geographical location

Geography too is no obstacle. The United Kingdom, Western Europe, the United States, Canada, Australia and New Zealand are already considered to be developed countries. Japan, Taiwan, South Korea, Hongkong and Singapore, force-fed on modern science and technology have become or are in the process of becoming developed countries. Russia, the Eastern European countries, from the point of view of being schooled in modern science and technology, have already covered part of the distance towards the common destination but are groping for a way to achieve a market economy and a truly free society. This leaves East Asia; the Indian sub-continent including Pakistan and Bangladesh; and parts of China, Africa and Latin America. Any one or more of these areas, by adopting the path of modern science and technology, can achieve freedom from poverty and take the first steps towards a better standard of living for themselves and future generations. This is the only way to go.

not natural resources

Japan has little by way of natural resources. Austria, Switzerland, Hongkong, Singapore and Taiwan are so small in area that one cannot expect them to have meaningful natural resources. Yet all these countries are prospering. What they have in common is human capital resources. It is time for us in In6dia to recognize that classical factors of production no longer hold true. In the last few decades, we have entered a knowledge based society and from now on, more than ever, it will be human capital that counts. The pace of growth in a given country can be aided by infusions of wealth from overseas but it is the people of each country which finally must put this wealth to creative and productive use. In the process, as we have shown, the people themselves—men, women and children—can become transformed, thus producing further wealth, and so on.

not East or West

Again, the case of Japan is interesting. At the very time, in the early twentieth century, when Rudyard Kipling was boasting about the enduring qualities of the British Empire, a curious phenomenon was happening on the other side of the globe! These people were not British or even European; they were not Christian but Buddhist and Shinto and they were not even Caucasian! Imperial Britain could not figure it out! When General MacArthur's fighters were destroyed on the ground in the Philippines by the Japanese Air Force, the general thought white mercenaries must have flown the Japanese planes!(1)

not agriculture or industry

This classification too has become outdated because agriculture itself, as we said earlier, has become an industry. Branches of production which fall between agriculture and industry go by the name of agro-industry. In all developed countries, the percentage of people engaged in agriculture or industry is progressively going down and that in service industries is going up. The point here is that the core concept behind even industries like the hotel industry or the tourist industry is that they are principally service industries. Bio-technology is, in other words, the industry of biology. In every field, the forces of science and technology remain the essential driving force.

or form of government

As we have already stated in respect of the earlier USSR and present day China, it is certainly of some consequence whether you have democracy and a free society or whether you have a totalitarian form of government. Science prospers best in a free climate but it will also provide development under a military dictatorship (earlier regimes in South Korea and Taiwan), civilian dictatorship (Hitler's Germany and Mussolini's Italy) or even a benevolent dictatorship (Singapore under Lew Kuan Yew). In the first half of the twentieth century, the USA under FDR, the USSR under Stalin and Germany under Hitler had one thing in common – each could make substantial economic progress only because of science and technology.

not even ideology

The World Development Report, 1996, quotes a paragraph about capitalism from The Communist Manifesto of Karl Marx and Friedrich Engels :

"Constant revolutionizing of production, uninterrupted disturbance of all social conditions, everlasting uncertainty and agitation... All fixed, fast-frozen relations, with their train of ancient and venerable prejudices and opinions, are swept away, all new-formed ones become antiquated before they can ossify. All that is solid melts into air..."

Then the Report proceeds to comment:

"Between 1917 and 1950, countries containing one-third of the world's population seceded from the market economy and launched a vast experiment in constructing alternative systems of centrally planned economies that transformed the economic and political map of the world. "(2)

The World Bank Report says that it is devoted to the transition of these countries back to a market orientation—a process aptly, if ironically, described by the Communist Manifesto's portrayal of the turbulent spread of capitalism in the nineteenth century

Both capitalism and communism could secure their own growth only with the help of the forces of modern science and technology but if the capitalists had realized that science meant humanity above all and the communists had accepted that science means freedom above all, a large part of the turmoil of the last 150 years might have been avoided. For the purposes of our own argument, once it is accepted that science represents only a pursuit of the truth, humanity and freedom also automatically become different aspects of the same theme.

the magic key

At different times in the course of history, different ideas or models have been quite seriously regarded as constituting a kind of panacea or magic key which would help mankind solve all its problems. For example, in our own times, for many people, especially in our country, this model has been religion. We have tried to show how religion cannot possibly provide an answer to man's many and growing material problems.

But there have been others. During the Middle Ages, for example, the notion of chivalry, believe it or not, was regarded as a magic key, capable of providing universal solutions. (3) Another example is that of the 1600s, at around the time of Shakespeare, when English society went through such stormy times, partly as a result of the new and increasing influence of science itself, that it was thought that something desperately needed to be done to resolve the complex social problems that were arising. For 200 years, language had been regarded as a panacea and was supposed to be capable of providing an answer to problems. The Royal Society, which was formed in 1662, itself to study science, was entrusted with the task of reporting whether a study of Latin would tell the nation what it needed to do!(4)

Yet another model was just simple human will. In his book Europe, Grandeur and Decline, A.J.P. Taylor says this about Napoleon:

The essence of the (French) Revolution was belief in man. Once you believe that man is naturally good, you must believe, too, that he can do anything. Napoleon certainly held this belief about himself. And no doubt man can do anything, if he goes the right way about it. The right way, as the events of the last century and a half have shown, is the way of science : the improvement of technique. The men of the French Revolution and Napoleon with them, supposed that they could master the world by will alone.

....Napoleon was following the wrong course, the further his will carried him, the greater was bound to be his final catastrophe.(5)

North vs South

It is often asked whether the world is capable of supporting its 7 billion people if poverty is banished worldwide and developing countries rise to the standard of living of the developed. One thing is certain. The march of science and technology cannot be stopped. In the twentyfirst century, it will spread to every corner of the globe and with it, the abysmally poor standard of living of the developing countries is bound to go up. There is practically no scope for it to go down. Technology is the great leveller and the great democratiser. Therefore, even if it were desired, it would be impossible to keep the poor down.

Does the world have resources to satisfy the needs of all its people? While natural world resources as known at present are undoubtedly limited, science itself will be instrumental in organizing more finds, ensuring better utilization, devising more miniaturization and of course, helping to create new, synthetic materials. Whether, therefore, the poor rise to the standard of living of the rich or whether some compromise will need to be worked out between rich and poor or whether all together can attain increasingly better standards of living for themselves once again can only be determined with the aid of science and science alone.

backlash against Science

In recent years, despite all that science has achieved, there has even been a backlash against science. Much of this criticism is misconceived and misdirected. Because we have so much science around us, it is only to be expected that there will be, in some cases, an excess of science or misplaced science. It is nobody's case that such excesses should be defended from criticism. In fact, they must be exposed and the excesses must then be curbed or eliminated altogether, as the circumstances may require.

But we cannot afford to throw the baby out with the bath water! Science is so much in evidence on all sides that it would be impossible to do without it. We cannot conceive of going back to the time of Stone Age man nor even to the conditions prevalent at the time of the birth of modern science, say, early 17th century in Europe. These were quite primitive conditions compared to the standard of living attained in all industrialized countries today.

Furthermore, while it is readily acknowledged that there have been excesses of science, yet it must be admitted that the excesses themselves may not have been noticed without the scientific mind. Ecology itself has become possible as a subject of study because of science.

using MoST as a tool

We have seen how our twin tools of science and technology could be used to analyze problems and situations. Approaching the end of this book, let us now once again use them to try and answer various other questions which are often raised. Pamela Philpose asks :

Have we as a nation of 840 million people, produced a single idea which has set bells ringing in New York or London? Or have we satisfied ourselves with being mere recipients of ideas formulated abroad? Why does the Indian brain swell to formidable proportions when soaked in the academic formulae of the West? Why is it that our own groves of academia are incapable of similar performance here?...Does the Gross National Product (GNP) of a nation determine its level of intellectual activity?(6)

Or, to quote a professor of physics, K.K.Datta, at Delhi University :

Let's face it, the scientific community and the overall world-view we have adopted and on which we have built our intellectual framework is set on the pattern of the post-Newtonian Western university model. We have failed to develop an alternative work-view.... Whether it is history, philosophy or physics, on what models do we base our work?(7)

Is it really possible to develop an alternative work-view? Are we asked to invent a new, wholly different modern science? Is it conceivable? Could this demand also not have been made on other countries which came after Europe in the history of modern science, countries such as the United States or Japan or in our own times, Hong Kong, South Korea or Taiwan and now China? The fact is it is neither necessary nor is it possible to re-invent modern science.

As for Indians blossoming overseas but failing to show any real merit in India itself, this question too should now be relatively easy to answer. It is one thing for Indians to slot into institutions that already exist in developed countries overseas. It is another thing altogether to be able to build those institutions in our own country.

We are not even a fully literate country. Our educational establishments leave a great deal to be desired. We are also unclear about the stellar role played by modern science in the development of the world and we ask, wistfully, if we cannot develop an entirely new alternative for ourselves. We are neither clear about our goal nor about the means of getting there.

At the least, it is necessary to have literacy. Then it is necessary to have education. Not merely education, but high-quality education; in other words, education predicated by, dependent on and fully informed by the philosophy behind modern science and technology. When we have done this, the institutions will automatically be built, the industries will come and the people will be transformed. There will be no need to leave one's hearth and home and settle overseas. There will be plentiful original contributions to research in science and developments in technology made from within our own country.

Which comes first? The people or the institutions? It stands to reason that the people of the country, its human or intellectual capital, must come first. Institutions are not conceived on their own. People need to develop institutions, not the other way round. However, in reality, once begun, there is a constant process of interweaving of people and institutions. People develop institutions, who develop people, who develop more and varied institutions and so on.

Knowledge of science is also necessary because of the type of society we are all entering. Communism is gone but Peter Drucker said that the 21st century would see large changes in even the concept of capitalism. Traditional economic resources like land, labour and capital would give way to resources like knowledge. Society would become divided into knowledge-workers and service-workers. (8)

Developed countries have already gone through the phase of heavy industrial development and are becoming what is variously called post-industrial society, mature societies and societies of the techtronic Age. If we in India are not to find ourselves overwhelmed by all these enormous changes, we must prepare for our own transformation without delay. And there is no other way of doing it than by truly getting to know about science.

astrology vs astronomy

Since millions upon millions of Indians depend so much on astrology, this may be the place in our book to compare its merits with astronomy. In a strange way, the meaning of the two words has become transposed in history. Plato himself coined the word astrology to mean reasoning (logos) about the stars as against astronomy which at that time stood for a mere ordering (nomos) of the stars.(9) Today, the two words represent the exact opposite of the meanings that they carried at that time.

Again and again in this book, we have examined different ideas, concepts and practices in India by their relative success or failure in terms of results. How have they benefited the people? Our criticism of the astrology of today must also follow the same course:

1. As we have said above, astrology is at least as old as astronomy – certainly older than modern astronomy – and yet it is unable to establish itself. It constantly demands acceptability by the scientific world whereas its achievements should, by now, have automatically gained acceptability for it.

2. Astrology often claims that it can benefit all mankind.(10) One wishes that it would benefit India which is desperately in need of help or even one single poor village and then speak of all mankind.

3. Floods and cyclones will never be predicted by astrology–but they are already being regularly predicted by astronomy

4. Astrology has not, and is unable, to develop its own tools e.g. man on the moon, spacecraft and satellites, telescope in space. These are all products of astronomy,

5. Astrology is valued by people because of its supposed powers of prediction. To do this, we may be looking in the wrong direction because more often it is necessary to look closely into the past (history) in order to predict or construct the future.

6. Historically, astrology has been a non-starter. Astronomy gave birth to all of modern science.

7. The study of astronomy can and does logically lead to other studies e.g. chemistry, physics, biology, zoology, botany, meteorology, metallurgy, geology and even the humanities. Astrology, after 2000 years, is itself floundering for existence and remains very much isolated.

8. Astrology assumes that individual events on earth are determined by the stars and the planets. The history of the developed world over the last 300/400 years has demonstrated that events are determined by man and his work and by this alone.

9. With astrology, there is automatic concern for one's own life and one's own good fortune. The simple fact is that the fate of one individual just does not count.

10. Finally, with astrology, there is the tendency to seek happiness for oneself and one's family. It may be that happiness lies in looking away from oneself— towards the happiness of another or the happiness of others.

what can the individual do?

We have devoted this book to a cataloguing of the nation's problems and an offering of general principles with which to help to solve these problems. But what is the individual to do? What can one person actually do? In one's everyday life, what is it that is involved in acquiring a modern mind? Earlier, it might even have been considered presumptuous for any outsider, including this author, to venture to offer these suggestions but in view of what we have discussed thus far, I hope that these will now be found worthy of consideration. What, therefore, should the individual do?

1. He should accept that, in our country, we have an urgent problem on our hands which calls for attention.

1. He should be prepared to accept science-technology as a method of change.
2. He should plan to cultivate a modern mind. He should look at problems, as well as opportunities, in a fresh light — not merely in terms of one religion vs. another religion
3. He should concentrate on the common problems of people, not on divisive issues.
4. He should accept that India is not necessarily the greatest country in the world —in fact, he should realize and acknowledge that India has thus far sadly been left behind in the race.
5. He should review his attitude to work as well as to study.
6. He should realize that all knowledge is one — that there are no separate truths for physics or astronomy or botany or sociology or morality or religion.
7. He should understand that when the global economy is upon us, the days of caste and creed are finally over.
8. He should treat women as fully equal partners of men – he should remember the half of India movement.
9. He should not wait for the next life—he should seek to

serve God now by serving his fellow man

10. He should avoid "groupism" and go by the majority, considering the interests of the nation; if the nation goes against the interests of man, he should consider the interests of humankind.

11. He should take another look at guru/shishya parampara. Instead, parents and adults should encourage self-reliance in children, thereby actively helping each generation to become better than the earlier one

12. He should understand that modernization does not stand for smoking, drinking, fast cars, the latest clothes, new electronics—it stands for punctuality, honesty, dependability, integrity, kindness, cleanliness, visual beauty and so on.

13. He should recognize that there is only one standard–whether in his dealings with God or with man.

14. He should read extensively, gathering both knowledge and wisdom. He should allow each book to evolve out of the one before.

the completion of change

Earlier in this chapter, we remarked how at different times in history, different general solutions like chivalry, language and human will itself were expected to provide a cure for all social ills. In our own times and in our own country, as we have tried to show in this book, we set a lot of store by religion. These expectations have been belied. What guarantee can there be, therefore, that modern science and technology will not also suffer a similar fate and that, like the other models mentioned here, it will also not similarly be eclipsed in the future? In history, there can, of course, be no guarantees but we can safely say that the prospects seem unlikely. Roughly one hundred years ago, there was neither the electric lamp nor the telephone. But can we think of a world a hundred or two hundred years hence without these conveniences? Modern science, now that it has been invented, can be expected to always remain with us.

In the past, civilizations have risen, reached their zenith, then declined and finally have fallen. Many have disappeared altogether. But this no longer applies. A civilization based on modern science and technology, cannot disappear—except, of course, if we destroy ourselves by a nuclear or similar holocaust. (But then, there is also always the possibility that Earth itself could be totally destroyed by a large asteroid at any time!). Therefore, a developed nation, once its men, women and children have been transformed (a future India?) cannot fall below a certain threshold and become a developing nation again. It cannot do this for the same reason that a literate man cannot become illiterate again. Working together, all of us, is this not the kind of glorious future we should try and secure for our beloved country?

NOTES

Chapter 1: India's problem: symptoms

1. E. R. Ramkumar, "Bleak Prospects for India's Children", Times of India, 10 January, 1989

2. P.C. Reddy, Times of India, 2 July, 2010

3. Times of India, 13 March, 2010

4. Times of India, 27 September, 2002

5. Times of India, 3 April, 1989,

6. The Economist, March 21-March 27, 2020

7. Dava Sobel, Galileo's Daughter, (New York: Penguin Books, 2000), p.201

8. Stanley A.Wolpert, Tilak and Gokhale, (Oxford University Press, 1991) p.130

9. Robert McCrum, William Cran and Robert MacNeil, The Story of English, (BBC Books/Faber and Faber, 1992) pp. 132-133

10. Boorstin, The Discoverers, (Penguin Books,1984), p.313

11. Dudley Seers and Leonard Joy, Eds, Development in a Divided World, (Penguin Books, 1971) p. 51

12. Carey McWilliams, California: The Great Exception, (University of California Press, reprinted 1999)

13. David Headrick, The Tools of Empire, (Oxford University Press, 1981), p.3

14. Allan Bloom, The Closing of the American Mind, (New York: Simon and Schuster, 1987)

15. William J. Bernstein, The Birth of Plenty, (New York: McGraw Hill, 2004) p. 32

16. Elizabeth Eisenstein, The Printing Press as an Agent of Change, (Cambridge University Press), p. 123

17. Nathan Rosenberg and L.E. Birdzell Jr., How the West Grew Rich (Mumbai: Popular Prakashan, 1987), p.5

Chapter 2 : What went wrong? How India, China and the Arab Muslim civilization missed out on the Scientific Revolution: a diagnosis

1. William J. Bernstein, The Birth of Plenty (New York: McGraw Hill, 2004),p,19, referring to Angus Maddison's Explaining the Economic Performance of Nations (Cheltenham, Elgar Publishing Press, 1995).

2. ibid, p. 3. Bernstein, referring this time to Angus Maddison's Monitoring the World Economy 1820-1992, says the take-off took place around 1820. He acknowledges that the Renaissance (circa 1450 AD) appears to some to be the pivotal point of the second millennium (1000 AD to 2000 AD) but did little to improve the conditions of everyday living. For us, however, the Renaissance remains the crucial point of take-off; the reasons for this will become clear later in the book.

3. William Ury, The Third Side, (New York: Penguin, 1999), p.62

4. Witold Rybczynski, The Concept of the Home, (New York: Penguin, 1987) p. 20. Later, we will have occasion to give examples of similar change in meanings of other words.

5. Elizabeth Eisenstein, The Printing Press as an Agent of Change, (Cambridge University Press, 1982) p.100.

6. ibid, p. 251

7. J.H. Plumb, The Penguin Book of the Renaissance, (Penguin Books, 1978), p. 10

8. J. Bronowski and Bruce Mazlish, The Western Intellectual Tradition, (New York: Harper Colophon, 1975) p. 108

9. Daniel Boorstin, The Republic of Technology (Ambika Publications, 1978), p.17; also Bronowski-Mazlish, The Western Intellectual Tradition, p. 124-125

10. Kirkpatrick Sale, The Conquest of Paradise (New York: Plume – Penguin Books, USA, 1991, p. 264

11. Arnold Pacey, The Maze of Ingenuity: Ideas and Idealism in the Development of Technology (Cambridge: MIT Press, 1976, p. 18)

12. Pacey, Maze, p. 19

13. Pacey, Maze, pp 54-86

14. Sale, Conquest, p. 57

15. Edited by Edward de Bono, Eureka! An Illustrated History of Inventions (New York: Holt, Rinehart and Winston, 1979), p.192

16. Richard D. Brown, Modernization, The Transformation of American Life, 1600-1865 (New York: Hill and Wang, 1976) p.112

17. Thomas M. Huber, The Revolutionary Origins of Modern Japan, (Palo Alto: Stanford University Press, 1981)

18. Yukichi Fukuzawa, The Autobiography of Yukichi Fukuzawa, (New York: Columbia University Press – UNESCO, 1960) p. 15

19. Priyatosh Mitra, The Mainspring of Economic Development (New York: St. Martin's Press, 1980) p. 61

20. Jindong Cai and Sheila Melvin, Beethoven in China (Penguin Group, Australia, 2015)

21. Ezra Vogel, Deng Xiaoping and the Transformation of China (Harvard University Press, 2011) p. 298

22. Pacey, Maze, pp. 187-188, quoting Irwin and Brett

23. Pacey, Maze, pp. 188-190

24. Pacey, Maze, pp. 277-278

25. Arvind Banavaliker, One India, One People, April 2005, article entitled How the Sailing Ship lost out to the Iron Steamer

26. William J. Bernstein, The Birth of Plenty, p. 172

27. Thomas Sowell, Conquests and Cultures (New York; McGraw Hill, 2004), p. 172

28. Sir Percival Spear, India (Michigan Press, 1961), quoted in Christopher Hibbert's The Great Mutiny (Penguin Books, 1988)

29. Amaresh Misra, War of Civilizations, India AD 1957 (New Delhi: Rupa and Co, 2008; Times of India, June 9, 2007

30. William Dalrymple, The Last Mughall (New York: Viking/Penguin, 2006) pp. 270, 274, 316-317

31. Thomas Sowell, Conquests and Cultures, pp 36 and 37

32. V.S. Naipaul, A Million Mutinies Now (New Delhi: Rupa and Co,

1990) p. 507

33. Daniel R. Headrick, The Tools of Empire, Technology and European Imperialism in the Nineteenth Century (New York: Oxford University Press, 1981) p.53

34. Daniel Boorstin, The Discoverers, (Penguin Books, 1984), p.188

35. Headrick, Tools of Empire, p. 58

36. Hernando de Soto, "El Otre Sendero" (The Other Path), Time, September 9,1999

37. G.Rattray Taylor, The Science of Life, A Pictorial History of Biology, Panther Edition, Thames and Hudson, London, illustration, p.10

38. J. Huizinga, The Waning of the Middle Ages (Penguin Books, reprinted 1990), p. 48

39. Charles Coultson Gillespie, The Edge of Objectivity (Princeton University Press,1960), p.66

40. Seyyed Hossein Nasr, Science and Civilization in Islam (New York: New American Library, 1968) p. 118 . All three examples appear on the same page.

41. Bernstein, Birth of Plenty, p. 103

42. Arthur Koestler, The Sleepwalkers: A History of Man's Changing View of the Universe (Penguin Books, 1979) p. 374

43. J. Bronowski, The Ascent of Man (Boston: Little Brown and Company, 1974)p. 202

44. Pacey, Maze, pp. 286-289

45. Boorstin, The Republic of Technology, p. 17

46. Huizinga, The Waning of the Middle Ages, p. 36

47. Boorstin, Republic of Technology, p. 17

48. Boorstin, The Discoverers, p. 62

49. Pacey, Maze, p. 288

50. S.A.A. Rizvi, The Wonder that was India, Vol. II (Sidgwick and Jackson,1987) p.225

51. Francis Fukuyama, The End of History and the Last Man (Penguin Books.1992) p.56-57

52. Eisenstein, Printing Press, pp. 226,219,217,229 and 123 respectively

53. Walter J. Ong, Orality and Literacy (London and New York: Metheun, 1982) p.117

54. Boorstin, The Discoverers, p. 512

55. V.S.Naipaul, India Today, 18 August, 1997

56. Michael Rothschild, Bionomics, Economy as Ecosystem (New York: Henry Holt & Co. 1992) p.9

57. Amitav Ghosh, interview, Economic Times, July 2008

58. Pacey, Maze, pp 284-285

59. John Keegan, A History of Warfare (New York: Vintage, 1994)p. 10-11

60. Barbara Tuchman, The March of Folly (New York: Ballantine Books, p. 152 and p. 156

61. Fawn Brodie, Thomas Jefferson, An Intimate History, (W.W. Norton & Co., 1974) p. 99

62. Urs Bitterli, Cultures in Conflict, (Stanford University Press, 1989), p. 113

63. Rybczynski. Waiting for he Weekend, p. 191

64. Brodie, Thomas Jefferson, p. 98

65. Brodie, Thomas Jefferson, p. 151

66. Braudel, Civilization and Capitalism, Vol III: The Perspective of the World, p. 513-514

67. Eugene Vanina, India International Quarterly, Spring 1997

68. Brodie, Thomas Jefferson, p. 150

69. Tuchman, The March of Folly, p. 215

70. Nasr, Science and Civilisation in Islam, p. 174

71. Nasr, Science and Civilisation in Islam, p. xii

Chapter 3: Science as Solution: treatment

1. The Economist, Pocket World in Figures, 2014 Edition, p. 159

2. Fernand Braudel, Civilisation and Capitalism, Vol.II: The Structures of Everyday Life (New York: Harper & Row, 1981), p. 205

3. Dr. V. Kurien, "Priority for Agriculture", Seminar at the Project for

4. Economic Education, Friedrich Neumann Foundation, 1991

    Eisenstein, Printing Press, p. 100 (quoting Garin, Italian Humanism)

5. Rajiv Gandhi, interview on board plane, date unavailable

6. Paul Johnson, Intellectuals (New York; Harper and Row, 1988)

7. Francis Fukuyama, The End of History and the Last Man, p.271

8. J.D.Bernal, Science in Society, Vol I: The Emergence of Society
    (Penguin Books, 1995) p.114

9. Times of India, 1 August, 1993

10. Boorstin, The Discoverers, p. 39

11. Boorstin, The Discoverers, p.39

12. Boorstin, The Discoverers, p.39

13. See Table 1, Chapter 1

14. Arthur Koestler, The Sleepwalkers, p. 107

Chapter 4: What is Science?

1. Prof. S.K.Ookerjee, The Times of India, 4 September, year unavailable,
    newspaper cutting with author.

2. Lewis Thomas, The Lives of a Cell (Viking Press, 1974) pp 101-102

3. Joel Mokyr, Technolgical Creativity and Economic Progress (Oxford
    University Press, 199), p. 81

4. Times of India, 24 February, 1985

5. Boorstin, The Discoverers, pp. 86, 92, 344, 420-421

6. Yukichi Fukuzawa, The Autobiography of Yukichi Fukuzawa,
    UNESCO 1960 Edition (Columbia University Press, p. 16-17)

7. Jonathan Miller, The Body in Question (London: Jonathan Cape,
    1974) Preface.

8. Eisenstein, Printing Press, p. 262

9. Boorstin, The Discoverers, p. 302

10. Arthur Koestler, The Sleepwalkers, (Pelican Books, 1979) p. 116

11. Schivelbusch, Wolfgang, The Railway Journey, The Industrialization of
    Time and Space In the Nineteenth Century, (University of California

Press, Oakland, California, 2014 edition)

Chapter 5: The ABC of Science – or Astronomy, Biology and Chemistry, a science primer.

1. Fernand Braudel, The Wheels of Commerce: Civilisation and Capitalism,15th-18th century, Vol II (William Collins, 1985) pp. 573-574

2. E.H.Carr, What is History? (Pelican Books, 1967) p.58

3. Bronowski and Mazlish, Western Intellectual Tradition, p 355

4. David Landes, The Unbound Prometheus (Cambridge University Press, 1989) pp.17-18

5. Boorstin, The Discoverers, pp. 16-17

6. Issac Asimov, Eyes on the Universe (Quartet Books, 1978) pp. 78,91,95, 102,106,111,114,124 and 161; donkey driver, The Universe (Time-Life Books) p. 166

7. Boorstin, The Discoverers, p.75

Chapter 6: Straddling Fences – from Science to the Humanities and back!

1. Arvind Das, The Times of India, 11 July 1993,The Past is Present and Absent.

2. George Kubler, The Shape of Time (Newhaven: Yale University Press,1962) p. 1

3. Isaac Asimov, Words from the Myths (New American Library, 1969) p. 18

4. Richard Feynman, What do you care what other people think! (New York: Bantam Books, 1989) p.11

5. E.H.Gombrich, Art and Illusion (Princeton University Press, 1989), pp 33-34

6. Gombrich, Art and Illusion, p. 39

7. Keith Irvine, The Rise of the Colored Races (New York: W.W.Norton and Co, 1970) p. 44

8.   Boorstin, The Discoverers, p. 103

9.   Rothschild, Bionomics, p.32

10. Rothschild, Bionomics, p.39

11. Boorstin, Republic of Technology, p. 19

12. Daniel J. Levitin, This is your Brain on Music (Plume Books, 2007) p. 11

13. Witold Rybczynski, Waiting for the Weekend (Penguin Books, 1992) p. 92 and p.194

14. Edward Said, Culture and Imperialism (Vintage, 1994) p. 93 and p.84

15. Orhan Pamuk, The Naïve and Sentimental Novelist (Penguin Books India Edition, 2011) p. 106

16. Shiva Naipaul, An Unfinished Journey (Hamish Hamilton, 1986)

17. Daniel Boorstin, The Discoverers, p. 287

18. ibid, pp. 153-154

19. ibid, p. 159

20. ibid, p.268

21. Jared Diamond, Guns, Germs and Steel (W.W.Norton & Co, 1998, pp. 405-408; Richard P. Feynman, "Surely you're joking, Mr. Feynman" (Unwin Paperbacks, 1986) p.338; Susan George and Fabrizo Sabelli, Faith and Credit, The World Bank's Secular Empire (Penguin Books, 1994) p.73-78

22. Arvind Das, The Republic of Bihar (Penguin Books, 1992) p. 90

23. Richard Feynman, What do you care what other people think? (Bantam Books, 1989) p.11

24. KQED Radio discussion on the Cincinnati Riots, April 17, 2001

25. Thomas Sowell, Conquests and Cultures (Basic Books, 1998) p.169-170

26. Henry Louis Gates, Two Nations, Both Black, Forbes, 14 September, 1992

27. Carlo Cipolla, Guns, Sails and Empires (Sunflower University Press/ Random House, 1988) p. 137

28. Sanjeev Prakash, The Woodcarvers of Nagina, India International

Centre Quarterly, No. 4/1985

29. Eisenstein, Printing Press, p.255

30. George Kubler, The Shape of Time, p.29

31. Eisenstein, Printing Press, p. 255

32. Charles Pye-Smith, Travels in Nepal, p.16

33. Quentin Crewe, In Search of the Sahara (London: Michael Joseph, 1983) p. 14

34. Paul Theroux, Riding the Iron Rooster (Penguin Books, 1989) pp. 370-371

35. The Times of India, 1 April, 1989

36. Mark Shands, Travels on an Elephant (Jonathan Cape, 1991)

37. Paul Theroux, The Happy Isles of Oceania (Penguin Books, 1992), p.476

38. Kirkpatrick Sale, The Conquest of Paradise (Plume Books, 1991) p. 104

39. Kenneth Clark, Civilisation (BBC/John Murray) p.271

Chapter 7: "FITTING ONE CIVILIZATION TO ANOTHER."

1. All comparisons are based on figures in the Economist's The Pocket World In Figures, 2014 Edition

2. The Times of India, 21 May, 1999

3. Richard D. Brown, Modernization, the transformation of American Life, 1600-1865 (Hill and Wang, New York) p. 4

4. Boorstin, The Discoverers, p. 72

5. Brown, Modernization, back cover and p.135 and p.60

6. David S. Landes, The Unbound Prometheus (Cambridge University Press, 1989) p. 24

7. Gombrich, Art and Illusion, p.81, p. 83 and p.68

8. Eisenstein, Printing Press, pp. 225-226

9. Eisenstein, Printing Press, p. 227 and p. 243

10. ames Gleick, Isaac Newton (Vintage Books, 2004), pp. 74-75

11. Alan Bloom, Closing of the American Mind, p. 180

12. David S. Landes, The Unbound Prometheus, pp. 17-18

13. J.H.Plumb, The Penguin Book of the Renaissance, 1978, p.53 and p.29

14. Pacey, Maze, p. 34 and p.37

15. Carol Adams, Ordinary Lives – A Hundred Years Ago (Virago, 1989) p.84

16. Mark Tully, No Fullstops, p. 271

17. Nirad Chaudhuri, The Times of India, Sunday Review, 17 November, 1991

18. Nirad Chaudhuri, The Times of India, Sunday Review, 17 November, 1991

19. Kenneth Clark, Civilisation, p. 64

20. Clark, Civilisation, p. 329-33

21. Walter S. Ong, The Presence of the Word (University of Minnesota Press, 1967) p. 54, p.63, pp 134-135

22. Eisenstein, Printing Press, pp. 131-132

23. Jos J.L.Gommans and Dirk H.A.Kolff, Warfare and Weaponry in South Asia, 100-1800

24. Jeremy Black, War and the World (Yale University Press, 1958) p.212

25. Kirkpatrick Sale, The Conquest of Paradise (Penguin Books-Plume, 1991) p.42

26. Ruth Benedict, The Chrysanthemum and the Sword (Houghton Mifflin Company, 1989) p.58

27. Times of India, March 2009, World Development Report, 2009

28. E.H.Carr, What is History? (Penguin Books, 1967), p.143

29. Masao Miyoshi, As We Saw Them, (Kodansha International, 1994) pp.99-101, 103-104, 113, 119, 137-141

30. Thomas Sowell, Conquests and Cultures (Basic Books, 1998) p. 341 quoting Eric Richards and Race and Culture, p. 2 and p.68

31. Times of India, 29 June, 1982. Several approaches to the newspaper for reproduction sadly did not produce even an acknowledgment. Newspaper cuttings with author.

32. A good part of this account has been summarized from Isaac Asimov's

Eyes on the Universe (Quartet Books, 1978)

33. Boorstin, The Discoverers, p. 312

34. Michael Krondl, The Taste of Conquest (New York: Ballantine Books) p. 95

35. V.S.Naipaul, A Writer's People, Alfred A. Knopf, New York/Toronto, 2008, pg 186

Chapter 8: Rallying the Nation: wooing the teachers, working with parents, involving the people.

1. John Dower, Embracing Defeat (W.W.Norton, 1999) p.248

2. The Economist, November 7, 2011

3. Sylvia Nasar, Grand Pursuit: The Story of Economic Genius (Simon and Schuster, 2011) p. 277

4. Raj Jain, Economic Times, May 25, 2009

5. ibid, Economic Times, May 25, 2009

6. ibid, Economic Times, March 30, 2011

7. ibid, Economic Times, May 25, 2009

8. ibid, Economic Times, May 25, 2009

9. Economic Times, May 31, 2011

10. Fortune magazine, July 2016

11. Sudhakar Ram, Time to Reinvent Work, Economic Times, March 8, 2010

12. J.A.Chowdhary, Times of India supplement on A.P., November 2011

13. Latha Jishnu, Business World, June 27, 2005

14. Richard D. Brown, Modernization (New York: Hill and Wang, 1976), pp. 28,51.54,60,115 and 126

15. The Economist, January 14, 2014 and August 23, 2014

16. Raj Jain, Economic Times, date unavailable

17. Gary P. Pisano and Willy C. Shih, Restoring American Competitiveness, Harvard Business Review, July-August 2009

18. Jagdish Bhagwati, The Manufacturing Fallacy, Economic Times, August 30, 2010

19. CNN interview with Gene Sperling, April 15, 2012

20. Times of India, June 10, 2012

21. a) Arthur Herman, Freedom's Forge (New York: 2013 Random House Trade Paperback). Interestingly, this brilliant author's equally fascinating book which preceded Freedom's Forge was Gandhi and Churchill ! b) I recently read in Blood and Ruins by Richard Overy, an excellent one volume account of World War II. Although the author also quotes FDR giving similar credit, he points out that volume output of military equipment during war was rather more complex.

22. John Chambers, Fortune, September 15, 2016

23. Citibank advertisement, Time 2016

24. Harish Damodaran, India's New Capitalists (Permanent Black, 2011)

25. Jeff Stemke, Economic Times, December 12, 2011

26. C.S.Ramalakshmi, Times of India supplement, November 2011

27. Steven Geiger, Economic Times, December 14, 2011

28. Kiran Karnik, Economic Times, December 12, 2011

29. Accessed from the internet

30. Accessed from the internet

31. Edward Dolnick, The Clockwork Universe (Harper Collins, 2011) pp, 13, 48 and 56

32. Boorstin, Republic of Technology, p. 17

33. Ezra Vogel, Deng Xiaoping and the Transformation of China (Harvard University Press, 2011) pp. 133, 143, 321,674 and 685.

34. Tim Brown and Roger Martin, Harvard Business Review, September, 2015

35. Management Today, May 1986 reporting on change at ICL Ltd.

36. Marius B. Jansen, The Making of Modern Japan, (Harvard University Press, Cambridge, Massachusetts, 2002), p.210

37. Eisenstein, Printing Press, p. 151

38. Witold Rybczynski, Waiting for the Weekend, pp.90-91

39. Ezra Vogel, Deng Xiaoping, p. 599

40. Some recommended books:

a. The Science of Life: A Pictorial History Of Biology, G Rattray Taylor, Thames & Hudson, 1967

b. Introducing Chemistry, Hazel Rossotti, Penguin Books, 1975

c. A History of Economics, John Kenneth Galbraith, Penguin Books, 1991

d. The Sleepwalkers, A History of Man's Changing Vision of the Universe, Arthur Koestler, Penguin Books, 1991

e. The Story of Maps, Lloyd A. Brown, Dover Publications, 1979

41. Thomas Friedman, Hot, Flat and Crowded (Farrar, Straus and Girrux, 2008) pp 314-315, 327, 335

42. Sunday Times of India, January 9, 2011

43. Laurence Steinberg, Benson Brown and Sanford M. Dombusch: Beyond the Classsroom: Why School Reform has failed and what Parents need to do (Simon & Schuster, 1997)

44. The Economist, October 17, 2009

45. Economic Times, March 12, 2011

46. Dr. A.P.J. Abdul Kalam, talk on Technology and Innovation, December 22, 2007

47. Dennis Danielson, The First Copernican (New York: Walker & Company,2006) p. 21

48. Sam Pitroda, Times of India, October 15, 2008

49. Himani Dalmia, "Feeding Hungry Hearts", Times of India, October 7,2009

50. Neeraj Kaushal, India's Child Nutrition Puzzle, Economic Times, 29 April, 2011

51. Time magazine, 4 April, 2011

52. Ajit Khilnani, The Idea of India (Hamish Hamilton, 1997) p.73

53. Michael Schulman, The Passionate Mind: Building up an Intelligent and Creative Child (New York: The Free Press, 1991), blurb.

54. "With Progress comes Diabetes", San Jose Mercury News, September

18, 2006

55. Friedman, Hot, Flat and Crowded, p. 18

56. Michael E. Porter, The Competitive Advantage of Nations (The Macmillan Press, 1990) p. 133

57. Time magazine, March 9, 2009

58. Friedman, Hot, Flat and Crowded, p. 18

59. Nicholas Philipson, Adam Smith, An Enlightened Life (New Haven and London, Yale University Press, 2010) p. 143

Appendix 1 to Chapter 8:

Forget Ideology, Consider Idea-logy! First appeared as an article by the author in the Bombay magazine, One India, One People, February 2004

Appendix 2 to Chapter 8:

1. Lester Thurow, Creating Wealth (Nicholas Brealey Publishing: 2000) p.135

2. J.K.Galbraith, A History of Economic Progress (Penguin Books,1991) p.69

3. Thurow, p. 18

4. ibid, p. 18

5. ibid, p. 19

6. p. 130

7. San Jose Mercury News, September 13, 2006

8. Times of India, June 17, 2007

9. Thurow, p. 135

CHAPTER 9: Conclusion

1. Time, August 7, 1995, p.40

2. World Development Report, 1996, From Plan to Market

3. Huizinga, Waning of the Middle Ages, p.66

4. Robert McNeal et al, Story of English, pp. 132-133

5. A.J.P.Taylor, Europe: Grandeur and Decline (Penguin Books, 1991)

6. Pamela Philpose, Intellectual Clones, The Sunday Observer, March 1-7, 1992

7. K.K.Datta, 1992. Unable to locate original article

8. Peter Drucker, Is Capitalism coming to an End, Spam magazine, May 1993

9. J.D.Bernal, Science in History: Vol.I (Penguin Books, 1969) p.196

10. Dr. B.V.Raman, Times of India, 28 January, 1982

ACKNOWLEDGMENTS

This book was the result of, say, 10 or 15 years of simply delightful labour. Labour in desperate search of some way. Several years of study of economics and law had still not shown me a way of approaching all knowledge. And then I discovered general science - something that I had run away from before. Here was a whole body of knowledge, a true colossus, the greatest man has ever created, standing right there before me - and all around me, waiting to be put to use.

I have benefited enormously from numerous discussions with Ketan and Sheila Kothari, Manish Kothari and Mamen Saura, Milind Gadekar, Hemant and Nasreine Canaran, Raj and Suha Velamoor, Namita Dalal, Ujwala Sriniwas, Raju Sunny and Suresh and the late Suhasini Mulgaonkar. Also with Jehangir Khambatta, Hannan Ezekiel and Hans-Jochen Moka, sadly all now deceased and no longer with us.

Finally, I should clarify that if there are any mistakes in the book in either the theorizing or in the interpretation of facts, the responsibility is entirely mine.

ABOUT THE AUTHOR

With an educational background of economics and law and after many years of questing, the author, Arvind Banavaliker, finally discovered general science for himself. He has written a column for a Mumbai magazine and has spoken often on this subject on All India Radio (AIR). He has lived in India for the greater part of his life, travelled abroad extensively and only recently has moved to the USA to be with his only daughter and her family.

INDEX

(Because of the constraints of automated production and despite several efforts, it has not been possible to achieve precise listing of the Index pages. Page numbers in the Index are correct but only approximately indicate the position in the book where the references are to be found.)